CONSERVATION, IDENTITY AND OWNERSHIP IN INDIGENOUS ARCHAEOLOGY

GUEST EDITORS:
Bill Sillar & Cressida Fforde

PUBLIC **ARCHAEOLOGY**

Table of Contents

Foreword *Neal Ascherson*	67
Editorial *Bill Sillar and Cressida Fforde*	69
Who's indigenous? Whose archaeology? *Bill Sillar*	71
The Ainu people of Japan: an indigenous people or an ethnic group? *Kaori Tahara*	95
Archaeology and the study of indigenous peoples in Siberia *Ole Grøn*	103
Of grizzlies and landslides: the use of archaeological and anthropological evidence in Canadian aboriginal rights cases *Jean Leclair*	109
Social scientists and native title cases in Australia *Peter Sutton*	121
Indigenous peoples' rights to their cultural Heritage *Lyndon Ormond Parker*	127
Strands of indigenism in the Bolivian Andes: competing juridical claims for the ownership and management of indigenous heritage sites in an emerging context of legal pluralism *Denise Arnold and Juan de Dios Yapita*	141
Museums and communities in Africa: facing the new challenges *Lorna Abungu*	151
Talking about others: archaeologists, indigenous peoples and heritage in Argentina *María Luz Endere*	155
The making of the Heart of the World: representation and the Kogi *Alan Ereira*	163
Social images through visual images: the use of drawings and photographs in the Western representation of the aborigines of Tierra del Fuego *Dánae Fiore*	169
What is a museum for? The Magüta Museum for the Ticuna people, Amazonas, Brazil *Constantino Ramos Lopes*	183
Artefacts, archaeologists, and American Indians *Joe Watkins*	187
Honor thy ancestor's possessions *Edward Halealoha Ayau*	193
Indigenous claims and heritage conservation: an opportunity for critical dialogue *Glenn Wharton*	199
Applied archaeology: revitalising indigenous agricultural technology within an Andean community *Ann Kendall*	205

Foreword

Neal Ascherson

With this publication, the journal at last reaches a milestone of distinction: its first 'Special' issue – at twice the normal length – devoted to a single topic.

Nothing could be closer to the concerns of Public Archaeology than the indigenous approach to the discipline, above all in post-colonial continents. It's true to say that this approach has transformed the self-understanding of archaeologists in Europe and North America, and will continue to do so. My hope is that this dedicated 'Special', guest-edited by Bill Sillar and Cressida Fforde, will become in itself a work of inspiration and reference.

Journal readers may need to have the current numbering of 'Public Archaeology' made clearer. This double-sized issue is registered as Volume 4, numbers 2 and 3. Volume 4, number 4 (single-sized again), should appear towards the end of this year. Early in 2006, we intend to publish another Special on the modern use of Egyptian imagery, edited by Professor Peter Ucko. That will be Volume 5, numbers 1 and 2.

Editorial

Bill Sillar and Cressida Fforde

One of the most dynamic aspects of public archaeology has been the demand by many indigenous peoples that they should be consulted about the excavation, study and display of their culture. In many areas, these demands have forced archaeologists to fundamentally reconsider both their aims and their methods. This has had a significant impact on the identification, research, protection and exhibition of the cultural heritage of indigenous peoples around the world. Archaeological research often focuses on the original inhabitants of a place and the subsequent changes that have occurred, whether as the result of internal developments, external influences or colonization. However, the identification of artefacts as 'indigenous' – and the implications inherent in the act of categorizing them – can be complex. For example, the classification of archaeological artefacts as indigenous (or belonging to a specific indigenous group) can affect disputes over land ownership and impact upon sensitive issues of modern political identities.

One or more groups of people can identify with artefacts, occupation sites, monuments or named places in the landscape as part of the legacy of their ancestors. For many indigenous groups, this is an inheritance they feel the need to protect, though to do so can be problematic and demanding. In some cases indigenous communities have worked with researchers and heritage managers to locate and conserve archaeological sites and other aspects of their cultural heritage. Such collaboration provides a valuable opportunity for archaeologists to learn more about the cultural meaning of places, structures and artefacts, and for archaeological investigations to further local peoples' understanding and connections with their past. It can also provide an important forum for indigenous people to inform the wider public about the history and present situation of their culture, and for the archaeologists to engage (or be engaged as a result of) indigenous support for the protection of ancient sites. However, archaeologists and heritage managers have sometimes been ignorant of indigenous concerns and, partly because of this, indigenous peoples have not always been sympathetic to the aims of archaeological research or cultural tourism. Concepts key to 'traditional' archaeology have sometimes been areas of contention. For example, indigenous views about 'protection' and 'conservation' may challenge the archaeological 'norms' of survey, excavation, site management and museum curation, and *vice versa*. For some indigenous people, archaeological work is viewed as little more than legalized grave robbing and land grabbing with the support and authority of national legislation.

Increasing awareness of indigenous views, concerns and demands have confronted archaeologists and heritage managers with difficult questions. For example, archaeology has traditionally imposed a professional obligation to protect the physical integrity of artefacts and some archaeologists have for this reason opposed indigenous requests to use or repatriate ancient materials. The use of public funds has promoted a professional commitment to supporting public access to artefacts, sites and research knowledge, but this may be complex when dealing with indigenous concerns that restrict access to information about, for example, sacred sites or ritual knowledge.

Furthermore, it is not always clear which modern populations are most directly identified with the archaeological remains, not only raising questions about who is or is not indigenous, and what authority, or ownership rights, such status confers, but also the role of archaeology in the defining process.

Archaeological research is a privilege, not a right. If we wish to continue to enjoy this privilege we will need to work with diverse communities and to demonstrate the relevance of archaeological research to their concerns. The developing dialogue between indigenous groups, archaeologists, heritage managers and museums is already transforming the discipline, and several papers in this volume refer to strategies to share decision making with regard to the aims and methods of research and the content and audience for public displays. The growing diversity of people employed as archaeologists and heritage managers, including some indigenous people, may also have a long-term effect in opening up the discipline and breaking down the 'them' and 'us' divides that characterize so much of this debate.

WHY THIS VOLUME?

The papers for this issue of *Public Archaeology* originate within the context of research and teaching at the Institute of Archaeology, University College London. With a wide range of staff and students involved in archaeology throughout the world we recognize the need to be aware of the continually developing issues that impact on all areas of archaeological practice. The mission statement adopted by the Institute includes both the intention 'to be internationally pre-eminent in the study, and comparative analysis, of world archaeology' and 'to ensure that the social, political and economic contexts of the practice of archaeology are taught and appreciated'. Since 1999 we have taught a third-year undergraduate option on 'Indigenous Archaeology', a course that focuses on indigenous peoples and their relationships to anthropological and archaeological investigations. One of the main questions that the course addresses is the very nature, and definition, of 'indigenism'/'indigenous' and its relationship, if any, to the evidence of the past as revealed by archaeology and/or oral history. The course uses case studies from around the world to discuss indigenous archaeology in all its complexity with the intention of fostering wider understanding in our students of the many issues they may meet in future archaeological work, not least encouraging them to consider the potential consequences of their work on local populations.

During the United Nations Decade for Indigenous People (1995–2004), in the spring of 2001, we also chose the theme of 'Indigenous Peoples and "Patenting" the Past' for the Institute's weekly research seminars. These seminars were organized by Peter Ucko, Bill Sillar, Jo Dullaghan and Natalie de Silva, who invited a range of indigenous speakers, lawyers and activists, as well as anthropologists and archaeologists, with the intention of focusing on the contested rights of ownership over materials and representations of the past of indigenous peoples (Ucko, 2002). In addition, we organized a series of weekly evening lectures entitled 'Moving Forwards with Indigenous Peoples to the 21st Century' in order to present these subjects in a public forum and extend the debate outside the university. Most of the contributors to this special issue presented papers within the undergraduate course, the research seminars or the public lectures held at the Institute of Archaeology.

Contact address: Institute of Archaeology, University College London, 34 Gordon Square, London WC1H 0PY, UK. Email: b.sillar@ucl.ac.uk; cressidaff@compuserve.com

REFERENCE

Ucko, P.J. Indigenous archaeology. *Papers from the Institute of Archaeology* 12 (2002) 1–11.

Who's indigenous? Whose archaeology?

Bill Sillar

ABSTRACT

The International Labour Organisation, the United Nations and various indigenous Organisations have raised and/or objected to diverse criteria through which indigenous groups have been defined and the rights that should be accorded to them. This paper discusses the implications of these issues in relation to archaeological research and heritage management and uses this to position the other papers in this volume. Specific themes that are addressed include: the impact of colonialism and nation-forming on indigenous groups; the continuing influence of 19th and early 20th century social evolutionary concepts on the representation of indigenous groups and the role of archival material from this period today; the contrasting processes of cultural continuity and assimilation within 'dominant' societies in which indigenous communities have participated, and the effects that this has had on more recent claims over land rights; the cultural differences that surround the concepts of individual and community ownership, particularly in relation to copyright; the role of academia, museums and the media in the representation of indigenous people in the past and the present.

WHO'S INDIGENOUS?

In recent years the concerns of many indigenous groups have gained wide publicity and organizations such as the United Nations (UN) have recognized the frequent infringement of human rights suffered by indigenous peoples. But, the fact that indigenous peoples are at last gaining some political power has meant that even their claim to be indigenous may now be treated with suspicion. Two of the most frequent questions that students ask are 'Why should indigenous peoples be given special rights?' and 'Who decides who is, and who is not, indigenous?'. When sitting in a classroom in London, listening to the many and varied demands made by indigenous people, and the special treatment and support offered to some indigenous people, these questions seem important and valid. Some students have therefore been surprised when visiting speakers have been taken aback, or offended, by these questions. It is perhaps ironic that people who were dismissed or marginalized as indigenous through classification systems imposed by explorers, colonial powers, nation states and academics are now using this same definition to fight to reclaim basic rights. But, it is even more ironic that people coming from areas of the world where descriptions such as 'Native' 'Aborigine' or 'Indian' have been, and frequently still are, terms of abuse, are now expected to prove or justify their indigenous status. When people are claiming specific, and sometimes exclusive, rights because they are 'indigenous', and increasing numbers of marginalized groups are 'becoming' indigenous (Hodgson, 2002: 1 p. 1037) it is legitimate to ask what is the basis of this claim. But, it is also important to ask: 'Who is asking the question?' 'Who is setting the definitions?' and 'For what reasons?'. All of the papers in this volume address the issues that surround previous categorization and current concepts of indiginiety and how these have affected past treatment of, and current demands by, indigenous peoples.

Archaeology is at the core of these debates, with the definition of 'indigenousness', the longevity of occupation and the continuity of cultural practices frequently resting on archaeological, historical and anthropological evidence. Yet, many indigenous people are suspicious of such academic pursuits, not least because archaeology and anthropology were themselves a part of the colonial process. These disciplines helped to categorize and describe indigenous peoples, information that was frequently used by colonial administrators as they deprived the indigenous inhabitants of their land, their rights and their dignity, and either sought to re-educate them to be subservient citizens or marginalize them at the edge of the dominant society's economic and social life.

Indigenous people are the descendants of the first occupants in each area of the world; there is obviously enormous diversity amongst all these different cultural groups, who have experienced different histories of expansion, conquest and colonization, and now have different aspirations and demands. The fundamental meaning of the term 'indigenous' as the original inhabitants of a particular place is relatively clear, but after many centuries of colonization, migration, intermarriage and acculturation, who is 'indigenous' today is frequently less clear. While many people in the world can claim descent from indigenous ancestors, it is not always clear who is included and who is excluded when discussing indigenous groups. Yet indigenous groups are demanding exclusive rights over human remains, artefacts and land, demands that prompt us to question the basis for these identity and ownership claims. At the start of the United Nations Decade for Indigenous Peoples in 1995, the UN provided a rough estimate of 300 million indigenous people in the world today, with the majority of these in India and China. But, as Arnold and Yapita (this volume) point out in their paper focusing on Bolivia, most statistics stating the number of indigenous people are unreliable, depending as they do on external categorizations, political expediency and a lack of detailed information. Arnold and Yapita also draw attention to how different groups in the Andean highlands have drawn upon different periods in history when constructing their diverse claims to indigeneity. Some place greater emphasis on their kinship and community of origin, whereas others place greater emphasis on racial differences and language use within urban and industrial settings, and political activism.

The meaning of terms such as 'Native', 'Indian', 'First Nation' or 'Aborigine' varies depending on the country or people being referred to and the context in which the terms are used (in academic discourse, national law, to sell arts and crafts or during a social conflict). Such variability, imprecision and flexibility is not surprising, given the wide range of groups and complex histories that are being referred to, but it does highlight one of the problems inherent in developing universal approaches to indigenous peoples' rights (Bowen, 2000). In the past, the African Commission on Human Rights has insisted that all Africans are indigenous to Africa and that no particular group could claim indigenous status, and in this volume Abungu makes a similar argument. However, Kenya declared the visually distinctive and politically powerful Masai as their indigenous population for the 1991 United Nations' Year of Indigenous Peoples, even though they probably only migrated into the region that is now Kenya some 300 years ago. Yet, like other indigenous groups, they have a history of cultural distinctiveness and marginalization by the nation state, they 'self-identify' as indigenous, and increasingly NGOs and others are referring to them as indigenous (cf. Hodgson, 2002). Like Pueblo societies who migrated from Anasazi sites, or Quechu-speaking communities that were relocated by the Inka State, these groups are no less 'indigenous' for having moved from their previous homelands, and yet it raises the question as to how movement affects a group's 'indigenous' rights and what it takes to transform them into 'colonizers'. Largely in response to the United Nations focus on indigenous peoples, the African Commission on Human Rights set up a Working Group on the Rights of Indigenous People/Communities in Africa in 2001; the report from this working group, which was adopted in November 2003, primarily identifies the term indigenous with nomadic subsistence modes:

> A misconception is that the term *indigenous* is not applicable in Africa as 'all Africans are indigenous'. There is no question that all Africans are indigenous to Africa in the sense that they were there before the

European colonialists arrived and that they have been subject to sub-ordination during colonialism. We thus in no way question the identity of other groups. When some particular marginalized groups use the term *indigenous* to describe their situation, they use the modern analytical form of the concept (which does not merely focus on aboriginality) in an attempt to draw attention to and alleviate the particular form of discrimination they suffer from.... those groups of peoples or communities throughout Africa who are identifying themselves as indigenous peoples or communities and who are linking up with the global indigenous rights movement are first and foremost (but not exclusively) different groups of hunter-gatherers or former hunter-gatherers and certain groups of pastoralists. (African Union, 2003: 62–63)

Perhaps academics should not be too quick to critique the precise justification used to claim indigenous status, as to do so would undermine the very real political and moral power that previously marginalized indigenous people are finally gaining at local, national and international levels. However, although it is understandable to use any methods available to fight for the rights and needs of all marginalized and vulnerable populations, we should be careful of grouping them all as 'indigenous populations'. Firstly there is a danger of equating indigeneity with poverty. The homeless, jobless and exploited peoples of the world include recent migrants, Creole and others, who may quite justifiably consider the use of indigenous, ethnic or racial identity claims to demand basic social and economic rights to be a divisive influence on a more fundamental class struggle. Although a primary aim of most secondary colonizers has been to acquire the wealth of the indigenous population (primarily their land, but also livestock, raw materials, labour and artefacts), some indigenous populations have managed to retain or regain some of their wealth. For instance, although the Pequots were so decimated by English colonists in 1637 that they were thought to be extinct, with their members killed or placed in slavery under the control of other Native American groups, those placed under the Mohegans eventually became known as the Mashantucket (Western) Pequots and have subsequently won back their reservation lands and now have one of the largest casinos in the USA, funding a major museum and making tribal members much richer than most North Americans. The Mashantucket Pequots, like the richer Saami herders, could hardly be called marginalized or vulnerable, but they are proudly indigenous. Secondly, archaeologists and other academics are increasingly being asked to give evidence in court to assess the legitimacy of indigeneity claims, where their evidence may be critical in making major decisions (Leclair, and Sutton, this volume), it may therefore undermine more legitimate claims if archaeologists are too carefree with the use of the term 'indigenous'.

DEVELOPING DEFINITIONS

In many countries of the world indigenous people continue to be among the poorest and most marginalized members of society who are particularly vulnerable to economic exploitation and disenfranchisement. It is for this reason that organizations such as the International Labour Organization and the United Nations have drawn attention to the predicament of such peoples. In raising awareness about indigenous rights these organizations have, at various stages, tried to describe and define indigeniety and their attempts to do so have been the source of debate and dispute, as various nation states, aid organizations and indigenous groups have first raised and then objected to the implications of diverse criteria (see Hodgson, 2002).

In the International Labour Organization's (ILO) Indigenous and Tribal Populations Convention 107 of 1957 'tribal and semi-tribal' populations were described as 'at a less advanced stage than that of other sections of the national community' (ILO, 1957: Article 1:l[a]) defining *semi-tribal* as those 'groups or persons who, although they are in the process of losing their tribal characteristics, are not yet integrated into the national community' (ibid.: Article 1.2). A key objective of the 1957 Convention was to 'facilitate ... their progressive integration into their respective national communities' (ibid.: preamble). This 1957 convention expressed the widely held assumptions of the period: that indigenous people were primitive, underdeveloped peoples who should be protected during the period of assimilation into the norms of civilized society. However, with an increasing participation of indigenous representatives in the ILO, Convention 107 was replaced in 1989 with a new Indigenous and Tribal Populations Convention, number 169. Convention 169 has probably been the most widely referenced, and influential, statement of indigenous rights, providing a basis for continuing campaigns at national and international levels. It removed the patronizing assumption that indigenous people would eventually abandon their customs and identities, in favour of asserting indigenous peoples' rights to regain their autonomy and maintain their distinct society. The 1989 Convention recognized the 'aspirations of [indigenous] peoples to exercise control over their own institutions, ways of life and economic development and to maintain and develop their identities, languages, and religions, within the frameworks of the States in which they live' (ILO, 1989: preamble). The ensuing Articles outlined a broad set of governmental responsibilities with regard to indigenous rights, including: a preference for customary legal solutions; recognition of the rights of indigenous peoples to ownership, possession and access to their traditional lands and resources; prevention of discrimination in the terms, practices and benefits of employment; government provision of adequate and appropriate health services and educational programmes in co-operation and consultation with the people concerned; and support for indigenous language instruction for children. Convention 169 defined Indigenous Peoples as:

(a) tribal peoples in independent countries whose social, cultural and economic conditions distinguish them from other sections of the national community, and whose status is regulated wholly or partially by their own customs or traditions or by special laws or regulations;
(b) peoples in independent countries who are regarded as indigenous on account of their descent from populations which inhabited the country, or a geographical region to which the country belongs, at the time of conquest or colonisation or the establishment of present state boundaries and who, irrespective of their legal status, retain some or all of their own social, economic, cultural and political institutions. [ILa 1989: Article 1.1]
(c) 'self-identification as indigenous, or tribal, shall be regarded as a fundamental criterion for determining the groups to which the provisions of the Convention apply' (ILO, 1989: 1. 2).

In 1982 the United Nations established a Working Group on Indigenous Populations which prepared a Draft Declaration on the Rights of Indigenous Peoples. Partly in response to the strong protest by the indigenous peoples throughout the Americas against 'celebrating' the 500th anniversary of Columbus's 'discovery' in 1492, the United Nations declared a Decade for Indigenous People (1995–2004), and in 2000 the UN established a Permanent Forum on Indigenous Issues.

The United Nations has been unable to develop a legally binding definition of indigenous peoples that the individual nation states and indigenous groups have been prepared to ratify, but the UN frequently quotes the definition proposed in 1986 by José Martinez Cobo (Special Rapporteur to the UN Economic and Social Council Sub-Commission on Prevention of Discrimination and Protection of Minorities):

> Indigenous communities, peoples and nations are those which, having a historical continuity with pre-invasion and pre-colonial societies that have developed on their territories, consider themselves distinct from other sectors of the societies now prevailing in those territories, or parts of them. They form at present non-dominant sectors of society and are determined to preserve, develop, and transmit to future generations their ancestral territories, and their ethnic identity, as the basis of their continued existence as peoples, in accordance with their own cultural patterns, social institutions and legal systems. (Cobo, 1986: 379)

Cobo (1986: 380) goes on to outline how to determine 'historical continuity':

> This historical continuity may consist of the continuation, for an extended period reaching into the present, of one or more of the following factors:
>
> (a) Occupation of ancestral lands, or at least part of them.
> (b) Common ancestry with the original occupants of these lands.
> (c) Culture in general, or in specific manifestations (such as religion, living under a tribal system, membership of an indigenous community, dress, means of livelihood, life-style, etc.).
> (d) Language (whether used as the only language, as mother tongue, as the habitual means of

communication at home or in the family, or as the main, preferred, habitual, general or normal language).
(e) Residence in certain parts of the country, or in certain regions of the world.
(f) Other relevant factors.

All this contrasts with the unequivocal final statement that emerged from the Consultation on Indigenous Peoples' Knowledge and Intellectual Property Rights, in Suva, in April 1995, where the indigenous representatives refused to be confined by any single definition and stated: 'We assert our inherent right to define who we are. We do not approve of any other definition'. Or the Report of the African Commission's working group on indigenous populations in 2003, which stated:

> This report does not aim at giving a clear-cut definition of *indigenous peoples,* as there is no global consensus about a single final definition. The global indigenous rights movement and the UN system oppose recurrent attempts to have a single strict definition. Other peoples of the world are not required to define themselves in similar ways, and the danger of a strict definition is that many governments may use a strict definition as an excuse for not recognizing indigenous peoples within their territories. For relevant comparison, it should be noted that the category *minority* is not defined in the UN Declaration on Minority Rights. (African Union, 2003: 62)

From this summary of influential international statements about identifying indigenous peoples a number of important issues can be identified:

- *Colonial origins*: indigenous groups are usually identified in contrast to secondary colonizers who have become the dominant society of modern nation states.
- *Less advanced*: attitudes to indigenous groups continue to be influenced by the 19th century social evolutionary concept of the 'primitive tribal savage'.
- *Descent and ancestry*: being able to prove kinship and descent from indigenous ancestors is assumed to be central to claiming indigenous rights.
- *Assimilation versus continuity*: adopting aspects of the 'mainstream' lifestyle is potentially seen as a loss of identity, and indigenous groups are defined partly in contrast to the wider national society through asserting a continuity of tradition and land use.
- *Conflict with the nation state*: the assertion of land claims and distinct native legal and political structures is inherently a challenge to the nation state.
- *Ancestral lands*: homelands and some specific places are important to the identity of most indigenous peoples.
- *Ownership and copyright*: the desire to reclaim not just land but other resources (both natural and cultural) and protect these through communal ownership.
- *Representation*: after centuries of categorization and manipulation by others many indigenous people object to external attempts to define and limit who belongs to their group, and assert the right to self-identification and the ability to maintain and develop their own culture including the importance of educating their children using their native language.

Each of these issues has implications in relation to the material remains of the past and the work of archaeologists; it is this relationship to archaeology that provides the focus for the discussion below, which also seeks to position the papers in this volume in relation to current debates over the rights of indigenous peoples.

COLONIAL ORIGINS AND THE PEOPLE WITHOUT HISTORY

Current debates over indigenous rights are primarily framed within the legacy of European colonial expansion and the emergence of nation states. A major definition of indigenous peoples is that they are distinct from those peoples who took their land and marginalized them from the structures of governance. The appropriation of indigenous peoples and their resources by 'foreigners' started with the colonial act of 'discovering' new lands and the renaming of 'native' places. During the process of colonization, indigenous groups were commonly subjugated, classified and regulated by external cultures, and this was frequently the defining process by which indigenous cultures were described and represented as 'other'. Perhaps the most significant 'difference' was religion, as it was a papal edict that provided a moral and legal justification for Christian nations to impose missionaries and obligations to trade on non-Christians; any resistance to this provided an excuse for full conquest. The papal decree or charter referred to as the bull *Romanus Pontifex* that Pope Nicholas V issued to King Alfonso V of Portugal, specifically sanctioned and promoted the conquest and colonization of non-Christians and their territories. On May 4th 1493 Pope Alexander VI issued bull *Inter Cetera*, which granted Spain the right to conquer the lands that Columbus had 'found', as well as any lands that Spain might 'discover' in the future, with the single proviso that Spain must not attempt to establish its dominion over lands that had already 'come into the possession of any Christian lords'. While pious Christians from Bartolomé de las Casas([1552] 1992) onwards have been important defenders of the rights of indigenous peoples, religious conversion has provided a central excuse for the destruction of indigenous social and religious structures. Indigenous belief systems regarding ancestral remains or sacred objects were dismissed as pagan superstitions and idolatrous practices, justifying their destruction or their removal to museums.

European colonizers encountered hunter-gatherers such as the San of South Africa, the Selk'nam of Tierra del Fuego and 250 or more language groups of Australian Aborigines, as well as large complex societies such as the Aztec and Inca states. From the colonizer's point of view, all these peoples were 'Natives', but different colonizing nations, encountering different societies at different times responded to these indigenous groups in many different ways. This focus on the colonial process can make the identification of indigenous peoples in Australia and New Zealand, where colonization took place relatively late and the primacy of Aboriginal and Maori occupation is well understood, seem much clearer than in places with written documents recording successive movements of different peoples in India and Europe, or the complexity of a sequence of expansionist states in Central and South America. Yet politics is stranger than fact. The British colonizers of Australia declared the land *terra nullius*, denying what we now know to be at least 40,000 years of occupation by aboriginal populations. Until 1967 Australian Aborigines did not have the vote and were not included in the census even though they were conscripted into the military. It was not until the Mabo decision of 1992, that the High Court of Australia conceded that the Aborigines had ownership of the lands prior to 1788, leading to a continuing debate about the return of Native Title (see Sutton, this volume). Whereas the British colonizers of New Zealand negotiated with the Maori chiefs and drew up the Treaty of Waitangi (1840), which at least guaranteed Maori citizenship and referred to Maori self-government. The Treaty, with its somewhat different wordings in the contemporary English and Maori versions, has returned to prominence with the setting up in 1975 of the Waitangi Tribunal, which has a mandate to identify and define the meaning of the principles of the treaty, including settling recent land claims. Earlier in North America the British had been forced to recognize the sovereignty of distinct Indian Nations over discrete territories, drawing up separate treaties such as the Treaty of Albany (1722) and Treaty of Lancaster (1744) with the Six Nations, and the Treaty of Logstown (1752) with the Delaware and Shawnee. In 1763 King George III issued a Proclamation that prohibited further settlement west of the Allegheny Mountains, and for those settlers seeking further land holdings this was one of the contentious pieces of British legislation during the war of independence. Even with the same colonizing power, the degree to which indigenous groups were recognized and negotiated with has been very different.

The distinction between indigenous peoples and others is a continuing reminder of the legacy of long-term processes of human colonization. However, the conditions of colonization are constantly changing (Gosden, 2004): the factors that influenced the first humans to move 'out of Africa', the movement of peoples and ways of life that characterize the development of agriculture and urban societies, the expansionist states of Europe, Africa, Asia and America, and the continuing economic and political incentives for migration today, have led to very different encounters between human groups in each specific situation. A major factor that characterizes the period of colonization by European and other states was the acquisition of indigenous land and the imposition of colonial rule; however, in cases such as the Andean Ayllus and Maori chiefs, indigenous elites retained some power during the colonial period and the decline in native jurisdiction was most fully realized during the succeeding periods of independence and nation building.

For many parts of the world the colonial period was characterized by the imposition of Western bureaucracies, particularly the use of written records. The traditional separation of the historical and anthropological study of colonial and later periods from the archaeological study of pre-history was justified both by the disjuncture between the study of pre- and post-European contact and the primacy that we give to the use of textual evidence, even though the place and many of the people were the same. Archaeologists have contributed to breaking down these boundaries in order to offer a critical appraisal of the colonial process in each specific instance and question the documentary records created by the colonizers through a detailed analysis of the archaeological evidence (Funari et al., 1999; Gosden, 2004). Recent years have also seen a re-appraisal of documentary evidence for a wide range of indigenous rebellions and resistance to colonization, including the using of colonial legal structures to fight for indigenous rights (e.g. Stern, 1987, 1993). Nowhere is the primacy of colonial texts stronger than within courts of law. Despite the care and precision with which reported speech is used in many oral cultures, most courts have considered this oral history as hearsay, in comparison with the validity given to the documents of the colonizers. However, the courts of many countries are now giving much greater legitimacy to both the oral traditions of indigenous groups and the use of archaeological evidence. As Leclair (this volume) describes in his analysis of legal disputes over native land claims, Canadian law has shifted to a cautious acceptance of oral histories as valid evidence; the identification and interpretation of archaeological evidence is also considered important, but concern is expressed because it may be insufficiently precise to establish proof of occupation by ancestors of a specific modern group. Archaeology provides an important source for understanding indigenous society prior to the colonial period, however identifying indigeneity implies an ability to categorize and separate prior local cultures from later 'intrusions' or the remains of native activities during the colonial period. Even distinguishing between the artefacts or human remains of indigenous peoples and colonizers is not always self-evident. The initial identification of Kennewick Man by Jim Chatters as of 'European type' (although latter dated to between 7200 and 7600 BC) has shown how what at first seem innocent analytical labels can bring with them highly loaded cultural values and assumptions (Hurst Thomas, 2000). Similarly, the handmade, unglazed pots originally referred to by Noël Hume (1962) as Colono-Indian ware and thought to be of Native American manufacture are now more commonly referred to as Colono ware and widely believed to have been largely made and used by African Americans, because of the similarities with some West African pottery and the preponderance at slave plantation sites (Ferguson, 1992). Equally, archaeologists have frequently referred to the artefacts and sites of successive periods as distinct cultures (e.g. the Satsumon as the pre-historic Ainu, named after a 'type-site' where the pottery was first identified, or the Anasazi as the ancient Pueblo society that originates from a Navajo term meaning 'enemy ancestors'). While there may be important debates over what the changes in the form and function of artefacts in successive phases mean in relation to cultural change, the terminologies frequently serve to separate indigenous peoples from their pasts. As the discourse between archaeologists and indigenous people shifts such categorization will become more problematic, as archaeologists feel less justified in imposing external classifications upon local understandings of oral history, ancestral remains and sacred sites.

PRIMITIVE SAVAGES? CATEGORIZING 'TRIBAL' PEOPLES

A central feature of 19th and early 20th century social evolution was the use of indigenous societies, encountered during the period of European colonial expansion, to illustrate and explain the 'early stages' in human development. Following the tradition of Lubbock's (1865) *Prehistoric Times; As Illustrated by Ancient Remains and the Manners and Customs of Modern Savage*, indigenous people provided the living examples to be compared with the archaeological evidence of 'our' primitive past.

Every social evolutionary typology identifies 'progress' within aspects of the economic, social and religious organization of past societies, leading from savage mobile hunter-gatherers to the hierarchy and specialization of urban civilization (e.g. Morgan, 1877). In fact, all these models reveal an ethnocentric bias of identifying the inequities of colonialism and capitalism (such as hierarchical societies, urban settlements, bureaucratic record keeping, industrialization and trade) as central features of social progress that mark the achievements of civilization. 'Tribal' groups were characterized as primitive because they had not 'achieved' the hierarchical organization and economic exploitation that characterized Europe. Although *The Origin of the Family, Private Property, and the State* (Engels 1884) offered a Marxist critique of the emergence of capitalism, the evolutionary categorization that it adopted also became the dogma of Soviet archaeological and anthropological investigations (Grøn, this volume). The Ainu of Japan, the Selk'nam of Patagonia, the Evenks of Siberia and Australian Aborigines have all been used as models for European and other prehistoric societies. To illustrate Darwin's Theory of Evolution, collectors vied for the body parts of indigenous populations to classify human diversity in museum displays (Fforde, 2004). Even today modern hunter-gatherers are frequently seen as direct analogies for Palaeolithic and Mesolithic societies, despite the fact that present-day hunter-gatherers have been marginalized onto the poorest land by settled agriculturalists, urban growth and industrialization (see Grøn, this volume). But these evolutionary categories were not used consistently, and it is primarily the 'otherness' of the native communities that was being identified. Thus the concept of 'tribe' is usually considered to be a stage during the social evolution from Band through Tribes and Chiefdoms to State societies (e.g. Service, 1962). However, in practice, the same term can be used for the vast Zulu state or small bands of Kung hunter-gatherers and it is used primarily to identify non-Europeans. A large percentage of the public today continue to view terms such as indigenous, aboriginal or tribal as implying a primitive life style. This raises important issues about the role of education and exhibitions in critically debating the connotations and uses of these terms in the past and the present (see below), and requires us to critically consider how we can best use the documents, museum collections and photographs that were created within a social evolutionary framework (see Fiore, this volume).

The people we refer to today as the Ainu were first written about by Japanese sources, referring to the inhabitants of Emishi using the Chinese character *Toi*, which can be translated as 'eastern barbarian'; even the name Ainu has been considered derogatory. In the past the Ainu have been described as descendants of European Stone Age people, and today both Japanese and foreign archaeologists use the Ainu as a parallel for the 10,000-year-old pre-agricultural Jomon. Yet the Ainu (or the Satsumon as archaeologists have named the prehistoric Ainu) were involved in agriculture and in using iron before the expansion of the Japanese state (Crawford and Masakazu, 1987; Fukasawa, 1998: 12–13). This suggests that the Ainu hunter-gatherer life style was partly the result of political pressures from the Wajin who demanded Ainu fishing and craft products. But this image of the Ainu as non-agricultural people is now central to their self-perception, which emphasizes hunting and the bear ceremony (Siddle, 1996: 37) and in this volume Kaori Tahara discusses changes in the aspirations of Ainu, from apparently seeking assimilation within Japanese society to increasingly working to maintain the features that differentiate the Ainu from mainstream Japanese society and preserve their cultural identity (see also Katarina, 1993).

The widespread influence of these social evolutionary ideas, particularly the classification of indigenous groups as the primitive bottom rung on the evolutionary ladder, provided a false legitimacy to a wide range of colonial and national policies. The 'primitive' life style of hunter-gatherers and nomads was, it was assumed, inevitably doomed to extinction; the question for the authorities was, how to manage this transition. The 'Indian Problem' was to be cured by one, or more, of the four major strategies: extermination, intermarriage with Europeans, assimilation by bringing into the national economy as labourers, assimilation through separation and re-education of the children. It is a sad comment on the depth of this colonial legacy that it is precisely the degree of resistance to these policies that is being used to assess indigeneity today. All of these policies were accompanied by the acquisition of much of the land occupied by indigenous groups. The land, like the people, needed to be 'improved' to become productive, so that through mining, planting, grazing and building the land could also contribute to 'progress'. This is the origin of the legal conception of *Territorium Res Nullius* or *terra nullius*, which stated that to be truly owned it was necessary that land be 'improved', whoever failed within some reasonable period to build upon, cultivate or otherwise transform their property from its natural 'state of wilderness' forfeited title to it. An argument that was justified with reference to ethnography and archaeology:

> What perhaps is most impressive in each of the cases we have discussed is this; that the dispossession by a newcomer of a race already in occupation of the soil has marked an upward step in the intellectual progress of mankind. It is not priority of occupation, but the power to utilize, which establishes a claim to the land. (Sollas, 1911: 383, quoted in Bowler, 1992: 728)

In 1810 Chief Justice John Marshall in the USA used *terra nullius* to argue that portions of Native American 'Indian Country' that were not cultivated by indigenous peoples might be construed as unowned and therefore open to claims by settlers. This began to be used as the basis for forming reservations – multiplying the number of Indians by the land they could use 'productively' and declaring this aggregate amount as sufficient for Indian needs, thus 'releasing' any surplus for acquisition by others (Churchill, 2002). The enclosure of land holdings, the mapping of boundaries and the granting of land titles, each of which legitimated the separation of indigenous people from their land, were considered essential aspects of these developments. In Australia the doctrine of *terra nullius* was upheld until as late as 1992 and only now are native title cases being considered by the Australian courts (Sutton, this volume).

DESCENT AND ANCESTRY: BLOOD QUOTAS AND LAND RIGHTS

One response to asking individuals what makes them indigenous is for the speaker to name their parentage back to their grandparents or further. As stated by the Khoi-San at the World Summit on Sustainable Development 'We are the original peoples tied to the land by our umbilical cords and the dust of our ancestors…' (Kimberley Declaration, 2002 – see Ormond-Parker, this volume). The highly emotive language that justifies indigenous peoples' identity claims and their access to their lands through the blood of their ancestors is no different to how the British aristocracy justify their ownership of their estates and inherited titles; indeed descent from one or more common ancestors is one of the strongest ties within human society. Yet, two centuries of anthropological studies of kinship have shown how complex and variable the reckoning of familial allegiance can be. As well as descent, membership of a kin group may also be achieved through marriage and adoption, and the naming and claiming of ancestors is always open to negotiation. Also, the degree to which indigenous societies were integrated or divided prior to colonization is difficult to assess as the processes of colonization and resistance were frequently an impetus for a restructuring of indigenous societies and a strengthening of ethnic identities (Smith, 1986; Shennan, 1989). For instance, Grøn (this volume) mentions how the Russian authorities fostered differences between the ethnic groups in Siberia.

Although many indigenous groups express a strong interest in an individual's parentage or clan membership, this has rarely required proof beyond the aural testimony of the individual and the shared knowledge within the group of lineage reckoning. This is partly the basis of the current approach of government departments in Australia, where indigenous programmes are recognized on the basis of decent, self identity and the community in which someone lives identifying them as indigenous. The current approach is a response to the traumatic history of the 'Stolen Generation' in Australia, which primarily removed children that were thought to be of mixed inheritance – typically those with an Aboriginal mother and a European father – to be socialized into white society. Ward Churchill (1999) claims that in the USA it was the treaties set up by the federal government that first began to use blood purity as an official strategy to differentiate between those who were 'more' and those who were 'less'

Indian. Most Native American groups traditionally intermarried and adopted others such as children and captives into the tribe, including the incorporation of Europeans and Africans during the colonial era. The idea of reckoning indigenous membership in terms of blood purity derives from European concerns over racial differences and attempts to develop 'objective' criteria to classify people for taxation and land allocation. The treaties set up between the USA and the Indian nations between the 1830s and the 1860s 'gave' larger plots of land to those of mixed blood or those who had intermarried with Whites (and were thus expected to farm the land more successfully), whereas 'pure' Indians were given smaller amounts of land that were to be held in common by the tribe (Churchill, 1999: 48–49). In 1887 the General Allotment Act was intended to dissolve this collective ownership of Indian land in favour of individual property rights. The practice of allotting these land-grants focused on a blood quota, with most federal authorities refusing land to anyone that was less than a half-blood member of a specific Indian group; however, while 'mixed bloods' were given their land directly, full-blood Indians were not yet considered competent and, as an interim measure, their land allotment was to be held in trust by local Indian agents for a further quarter century (Churchill, 1999: 49–50). However, in 1934 the Indian Reorganization Act (IRA) legitimated the continuation of Indian reservation lands to be administered by federally designated tribal councils. The IRA constitutions for reservation lands applied the prevailing federal standard to define tribal membership by blood with a quarter-blood usually stated as the minimum. In time, this was reinforced by the tribal councils who felt the need to limit the number of people eligible for health care, benefits and land rights, etc. In 1990 the Act for the Protection of American Indian Arts and Crafts proposed that only people with at least one-quarter Indian blood or enrolled in a federally recognized tribe could describe themselves as 'Indian' for the purpose of authenticating the making and marketing of Native American crafts and artwork (Churchill, 1999). (Similarly when the National Indigenous Arts Advocacy Association (NIAAA) of Australia developed a Label of Authenticity for Aboriginal art in 1999, concerns were raised about how indigenous artists would, or should, validate their 'authenticity' to others.) Thus some Native American concepts of who is, or is not an Indian have gone beyond a flexible concept of tribal membership to internalize some Euro-American concepts of racial purity.

Ward Churchill's (1999) review of the origins and development of blood quota as a measure of authenticity has gained a particular poignancy, as his own claims of Native American ancestry have been called into question in recent months. Churchill is a professor of ethnic studies at the University of Colorado, who has come into greatest prominence through suggesting that the 11 September 2001 attack on the World Trade Center was both a response to and a consequence of US violations of international law, disregard for human rights and violence abroad. Churchill claims descent from both the Keetoowah tribe on his mother's side and the Creeks on his father's. Although the Keetoowah Band requires that: 'a person must be 1/4 degree of Cherokee Indian ancestry or above to be a member of the United Keetoowah Band', in 1994 the Boulder campus chancellor of the University of Colorado concluded that in relation to employment the Universities policy considered self-identification as the most reliable indicator of ethnicity. However Colorado's Standing Committee on Research Misconduct is currently (May 2005) debating whether Professor Churchill has attempted to 'gain a scholarly voice, credibility, and an audience for his scholarship by wrongfully asserting that he is an Indian' (http://www.colorado.edu/news/reports/churchill/report.html).

In Tasmania the assumption that blood purity was central to indigenous status was used to claim that the death of Truganini, the 'last Tasmanian', marked the extinction of Tasmanian Aborigines in 1873. However, in the 1970s, descendents of indigenous Tasmanians who had married white settlers campaigned for the return of Truganini's body, which was eventually cremated in 1976. It is now widely accepted within the Tasmanian community that some 10,000 people have Aboriginal heritage. This has resonances within Fiore's article (this volume) as it is has been claimed that the Yámana Indians from Tierra del Fuego and the Taino Indians of Cuba were also extinct. This may be because it is easier to be sympathetic about the fate of the dead than acknowledge the rights of the living, but when descendents are now geographically spread with diverse life experiences and cultural identities it is also less clear what rights can or should be returned to them.

Lineal descent has gained an added significance within North American archaeology as the Native American Graves Protection and Repatriation Act (NAGPRA) states that human remains and artefacts can be reclaimed if the applicant can show either lineal descent or cultural affiliation with the burial.

> A lineal descendant is an individual tracing his or her ancestry directly and without interruption by means of the traditional kinship system of the appropriate Indian tribe or Native Hawaiian organization or by the common law system of descendence to a known Native American individual whose remains, funerary objects, or sacred objects are being requested under these regulations. This standard requires that the earlier person be identified as an individual whose descendants can be traced. (NAGPRA, 1990: section 10.14)

As Ormond-Parker (this volume) discusses in relation to human remains held within British institutions, claims for repatriation to descendant families are only possible if there is also a full and frank disclosure of all the documentation relating to the collections.

ASSIMILATION VERSUS CONTINUITY: GOING NATIVE IN THE NATION STATE

Another factor that distinguishes indigenous communities from other citizens of a country is continuity of some aspects of their traditional life style. In contrast to this, a major aim of many nation states in the 19th and 20th centuries was to incorporate their citizens within the norms of national society, and frequently the distinctive languages, laws, religions and economies of indigenous peoples were seen as a challenge to this aim. For this reason many nations adopted explicit policies to transform 'undesirable' aspects of native culture and incorporate indigenous people into the national economy. Frequently state education policies have been a primary tool used to bring indigenous children into the norms of national society and modernity (see Arnold and Yapita, this volume). As Tahara Kaori highlights in her discussion of the Ainu (this volume), some indigenous people adopted the aspirations of the time and sought assimilation, however many others worked to maintain indigenous identities through active or passive resistance to these policies. Although indigenous people today articulate with national and world economies, many communities have adapted and maintained aspects of their cultures and some have sought to reaffirm their identities by retrieving abandoned traditions. But while the more traditional San of Southern Africa are able to use their distinctive life style and dress to argue for land rights and local self-governance, those San who have been incorporated into the urban economy and class segregation do not fit into essentialist models of indigenous groups; the rural and urban San have been able to combine resources in developing a pan-San indigenous movement but their distinctive histories and aspirations also raise tensions (Sylvain, 2002).

One of the most devastating influences on indigenous cultures has been the forced removal of children from their families, such as the Indian boarding schools of the USA where separation from Native American families was accompanied by a ban on speaking native languages and wearing indigenous dress, and where indigenous beliefs and histories were replaced by the doctrines of Christianity as well as forced labour. By the 1920s approximately 80% of Native American children in the USA were sent to boarding schools to be acculturated away from family and tribal influences (Hurst Thomas, 2000). Similarly from the 1800s till as recently as the 1960s, over 100,000 Aboriginal children were systematically removed from their parents and placed with white families in a policy that was actively supported by the British and Australian governments. Article II of the convention on the Prevention and Punishment of the Crime of Genocide, adopted by the United Nations in 1948, includes the forcible transfer of children from one group to another in its definition of genocide. In May 1995 the Australian National Inquiry into the past and present practices of separation of Aboriginal and Torres Strait Islander children from their families was established, supporting a very wide-ranging re-appraisal of the treatment of Aborigines in Australia. The resulting books recording individual experiences and reactions to the history of the Stolen Generations have recently been recognized as one of nine significant items of documentary heritage inscribed as Australia's contribution to UNESCO's Programme to protect and promote documentary material.

Where indigenous communities maintain continuities with earlier cultural practices these are often in spite of colonial policies that either removed indigenous people from their land and their families or marginalized them on poor quality reservation lands. It is therefore particularly ironic that it is now becoming a feature of legal battles for indigenous land rights in both Canada and Australia that the courts seek evidence for continuities in social, economic and religious practices within indigenous communities to justify rights of access to land (Leclair, Sutton, this volume). In a reversal of the assimilation policies of earlier periods, indigenous peoples now gain rights by asserting their cultural distinctiveness. Archaeologists, anthropologists and historians may be drawn in to identify evidence of continuity of cultural practices. Similarly the request for the return of human remains under the Native American Graves Protection and Repatriation Act of the USA stipulates that the applicant has to show some aspect of continuity of cultural affiliation in order to claim the remains. These claims can use the following types of evidence: 'Geographical, kinship, biological, archaeological, anthropological, linguistic, folklore, oral tradition, historical or other relevant information or expert opinion' (NAGPRA, 1990: section 10.14).

Archaeologists, anthropologists and heritage professionals could all have an important role to play in supporting indigenous efforts to maintain cultural continuity through promoting local languages (Arnold and Yapita, this volume), developing relevant aspects of indigenous economic activities (Kendall, this volume) educating future generations about their culture and history (Ramos Lopes, Abungu, this volume). Such efforts at maintaining and revitalizing indigenous culture are upheld as a right under the UN's Draft Declaration on the Rights of Indigenous Peoples (Article 12). While many museums played an important role in the nation building of the 19th and 20th centuries, Abungu (this volume) asserts their potential in revitalizing an interest in local cultural traditions for future generations of African children.

CONFLICT WITH THE NATION STATE

Many nation states emerged within the context of liberal reform where the descendents of the original colonizers demanded to be freed from the economic and legal control of the colonial power. In many areas, such as Peru and Bolivia, once independence had been achieved new laws were enacted that consolidated settlers' land ownership, and removed much of the authority of native leaders and the distinctive legal protection extended to native communities in an effort to draw them into the national economy. For this reason any demand to 'indigenous rights' is inherently a challenge to National Sovereignty because it is a claim of primacy and a demand to rights that pre-date the forming of the modern state, its national laws, and the written titles of land ownership (see Leclair, and Sutton, this volume).

At the time of independence 'Indian Title' was well-recognized by the founding fathers of the USA and Thomas Jefferson (1793) conceded that 'The Indians [have] full, undivided and independent sovereignty as long as they choose to keep it, and ... this might be forever'; only the voluntary sale of title or concessions given through treaties could extinguish title or sovereignty (Catanzariti, 1992: 272). However, in 1831, Chief Justice John Marshall made a rather different ruling in the case of the *Cherokee v. Georgia*. After conceding that the arguments 'intended to prove the character of the Cherokees as a state, as a distinct political society, separated from others, capable of governing itself, has ... been completely successful', Marshall went on to observe:

> Though the Indians are acknowledged to have an unquestionable and, heretofore, unquestioned right to the lands they occupy until that right shall be extinguished by a voluntary cession to our government, yet it may well be doubted whether those tribes which reside within the acknowledged boundaries of the United States can, with strict accuracy, be denominated foreign nations. They may more correctly, perhaps, be denominated domestic dependent nations. They occupy a territory to which we assert a title independent of their will, which must take effect in point of possession when their right of possession ceases. Meanwhile, they are in a state of pupilage. Their relation to the United States resembles that of a ward to his guardian. (Marshal, 1831)

Although it could be argued that the very existence of a treaty suggests that both nations were equivalent sovereign states, this ruling clearly expresses the 'problem' that the newly formed Nation of the United States had in dealing with claims for self-determination within their national boundaries. These arguments remain pertinent to the power and authority of the native nations within the USA and were recently quoted by Justice Thomas in relation to the case of the US v. Billy Jo Lara, where he concluded 'The Court should admit that it has failed in its quest to find a source of congressional power to adjust tribal sovereignty. ... We might find that the Federal Government cannot regulate the tribes through ordinary domestic legislation and simultaneously maintain that the tribes are sovereigns in any meaningful sense. But until we begin to analyze these questions honestly and rigorously, the confusion that I have identified will continue to haunt our cases' (Thomas, 2004: 13).

When national institutions and laws fail, indigenous peoples may try to use international bodies to place pressure on their national government to recognize their 'indigenous' status (see Ormond Parker, and Tahara, this volume). Organizations such as the United Nations are in the process of generating international norms that seek to define and protect the rights that indigenous people should have over their cultural practices and material heritage. Through this process a new generation of indigenous peoples has grown up who are knowledgeable and competent in the areas of international diplomacy and legislation. However, one of the great hopes of the United Nations International Decade of the World's Indigenous People, which ended in December 2004, was the adoption of an international declaration for the protection and promotion of indigenous peoples' human rights. The working group met for its 10th session in Geneva in September 2004, but the adoption of the declaration was blocked by several governments. Two of the major sticking points have been Article 3: 'Indigenous peoples have the right of self-determination. By virtue of that right they freely determine their political status and freely pursue their economic, social and cultural development' and references in several places within the draft treaty to the collective rights of indigenous peoples. These demands to self-determination, collective rights and indigenous law are seen as a particular challenge to the authority of the nation state (Arnold and Yapita, this volume). The United Kingdom's government has been accused of acting in concert with the USA, Canada, New Zealand and Australia to prevent the concept of collective rights being enshrined in the declaration (Whall, 2002). To date no indigenous group has made any serious attempt to succeed from the nation states within which they have been incorporated; on the contrary, indigenous groups have largely worked through the legal frameworks of their nation states, relying on the moral pressure of international agreements and media coverage to place pressure on their governments and judicial systems to recognize indigenous rights (see Leclair, Sutton, Ormond-Parker, Tahara, this volume).

ANCESTRAL LANDS: WHO CONTROLS INDIGENOUS HERITAGE?

In recent years indigenous activism at national and international levels has led to a renewed focus on indigenous rights and the return of land to indigenous groups in many parts of the world. This has resulted in several prominent court cases, although providing strong evidence for a legal case that can demonstrate specific links between present-day indigenous groups and the pre-colonial occupants of the land is complicated (Leclair, Sutton, this volume). It is widely recognized that attributing artefact groups or 'archaeological cultures' to specific peoples in the past, and then to their living descendents today, is extremely difficult and politically risky (Shennan, 1989: Jones, 1997). This has enormous implications for the use of archaeological evidence and the testimony of archaeologists in court. Leclair describes how Bruce Trigger's advice that archaeologists should not accept oral histories uncritically, was applied in a very different context when it was cited extensively to undermine the use of oral tradition during a legal challenge to First Nation land claims in Canada. In another case, Richter's interpretation of archaeological evidence relating to Five Nations trading practices across the St Lawrence River became central to a legal claim over the right to continue cross-border international trade unhindered by importation duties (Leclair, this volume). No archaeologist can predict how their research, analysis and interpretation will be used by others, but archaeologists need to be more considerate of the wider forum within which our work may be used. At the other end of the scale some anthropologists and archaeologists have worked actively with indigenous groups to support their claims, and Leclair also points out that within a court of law this may mean that these individuals will lose their potential status as expert witness because they have become too associated with the plaintiff's cause. An archaeologist's or anthropologist's primary duty to the well-being and care of the people they are working with may be best served by the clear reporting of evidence and the sensitive interpretations of their situation, but not by pushing ambiguous data to their interpretative limits.

The 'old' nations of Europe have frequently drawn upon their distinctive pasts to develop a sense of national unity, and during the process of gaining independence from colonial powers many 'new' nation states appropriated the heritage of their indigenous peoples as emblems of the state. This can be seen with regard to how Peru has portrayed the Inka as symbolic precursors of the modern nation state, how Mexico has adopted symbolism from the Aztecs and the Maya, or Rhodesia was transformed into the nation of Zimbabwe. For Bolivia it has been the site and culture of Tiwanaku that has provided the key symbols for nation building and, in this volume, Arnold and Yapita discuss some of the tensions that this raises for indigenous Bolivians who also identify with Tiwanaku and have revived ceremonies at the site and recently campaigned to return one of the enormous monolithic statues from the national capital of La Paz back to Tiwanaku. Similarly, Endere describes a revival of indigenous ceremonies and rituals at 'national monuments' in Argentina, and on some occasions the indigenous groups demand exclusive use of the sites so that these rituals can be undertaken in secret. Endere also discusses changes in law, policy and approach to indigenous heritage in Argentina, debating the important question of who owns and manages 'national' heritage when it is within the territory of specific indigenous groups and seen as 'their' heritage. This may include sites that were not previously known about by the group or necessarily constructed by their ancestors. For instance the three and a half million year old hominid tracks in the volcanic ash at Laetoli, Tanzania, discovered by Mary Leakey, have been adopted by the local Masai who revere them and guard them on behalf of the Antiquities Unit of Tanzania (Stanley-Price, 2000).

It should be remembered that the 'conservation' of some World Heritage Sites and National Parks has been achieved by removing indigenous inhabitants. Many National Parks were created to preserve 'wildernesses', a concept similar to that of *terra nullius* that assumes a lack of permanent buildings and fences meant that the land was unaffected by the presence of humans and would be better protected by removing indigenous residents and preventing nomadic groups from using the area. For instance, Yellowstone National Park was created by expelling the resident Shoshone, and Blackfeet were removed from Glacier National Park, helping to develop an approach that has been exported to many other parts of the world (Spence, 1999). The conservation of archaeological sites and landscapes and their recognition as National or World Heritage has occasionally resulted in the removal of ownership and control from the local population who originally constructed them and previously maintained them (Endere, this volume). It is not surprising that indigenous people sometimes consider earlier archaeological work to have been little more than legalized grave robbing and land grabbing with the support and authority of national legislation to back it up (Watkins, this volume). This insult is compounded when information at the site describes the people who built and used it in some period of deep prehistory without discussing any links with the cultural traditions and the concerns of the living communities (Endere, this volume). In 2000 the Timbisha Shoshone Indians of California and Nevada regained 7600 acres of land, some of it within Death Valley National Park, to be held in trust by the USA for the benefit of the Tribe in recognition of 'the contributions by the Tribe to the history, culture, and ecology of the Park and surrounding area' (Timbisha Shoshone Act, 2000). The Tribe and the National Park Service will manage the Park land co-operatively, including a provision to temporally close parts of the park when the tribe wish to carry out traditional cultural and religious activities. This is the first time that Native American ownership has been recognized within a National Park and Congress also stated that portions of lands previously designated as 'wilderness' would be recognized as Timbisha Shoshone Natural and Cultural Preservation Area.

At the centre of these debates is the question of how national bodies that own, manage and/or publicize 'national' heritage can work with indigenous groups to include concerns about ownership and access to 'their' heritage. This may require a dualistic approach such as that of Norway, where successive Cultural Heritage Acts since 1978 have included legal protection for any Saami cultural remains over 100 years old, whereas most historical remains must be older than the reformation in 1537 to be given automatic protection. Or they may relate to specific territories such as Nunavut, Canada's newest and largest territory, established in 1999 to be a homeland for the Inuit, where the conservation of the archaeological heritage comes under the remit of the Department of Culture, Language, Elders and Youth, which aims to create 'a territory of strong, self sufficient communities that reflect traditional values and culture'. In relationship to World Heritage Sites the idea of an Indigenous Peoples Council of Experts was presented to the 24th session of the World Heritage Committee by representatives from Australia, Canada and New Zealand. The initiative was taken by indigenous peoples wishing greater involvement in the development and implementation of laws, policies and plans for the protection of their knowledge, traditions and cultural values relating to their ancestral lands, within sites now designated as World Heritage properties. This proposal was turned down by UNESCO's World Heritage Committee in December 2001; however, the debate about how to include indigenous peoples has had some influence on UNESCO's Convention for the Safeguarding of the Intangible Cultural Heritage adopted in 2003. This defines intangible cultural heritage as

> the practices, representations, expressions, as well as the knowledge and skills, that communities, groups and, in some cases, individuals recognise as part of their cultural heritage. It is sometimes called living cultural heritage, and is manifested inter alia in the following domains: oral traditions and expressions, including language as a vehicle of the intangible cultural heritage; performing arts; social practices, rituals and festive events; knowledge and practices concerning nature and the universe; traditional craftsmanship. The intangible cultural heritage is transmitted from generation to generation, and is constantly recreated by communities and groups, in response to their environment, their interaction with nature, and their historical conditions of existence. It provides people with a sense of identity and continuity, and its safeguarding promotes, sustains, and develops cultural diversity and human creativity. (UNESCO, 2003)

OWNERSHIP AND COPYRIGHT: WHO OWNS INDIGENOUS KNOWLEDGE?

There is currently a heated debate over the rights indigenous peoples should have to own and protect their resources, including genetic materials, artistic designs, music, ceremonies, artefacts or sacred sites. These issues have been debated particularly strongly within the World Intellectual Property Organization (WIPO), which has been discussing the protection, promotion and preservation of traditional cultural expressions for at least two decades. However, this debate has not yet resulted in a consensual policy at WIPO, largely because it raises major challenges in relation to most copyright law. The Western ideal of 'invention' identifies adaptations in creative art or technical advancement as individual originality. Copyright laws have been formulated to protect the innovative creations of specific authors for a prescribed period in order that the author can gain economic benefit from their innovation. This can be contrasted with those indigenous groups who consider the making of art or the breeding of plants and animals as a communal obligation. Here individual creativity may be acknowledged, but it is also the individual's duty to preserve the communal resource through appropriate use and by passing it on to succeeding generations within the group with an emphasis placed upon protecting customary knowledge and skills and occasionally restricting who uses them. However, copyright law has been developed to encourage rapid innovation, not to restrict access to collectively owned traditional knowledge and protect it from inappropriate borrowing (Blakeney, 1999).

Perhaps the best known of these debates has been in relation to Aboriginal art in Australia. The form and style of Aboriginal art may be constrained by other members of the community to prevent the misuse or misrepresentation of the imagery, particularly where the designs are sacred or meaningful within a specific context. Aboriginal artists are free to create original pieces of commercial work, but the style and content of certain images may belong to a specific group and the context and use of the images may be constrained by traditional rules. Although there has been a long history of misuse and unauthorized reproduction of works of Aboriginal art, a number of cases in the Australian courts have extended some protection to Aboriginal artists through the Copyright Act. In 1988 Johnny Bulun Bulun and 13 others sued a T-shirt manufacturer who had used their designs. Although this case did not proceed to judgement, the out-of-court settlement for US$150,000 was widely reported. In 1994 the copying of an Aboriginal design to decorate carpets led to a court case in which a large award of damages established that copying a part or the whole of an Aboriginal work was a copyright infringement. However, it was the view of the recently disbanded Aboriginal and Torres Strait Islander Commission that, despite these developments, effective protection of indigenous intellectual property was beyond the scope of existing laws. Problems with the application of copyright law can be seen in the case of The Reserve Bank of Australia being sued by the Galpu clan for using the design of a morning star pole on a commemorative banknote. Although the pole had been created by an initiated member of the clan, the Galpu asserted that the artist was under obligation to the clan to prevent the design of the pole from being used in inappropriate contexts. In this case the Judge expressed sympathy for the Clan's concerns, but stated that Australia's copyright law did not provide adequate recognition of Aboriginal community claims to regulate the reproduction and use of works that are essentially communal in origin (Blakeney, 1999). As another example, Blakeney (1999) discusses the painted images of the Wandjina, the Creation Ancestors of the Kimberley Aboriginal People, which form a notable part of the Kimberley area rock art. These images may be retouched or painted today, provided that appropriate deference is given to the ancient spirits. Although the Kimberley Aborigines believe that inappropriate treatment of these images will cause death and devastation, there is currently no law to prevent the use of these images by commercial enterprises.

Knowledge about 'wild' plants with specific properties has been maintained within many indigenous communities, similarly crops and animals have been nurtured and developed during the thousands of years of labour involved in their domestication. This raises the question as to who should have the right to control or own modifications of these in the future. The 1975 European Patent Convention forbade the patenting of plant varieties both because small changes in plant varieties could not be easily patented as 'inventions' and because the freedom of farmers to breed and develop plant varieties was considered essential for food security and crop protection. The European Patent Office (EPO) started to grant some patents on plants and animals in the early 1990s, but in 1995 Greenpeace successfully brought a case against a patent on GM plants and the EPO's Court of Appeal confirmed its original ruling that plant varieties could not be patented. In 1998, in response to pressure from the biotech industry, the European Union (completely separate from the EPO) enacted a directive that explicitly allowed the patenting of living organisms, such as plants and animals (Directive 98/44/EC on the legal protection of biotechnological inventions) in direct conflict with those of the European Patent Convention. Restrictions on the patentability of plant varieties are not present in the patent laws of the USA, Japan or Australia. Previously, directives from Trade-Related Intellectual Property Rights (part of the World Trade Organization) required all countries to extend their patenting to include micro-organisms and microbiological processes, but permitted countries to exclude plants and animals and stipulated two major exceptions – breeders should be allowed free access to registered varieties during the period of experimentation, and farmers should be allowed to reproduce varieties for seed and even to sell the seed as long as this was not the main business of the farm. However, further revisions in 1991 to the International Agreement on Plant-Variety Protection (UPOV) allow nations to revoke either of these exemptions and in 1994 the US eliminated the farmer's exemption (Brush and Strabinsky, 1996: 15). Recently farmers in the USA have been obliged to sign contracts that forbid them from replanting the seed they have grown, and Monsanto have taken farmers to court for re-sowing Roundup Ready Soybeans and even crops that have hybridized with their strains. Apparently unaware of George Washington's advice 'It is miserable for a farmer to be obliged to buy his Seeds; to exchange Seeds may, in some cases, be useful; but to buy them after the first year is disreputable.' (George Washington to his farm manager William Pearce, 16 November 1791). Multinational seed companies have used patenting law to gain rights over traditional crops; sometimes forcing farmers to pay for growing crop varieties based on local domesticates (Shetty, 2005), such 'improved' varieties are usually dependent on the use of expensive chemical fertilizers and pesticides (Kendall, this volume).

However, many indigenous and small-scale farmers have resisted these movements. For instance, the Bolivian government's attempt to introduce a Genetically Modified potato strain resistant to Cyst Nematode was thwarted by protest from politically active peasant farmers, who demanded that greater attention be paid to existing local varieties. At a meeting in Mexico in November 2004, environmental activists and indigenous representatives complained that the 15 research centres of the Consultative Group for International Agricultural Research, who hold seed banks of all the main crop varieties in the world, were building overly strong links with large biotechnology corporations giving them free access to indigenous crop varieties that were being genetically modified to develop expensive commercial strains. Perhaps in response to the protest in Mexico, the International Potato Centre (CIP) in Lima, Peru, recently returned commercial rights over potato varieties to Quechua-speaking farming communities. The 206 potato varieties will be 'repatriated' from CIP's collections to be maintained in a 'potato park'. As well as providing food for the six communities that jointly own the land in southern Peru, the 15,000 ha park will serve as a 'living library' of potato genetic diversity (Shetty, 2005). The agreement, which is the first of its kind, aims to ensure that the control of genetic resources is kept with local people, that it does not become subject to intellectual property rights in any form, and that the diversity of Peruvian potato varieties is maintained. This could lead to similar deals elsewhere to return rights in major crops to the communities that domesticated them. While archaeologists have been very vocal about the trade in antiquities (which impacts on our own resource and livelihood) we have largely ignored the important political implications of our research into domestication, offering little criticism of commercial companies that have claimed ownership of indigenous crop varieties through relatively minor changes.

These arguments over copyright have also affected the ongoing debates about the ownership of human remains. Ormond-Parker (this volume) describes how the Australian Law Commission, following an earlier ruling in Britain, have overturned earlier assumptions that the human corpse was not an object of property and declared that body parts and DNA may be retained by institutions that have modified the sample through their skills and expert work. Like GM crops, access to the technical skills can be a route to claim the originality and inventiveness that justifies ownership, an argument that seems to echo previous claims that indigenous people's lands were *terra nullius* and could be claimed by settlers able and willing to 'improve' them using 'alien' technologies. Ormond-Parker considers the argument that genetic research may have benefits far beyond the indigenous community, but he highlights how rarely indigenous people have gained any benefit from such research. Only when indigenous people have given their 'free, prior, and informed consent' can such research be justified.

Conflicts over the ownership of human remains and artefacts, particularly grave goods, are now a familiar issue within archaeology and museum practice (Fforde *et al*., 2002). One of the best-reported examples has been the ongoing work to repatriate the Zuni *Ahayu:da* (the 'twin deities' *Uyuyemi* and *Maia'sewi*). The Zuni believe that after formal use these cylindrical wooden sculptures should be allowed to disintegrate and return to the land, their removal and conservation in museums was considered to be a major cause of tribal decline. The Zuni were prepared to take a long-term approach to retrieving the *Ahayu:da*, negotiating with museums and collectors for their return and arranging a secure facility for their retention (Merrill *et al*., 1993; Ferguson *et al*., 2000). In this volume Edward Halealoha Ayau describes the reasons for reclaiming four wooden sculptures that had been removed from the burial cave of a high-ranking Hawaiian chief. These ancestral deities, *ki`i aumākua*, had been part of a funerary assemblage in a burial cave and were removed from the cave to the Bishop Museum in 1905. *Hui Mālama I Na Kūpuna O Hawai'i Nei* (Group Caring For the Ancestors of Hawai'i) placed the *ki`i aumākua* back in the original cave. Sadly this cave has since been desecrated a second time and many of the funerary items were removed again. This raises important questions about the need to secure repatriated artefacts to prevent further theft. In other cases the communal ownership of artefacts and their return to indigenous owners has been upheld and protected by the law. For instance, the Aymara people of Coroma, Bolivia, own a wide range of ancient fine ceremonial weavings, which have been used to defend community land claims (Bubba, 1997; Arnold and Yapita, this volume), and the responsibility for caring for these rotates among families who take on positions of authority in the community. In the late 1970s, a number of these sacred garments were sold by individual community members put under pressure by North American art dealers. As both the USA and Bolivia are parties to the UNESCO conventions on cultural property, which prohibit commerce in items that are held communally and constitute spiritual and cultural patrimony, the sale by individual community members was deemed illegal and the items were eventually returned to Coroma (Zamora, 1996).

There is a widely accepted ethic that archaeologists have a duty to promote public access to sites and publish the results of their research; this ethic is particularly strong both because the research is frequently publicly funded and because the process of excavation destroys evidence. For instance, the Society for American Archaeology stresses that archaeologists should 'advocate use of the archaeological record for the benefit of all people' (SAA, 1996). But, this ethic is challenged by indigenous groups, who assert that access to sacred sites or ritual knowledge is an exclusive right belonging to certain members of the indigenous group. For instance, the Hopi have prevented the release of archaeological and oral history reports for scholarly research or public interest, restricting them to use within the tribe (Ferguson *et al.*, 1995). The prevention of public dissemination of confidential information can also be endorsed by the court, for instance in 1976 the Australian court prevented the sale of the book *Nomads of the Desert* by the anthropologist Dr Mountford, which included descriptions and photographs of Pitjantjatjara sites, artefacts, totemic geography and art. The court believed that disseminating this information was a breach of confidence and it went on to state that 'revelation of the secrets to their women, children and uninitiated men may undermine the social and religious stability of their hard-pressed community' (McDonald, 1997). Here, indigenous desires to retain ownership of knowledge conflicts with our ethic to promote the public dissemination of knowledge (Tarlow, 2001).

MAINTAINING CULTURE OR PRESERVING MATERIAL CULTURE?

Archaeologists, heritage managers and conservators all profess as a primary aim their intention to preserve the material remains of the past. This can be compared with the continuing struggle of most indigenous people to preserve their culture. Frequently these two approaches are very closely allied, with archaeologists and indigenous groups working closely together to preserve ancient sites. However, there are times when the potential shared interests of these groups are confronted by somewhat different priorities. In this volume Wharton describes how indigenous responses to conservation have sometimes objected to the focus upon preparing objects for static display rather than for cultural use, but he also highlights how museums have frequently preserved the patina and damage on indigenous remains, whereas European paintings, weavings and sculptures are restored to the original glory of the 'artists intent'. These differences in conservation practice appear to reflect a bias in how museums represent indigenous and Western cultures.

There may be times when the priorities of indigenous communities will seem at odds with our concerns to preserve the vestiges of past activities. In Sri Lanka a statue of the Buddha, which had been defiled by a tourist sitting on it, was 'restored' by washing it with milk, a process that removed centuries-old painted decoration (Wijesuriya, personal communication, 2001). Those of us concerned for the preservation of the evidence of past activities may be horrified by this, but this act of ritual purification is understood to have restored the statue back to its divine state (cf. Wijesuriya, 2001). Wharton highlights how various indigenous groups may have extremely different ideas about what should and what should not be conserved for posterity, and there are also differences of opinion within indigenous communities. Ayau (this volume) echoes the Zuni in stating that 'our duty is to assure that the *iwi kū puna* and *moepū* (ancestral remains and funerary items) are properly buried and protected so that the centuries-long process of deterioration and eventual absorption back into the land may take place undisturbed, so that the cycle of life can be renewed'. As Ayau acknowledges his recovery of traditional Hawaiian *indigenous* views on cultural 'conservation' processes (the removal of funerary goods from the defilement of public display in museums to be entombed again within the sacred context of a burial cave) may be described as 'destruction' by *Western* notions of 'conservation' of the material fabric of art and artefacts, but he considers it an obligation to his ancestors to restore funerary items to their original context, and in so doing help to preserve Native Hawaiian cultural values. However, the act of removing the wooden sculptures from the Bishop Museum was not considered desirable by all indigenous Hawaiians, some of whom argued that the preservation of the statutes was an opportunity to educate their children about Native Hawaiian culture. While Ayau argues that the only way to revive and maintain Hawaiian culture is to respect the intentions of the ancestors, others see the survival of the ancestral statues within the museum as a potential focus for young Hawaiians to see the achievements of their ancestors and nurture a desire to maintain their culture. A very similar situation is described by Watkins (this volume) with regard to the artefacts recovered from excavations in the Spiro Mounds, Oklahoma, where the Caddo tribe (who would wish to display the artefacts to educate their children) and the Wichita (who would choose to rebury them) have equivalent claims to be the descendents of the people who originally made and buried them.

The complex relationship between conserving artefacts and maintaining culture resonates through Kendall's article (this volume). Kendall had no doubt that it was more important to bring Native Andean agricultural systems back into active use by rebuilding them, and she was able to persuade the Peruvian National Institute of Culture that it would be better to reconstruct the Inka canals and terraces rather than preserve the partial archaeological remains. This is combined with an appreciation of the appropriateness of indigenous technology, using local materials and techniques that can be economically maintained by community members willing to contribute their labour. In Andean communities the maintenance of canal systems has traditionally been a major focus for rituals and a reaffirmation of community organizations (Isbell, 1985), and Kendall describes how the archaeological project's renovation of a disused canal system also provided a renewed focus for social cohesion within the community. However, there is a further issue: the intensified agricultural production results in increased yields, just as it would have done for the Inka, but it is labour intensive and the 21st century economy does not value the produce as highly. Maintaining or reviving indigenous cultural practices may be as important as conserving ancient artefacts, but it is only feasible if it is socially desirable and economically viable for the modern community.

Museums have traditionally been repositories for artefacts removed from their original cultural context. However, more recently museums have emerged as an additional locus for indigenous identity, and their collections and exhibitions can play a very active role in the maintenance or revival of indigenous culture, customs and crafts. Museums that incorporate the intentions behind UNESCO's Convention for the Safeguarding of the Intangible Cultural Heritage into their function may see a major role for themselves in maintaining skills and design practices for future generations. In this volume Ramos Lopes discusses how the creation of an ethnographic museum in the Amazon became a major focus for the cultural identity and activism of the Ticuna Indians. His account describes how this museum was a powerful source of indigenous pride and affirmative action, but that it was also seen as a threat by settler society at a time when the Ticuna were working to retain and regain some of their landholdings. In this case it was the Brazilian State military that provided essential protection to the Ticuna. The museum also provided a focus for the development of international relations and helped to draw attention to the Ticuna cause. Abungu describes a similar role for museums in Africa, but she highlights that museums will have to change if they are to support community involvement. Museums have tended to treat their own collections as 'sacred objects', restricting access to the curatorial priests and initiated researchers and excluding visitors from contact with the artefacts through prominent display of the sacred prohibition 'do not touch'. Similarly indigenous beliefs can also impose taboos about who should see or handle particular items held in museum collections (such as some Australian Aboriginal bull roarers). There is obviously a need to be creative in rethinking which restrictions matter and how the display and/or the active use of artefacts can help to retain their cultural significance. For instance, recently the Cambridge Museum of Archaeology and Anthropology accessioned a set of Naga shamanic equipment; however, the ownership of this collection continues to reside with the Naga who can request the return of the equipment when it is needed and who have imposed conditions upon the museum as to which items can be stored or displayed together and which must be kept apart (Anita Herle, personal communication, 1994).

REPRESENTATION OF INDIGENOUS PEOPLES: WHO SPEAKS FOR WHOM?

Indigenous peoples have frequently been delimited, defined and displayed by external authorities, so it is no surprise that indigenous representatives at Suva reacted against further external definitions and stated: 'We assert our inherent right to define who we are. We do not approve of any other definition'. But, such assertive statements, and their use of highly emotive language to make political demands, may be challenged on the grounds that it is frequently unclear as to who has the authority to speak for indigenous groups. Different groups have diverse traditions for selecting leaders and spokespersons. Like internal indigenous legal systems these may not conform to national norms of democratic election. For instance, as Arnold and Yapita (this volume) briefly mention in relation to Bolivian Ayllus, there may be distinct gender structures and a heavy reliance on kinship alliances. Some groups have developed more recent representative organizations in the form of NGOs or cultural associations, whereas others have never recovered internal structures of governance appropriate to the shifting nature of their populations since the colonial impact and are largely represented by activist individuals or external aid agencies. Arnold and Yapita describe some of the tensions between traditional community elders and political activists of urban groups in Bolivia today.

Hui Mālama I Nā Kūpuna O Hawai'i Nei (Group Caring For the Ancestors of Hawai'i) was formed in December 1988 by Native Hawaiians to protest against the archaeological disinterment of over 1000 burials in preparation for the construction of a Ritz Carlton Hotel. More recently, the Bishop Museum has suggested that it may also request to be recognized as a Native Hawaiian organization pursuant to NAGPRA. The Bishop Museum, founded in 1891 in the name of the Princess Pauahi Bishop, whose collections it contains, has acted as steward of the Native Hawaiian collections and some of its staff (although not the current director) are Native Hawaiians. Ayau has protested at the conflict of interest that will be inherent if a museum that is a repository of Native Hawaiian collections is also the critical monitor of appropriate cultural practice (Ayau, 2004). Who can judge the degree to which either of these organizations are representative of Native Hawaiians, living or dead?

But what of archaeologists and anthropologists, who are sometimes placed in the privileged position of 'experts' on indigenous cultures within court cases? In some cases their professional training gives them an ability to sum up a variety of data and describe patterns in behaviour or material culture in a way that the courts will accept as relevant (Sutton, this volume). But, unless trained in forensic work, few of us would feel prepared to present our academic work in such a context. This has been particularly frustrating for some indigenous groups, which have had to request or pay 'experts' to present their own culture to the courts. Frequently, changes in the law have benefited the experts in providing further work. For instance, NAGPRA resulted in paid employment for archaeologists and curators in registering Native American collections; similarly Tahara (this volume) describes how the Act to promote Ainu culture has created more work for academics. It can be little surprise that indigenous groups have frequently preferred to use moral pressure or media publicity rather than the much more expensive and time-consuming route of the courts (Ormond-Parker, this volume), such as the Kayapo's successful use of media interest in themselves and their confrontation with miners and loggers to pressurize the Brazilian government and the World Bank to change policies and help to protect a series of reserves totalling roughly the area of Scotland (Turner, 1992).

The public perception of indigenous people has largely been constructed through the writings, drawings, photographs and collections used to create museum displays, films and publications. Today we all 'consume' images of indigenous people through magazines, television programmes, music and the tourist industries. These representations may be produced by indigenous peoples, have the co-operative involvement of indigenous peoples or be produced by external agencies, but whoever produces them there are further issues about who controls the representations, who distributes them and who benefits from them.

Alan Ereira (this volume) discusses the production and editing of his influential film *From the Heart of the World* and his deliberate attempt to be true to the intentions lying behind the Kogi's original request to be filmed by highlighting their isolated status in relation to wider Columbian society and their request to us, 'the younger brother', to respect and protect their cultural traditions, their environment and their isolation. Ereira acknowledges that he sometimes deliberately excluded a few disruptive details (such as a shot of saplings growing in *coca cola* cans (personal comment 2002)) and agreed to Kogi suggestions (such as the use of a newly constructed gate to represent the gulf between 'us' and 'them') to make the film much more true to the Kogi's own vision that the film should be deliberately advocatory. The wide-ranging effects of this film have included the setting up of the Tairona Heritage Trust, which used its resources to help buy-out recent settlers to provide land for the Kogi until such time as the Colombian state also came to support this policy (Ereira). However, since the making of the film the situation in the Sierra has changed fundamentally, with paramilitaries and the army vying for control of the region, although this did not gain international media attention until eight tourists were kidnapped at the end of 2003. The film also contributed to the public image of indigenous peoples as being respectful of the environment. The image of indigenous peoples as guardians of the environment may have contributed to some of their enhanced political power in recent years (Leclair, this volume), but it is just as dangerous and partial as the previous stereotype of the primitive savage. The archaeological record attests to large-scale processes of deforestation, soil erosion and occasional faunal extinctions brought about by human activities throughout much of the world prior to European colonization (Bahn and Flenley, 1992). Yet many indigenous groups do have a close engagement with their land and are understandably critical of the impact of large-scale agriculture, industrialization, mining, dams and pollution. In some cases indigenous technology and land management was more productive and able to sustain a larger population prior to the impact of colonization and the imposition of European agricultural techniques (Uribe Botero, 2005–07; Kendall, this volume). The question facing archaeologists, museums and the media is how to explore these issues in a nuanced and critical way that includes the presentation of indigenous people's views without constructing false stereotypes – and all within the short space of a newspaper article, a display case or a short documentary. As the Kogi now have access to equipment to make their own films through the 'Indigenous Media Project' it will be instructive to see if they choose to present an idealized vision of traditional Kogi society or if, like films made by other indigenous groups, they focus more strongly on active identity construction and areas where they are in conflict with local and national society (Turner, 1992). The process of creating and disseminating films and other representations is now an active aspect of many indigenous groups contributing to the maintenance and change of society, and Turner (1992: 7) reports that some of the younger Kayapo chiefs gained their chieftainship partly because of the renown and mediating skills they developed as camerapersons.

Public archaeology is primarily concerned with promoting access to sites, artefacts and information about the past. But, when dealing with the past and the present of indigenous peoples, the usual concerns over who decides what to display and who has access to the display become ever more pertinent. Every museum exhibition, whatever its overt subject, inevitably draws on the cultural assumptions of the people who make it. For this reason more and more exhibitions are being produced in close co-operation with representatives from diverse groups, in order to encourage self-critical internal discourse prior to finalizing the exhibit. The collections within museums are the primary resource and *raison d'être* for most museums, but they are also a problematic inheritance when it was precisely these objects that were used to construct earlier representations of indigenous groups as 'primitive'. For this reason many museums are reconsidering how they use these problematic collections and how their displays will be understood and received by different audiences today. Perhaps one of the most well-known examples of this issue has been the full-sized figures modelled on the bodies of Khoisan living in Cape Town in 1910, that were used in a representation of bushmen around a camp fire at the Cape Town Museum. The museum became increasingly embarrassed by the evolutionary stereotypes that it was displaying, but the popularity and historical significance of the display meant that the figures could not simply be disposed of and needed to be re-contextualized (Lane, 1996; Davison, 2001). The same issue of re-evaluating images that were created at the time of social evolutionary dogma confronts Danie Fiore in her article discussing the photographs and drawings of Indians of Tierra del Fuego, particularly when dealing with the 'then' and 'now' photos of indigenous people apparently persuaded to abandon traditional body paint and masks and don the European-style clothing of 'successful' assimilation. There is a need to consider the original purpose of these images (created by explorers, missionaries and anthropologists) and the degree to which they justified and constructed the image and ideal of the civilized 'white-man' as much as the 'Indian', and Fiore goes on to consider the use of these images in a modern self-critical exhibition. But, there may also be a problem if museums see their role as primarily one of promoting tolerance if this implies 'pacifying activism'. Throughout Africa some culture houses have played an important role in providing a platform for traditional elites to challenge the authority of national politics. This raises further questions about the audience that museums address – can they be relevant to local community and international tourism at the same time, and how should we measure the success or failure of a museum's activities? (See also Abungu and Ramos Lopes, this volume.)

DEBATE OR DISPUTE?

While writing this introductory article, I have been very conscious of the curious responsibilities of the editors of an academic journal when discussing issues of such emotional and political strength. It is surely the purpose of academia not simply to pander to the norms, prejudices or stereotypes on a given subject, but to seek out the contradictions, problems and pitfalls of current practice. As Leclair discusses, we should be aware when legal decisions and sensitivity over indigenous politics are restricting justifiable debate. As discussed in this article, indigenous demands are a major challenge to many of the most fundamental assumptions and practices of archaeology and heritage management. But, while I am keen to develop an informed discussion, I do not think it should be our role to create contestation through our own polemic. As is probably clear from this text, I am broadly sympathetic to many of the concerns of indigenous peoples and appreciative of the difficulties inherited from past conflict as well as current issues. Yet, at the beginning of the 21st century it is rarely clear how the return of indigenous peoples' rights can best be achieved, as even in relation to specific situations it is difficult to identify to whom such rights would now apply, or the impact returning such rights will have on others. What is clear is that archaeological remains and the rich heritage of indigenous peoples will remain at the centre of these debates. I hope that the papers in this volume will contribute to the increasing awareness within the archaeological community that these are issues that affect our practice and require our consideration.

ACKNOWLEDGEMENTS

This paper and this volume would not have come into being if I had not been asked by Peter Ucko to help co-ordinate a third-year undergraduate course on Indigenous Archaeology with him. I owe enormous debts to Peter for being both an unstinting provocative critic and a kind and supportive colleague. The many and varied contributors to that course and the seminar series from which the collection of papers in this volume emerged gave me a wide-ranging introduction to the complex relationship between indigenous peoples and archaeological practice. I greatly appreciate all the time and energy that speakers and students have given to discussing and debating these issues with me. I am particularly grateful to Peter Ucko, Cressida Fforde and Lyndon Ormond-Parker for taking the time to offer useful comments on an earlier version of this paper.

Bill Sillar is a Lecturer at the Institute of Archaeology, UCL, where he co-ordinates an MA in Artefact Studies and a course on Indigenous Archaeology. He previously taught at the University of Wales, Lampeter. Bill's research has focused on how people make and use material culture to shape the world they live in. His PhD (Cambridge 1994) was based on research into the production, trade and use of pottery in Peru and Bolivia. He has also undertaken archaeological work at Raqchi, near Cuzco, Peru, studying the changing fortunes of the site and the community in relation to successive expansionist states (Wari, Inka and Spanish).

Contact address: Institute of Archaeology, University College London, 34 Gordon Square, London WC1H 0PY, UK. Email: b.sillar@ucl.ac.uk

REFERENCES

African Union. *Report of the African Commission's Working Group of Experts on Indigenous Populations/Communities* (2003) http://www.iwgia.org/sw2186.asp

Ayau, E.H. Bishop Museum doesn't qualify as a claimant to artifacts. *Star-Bulletin* Hawaii, 29 August (2004).

Bahn, P. and Flenley, J. *Easter Island, Earth Island: A Message from our Past for the Future of the Planet.* Thames and Hudson, London (1992).

Bartolomé de las Casas. *A Short Account of the Destruction of the Indies.* Translated by Nigel Griffin. Penguin Classics, London [1552] (1992).

Blakeney, M. *Intellectual Property in the Dreamtime – Protecting the Cultural Creativity of Indigenous Peoples.* Seminar presented at the Oxford Intellectual Property Research Centre, 9 November (1999) http://www.oiprc.ox.ac.uk/EJWP1199.html

Bowen, J.R. Should we have a universal concept of 'indigenous peoples' rights? Ethnicity and essentialism in the twenty-first century. *Anthropology Today* 16 (2000) 12–16.

Bowler, P.J. From 'savage' to 'primitive': Victorian evolutionism and the interpretation of marginalized peoples. *Antiquity* 66 (1992) 721–729.

Brush, S.B. and Strabinsky, D. (eds) *Valuing Local Knowledge: Indigenous People and Intellectual Property Rights.* Island Press, Washington DC (1996).

Bubba, C. Los rituales a los vestidos de María *Titiqhawa*, Juana *Palla* y otros, fundadores de los ayllus de Coroma. In Bouysse-Cassagne, T. (ed. Compiler) *Saberes y memorias en los Andes. In Memoriam Thierry Saignes.* CREAL-IFEA, Lima (1997) 377–400.

Catanzariti, J. *The Papers of Thomas Jefferson.* Princeton University Press, Princeton NJ 25 (1992).

Churchill, W. The crucible of American Indian identity: native traditions versus colonial imposition in postconquest North America. In Champagne, D. (ed.) *Contemporary Native American Cultural Issues.* Altamira Press, Walnut Creek (1999) 39–67.

Churchill, W. The law stood squarely on its head: U.S. legal doctrine, indigenous self-determination and the question of world order. *Oregon Law Review* 81 (2002) 663–706.

Cobo, J.M. *The Study of the Problem of Discrimination against Indigenous Populations.* United Nations Document E/Cn.4/Sub.2/1986/7/Add.4. (1986).

Crawford, G.W. and Masakazu, Y. Ainu ancestors and prehistoric Asian Agriculture. *Journal of Archaeological Science* 14 (1987) 201–214.

Davison, P. Typecast. Representations of the Bushmen at the South African Museum. *Public Archaeology* 2 (2001) 3–20.

Engels. *The Origin of the Family, Private Property, and the State.* Pathfinder Press, New York, [1884] 1972.

Ferguson, L. *Uncommon Ground: Archaeology and Early African America 1650–1800.* Smithsonian Institute Press, Washington DC (1992).

Ferguson, T.J., Dongoske, K., Yeatts, M. and Jenkins, L. Working together: Hopi oral history and archaeology, Part I: the role of archaeology. *SAA Bulletin* 13 (1995) 12–15.

Ferguson, T.J., Anyon, R. and Ladd, E.J. Repatriation at the Pueblo of Zuni: diverse solutions to complex problems. In Hihesuah, D.A. (ed.) *Repatriation Reader: Who Owns American Indian Remains.* Bison Books, University of Nebraska Press, Lincoln NB (2000) 239–265.

Fforde, C. *Collecting the Dead: Archaeology and the Reburial Issue.* Duckworth, London (2004).

Fforde, C., Hubert, J. and Turnbull, P. (eds) *The Dead and their Possessions: Repatriation in Principle, Policy and Practice.* One World Archaeology, Routledge, London (2002).

Fukasawa, Y. *Ainu Archaeology as Ethnohistory: Iron Technology Among the Sara Ainu of Hokkaido, Japan, in the 17th Century.* BAR, London (1998).

Funari, P.P.A., Hall, M. and Jones, S. (eds) *Historical Archaeology: Back from the Edge.* Routledge, London (1999).

Gosden, C. *Archaeology and Colonialism: Cultural Contact from 5000BC to the Present.* Cambridge University Press, Cambridge (2004).

Hodgson, D.L. Comparative perspectives on the indigenous rights movements in Africa and the Americas. *American Anthropologist* 104 (2002) 1037–1049.

Hurst Thomas, D. *Skull Wars: Kennewick Man, Archaeology and the Battle for Native American Identity.* Basic Books, New York (2000).

International Labour Organization. *Indigenous and Tribal People's Convention 107*. (1957).

International Labour Organization. *Indigenous and Tribal People's Convention 169*. (1989).

Isbell, B.J. *To Defend Ourselves: Ecology and Ritual in an Andean Village*. Waveland Press, Prospect Heights IL (1985).

Jones, S. *The Archaeology of Ethnicity: Constructing Identities in the Past and the Present*. Routledge, London (1997).

Katarina, V. *The Return of the Ainu: Cultural Mobilization and the Practice of Ethnicity in Japan*. Harwood Academic Publishers, Amsterdam (1993).

Kimberley Declaration. *International Indigenous Peoples Summit on Sustainable Development*. Khoi-San Territory, Kimberley, South Africa, 20–23 August (2002). http://www.iwgia.org/sw217.asp

Lane, P. Breaking the mould? Exhibiting Khoisan in Southern African museums. *Anthropology Today* 12 (1996) 3–10.

Lubbock, J. *Prehistoric Times, as Illustrated by Ancient Remains and the Manners and Customs of Modern Savages*, 3rd edn, Williams and Norgate, London (1865).

Marshall, J. *Cherokee Nation v. State of Georgia*. Chief Justice Marshall's delivery of the opinion of the Court (1831) http://www.ku.edu/carrie/docs/texts/cherokee.htm

McDonald, I. *Protecting Indigenous Intellectual Property*. Australian Copyright Council, Sydney (1997).

Merrill, W.L., Ladd, E.J. and Ferguson, T.J. The return of the Ahayu:da: lessons for repatriation from Zuni Pueblo and the Smithsonian Institute. *Current Anthropology* 34 (1993) 523–567.

Morgan, L.H. *Ancient Society*. Holt, New York (1877).

Mountford, C.P. *Nomads of the Australian Desert*. Rigby, Melbourne (1976).

Noël Hume, I. An Indian ware of the colonial period. *Quarterly Bulletin, Archaeological Society of Virginia* 17 (1962) 1–14.

Service, E.R. *Primitive Social Organization: An Evolutionary Perspective*. Random House, New York (1962).

Shennan, S. Introduction: archaeological approaches to cultural identity. In Shennan, S. (ed.) *Archaeological Approaches to Cultural Identity*. Routledge, London (1989) 1–32.

Shetty, P. Peruvian 'potato park' to protect indigenous rights. *Science and Development Network*. http://www.scidev.net/News/index.cfm?fuseaction=readNews&itemid=1859&language=1 19 January (2005).

Siddle, R. *Race, Resistance and the Ainu of Japan*. Routledge, London (1996).

Smith, A.D. *The Ethnic Origins of Nations*. Blackwell, Oxford (1986).

Society for American Archaeology (SAA). *Principles of Archaeological Ethics*. Adopted 10 April (1996). http://www.saa.org/aboutSAA/ethics.html

Sollas, W.J. *Ancient Hunters and their Modern Representatives*. Macmillan, London (1911).

Spence, M.D. *Dispossessing the Wilderness: Indian Removal and the Making of the National Parks*. Oxford University Press, Oxford (1999).

Stanley-Price, N. *The Palaeolithic, Preservation and the Public*. Archaeology International. Institute of Archaeology, UCL, London (2000) 53–56.

Stern, S.J. (ed.) *Resistance, Rebellion, and Consciousness in the Andean Peasant World: 18th to 20th Centuries*. University of Wisconsin Press, Madison WI (1987).

Stern, S.J. *Peru's Indian Peoples and the Challenge of the Spanish Conquest*. University of Wisconsin Press, Madison WI (1993).

Sylvain, R. 'Land, water, and truth': San identity and global indigenism. *American Anthropologist* 104 (2002) 1074–1085.

Tarlow, S. Decoding ethics. *Public Archaeology* 1 (2000) 245–259.

Timbisha Shoshone Act Public Law 106–423: To provide to the Timbisha Shoshone Tribe a permanent land base within its aboriginal homeland passed by Congress and signed by President Clinton 1 November (2000) http://thomas.loc.gov/home/thomas.html

Thomas, J. *United States, Petitioner v. Billy Jo Lara*. Supreme Court of the United States No. 03. 107. 19 April (2004) http://supct.law.cornell.edu/supct/pdf/03-107P.ZC2

Turner, T. Defiant images: the Kayapo appropriation of video. *Anthropology Today* 8 (1992) 5–16.

United Nations. *Draft Declaration on the Rights of Indigenous Peoples*. United Nations Document E/CN. 4/Sub.21994/2/Add. 1(1994) http://www.unhchr.ch/indigenous/groups-01.htm

United Nations Educational Scientific and Cultural Organization (UNESCO). *Convention for the Safeguarding of the Intangible Cultural Heritage* (2003). http://unesdoc.unesco.org/images/0013/001325/132540e.pdf

Uribo Botero, E. Natural resource conservation and management in the Sierra Nevada of Santa Marta. Case study document CEDE (2005-7). http://economia.uniandes.edu.co/~economia/archivos/temporal/D2005-07.pdf

Washington, G. *The Writings of George Washington from the Original Manuscript Sources*. 34. Electronic Text Center, University of Virginia Library. http://etext.virginia.edu/washington/fitzpatrick/

Whall, H. *Indigenous Self-Determination in the Commonwealth*. Occasional Papers Commonwealth Policy Studies Unit, Institute of Commonwealth Studies, University of London, November (2002).

Wijesuriya, G. Pious vandals – restoration vs. destruction. In Layton, R., Stone, P.G. and Thomas, J. (eds) *Destruction and Conservation of Cultural Property*. Routledge, London (2001) 256–263.

Zamora, C.B. Collectors versus native peoples: the repatriation of the Sacred Weavings of Coroma, Bolivia. *Museum Anthropology* 20 (1996) 39–44.

The Ainu of Japan:
an indigenous people or an ethnic group?

Kaori Tahara

ABSTRACT

In 1997 the Japanese Parliament ratified the Act for the *Promotion of Ainu Culture and the Dissemination and Advocacy for the Traditions of the Ainu and Ainu Culture*; this act officially designates Ainu culture and language for restoration and promotion in Japan. However, despite demands from Ainu people to be recognized as an indigenous group, the Japanese government designates the Ainu only as an 'ethnic minority'. Generally, the Japanese define Ainu people as descendants of those who assumed Ainu culture in Hokkaido during the period of Japanese colonization (from the 13th/14th centuries to the middle of the 19th century). A primary consideration today is to identify and date the origins of Ainu culture (which can then be conserved in accordance with the 1997 Act). Most Japanese academics agree that the Ainu people are the prior inhabitants of Hokkaido, but they also consider Hokkaido 'Japan's inherent territory'. At present, the Japanese authorities seem to consider the term 'indigenous' to mean a population who had prior possession of land, but who now have no right to it or its natural resources. However, many Ainu continue to demand recognition as an 'indigenous people', rather than an ethnic minority.

INTRODUCTION

The perception of Ainu culture in Japanese society today has improved since the Nibutani Dam Case in 1997, which led to a legal recognition of the Ainu (Tahara, 1999), the abolition of the 1899 *Act for the Protection of Former Aborigines*, and the enactment of a law for the *Promotion of Ainu Culture and for the Dissemination and Advocacy for the Traditions of the Ainu and the Ainu Culture* (1997 with amendments in 1999). The aim of the new law was 'to realize a society in which the ethnic pride of the Ainu is respected and to further develop the national culture by implementing measures that promote Ainu culture'. As a result, Ainu culture and language are now legally designated for restoration and promotion. On the other hand, the definition of Ainu people remains confined to the status of an ethnic minority. During the deliberation of the bill, the government discussed the Ainu people as a people with 'ethnic pride'; the description of them as an indigenous group is expressed only in one of the five Supplementary Resolutions of the Cabinet Committees of the House of Representatives and Councillors. In this supplement to the bill recommendations are made regarding appropriate measures to promote Ainu culture and this includes a recommendation 'to make efforts to disseminate the knowledge about Ainu traditions, including the indigenous nature of the Ainu, which is a historical fact'. This part of the bill is not legally binding, although it is expected to be used as a guideline for the executive authority. This limitation disappointed the Ainu, who have strongly demanded indigenous status since 1984.

Generally, the Japanese define Ainu people as descendants of those who assumed Ainu culture in Hokkaido from the 13th or the 14th centuries to the middle of the 19th century, during the Japanese colonization of this island. Now, the issue is to determine to what date this culture can be traced back. However, defining Ainu identity always evokes controversy amongst the Japanese authorities and academics, as well as the Ainu people themselves, because the way in which each group chooses to define the 'Ainu' depends upon their own interests. In this article, I would like to clarify the various definitions of Ainu by looking at those held by Ainu people, Japanese academics (particularly archaeologists and anthropologists) and the Japanese authorities.

A BRIEF HISTORY OF THE AINU

The earliest historical documents mentioning the Ainu affirm that they lived on Hokkaido island (the second largest of the four main islands of modern Japan north of Honshu). Hokkaido was called Yezo or Ezo until 1868. Japanese immigration on to the island of Ezo is first documented in the 15th century. In 1432 a retainer clan, the Andos (later renamed Kakizaki and then Matsumae) from the north of the Japanese mainland crossed the Strait of Tsugaru, which divides the mainland of Honshu from Ezo island. The Japanese settled on the Oshima peninsula in the south of Ezo, where they constructed several forts and made their livelihood by trading with the Ainu. Following the murder of an Ainu youth in 1457, Ainu troops led by their chief, Koshamain, rose against the Japanese and destroyed the forts in the south of Ezo. However, many of the Ainu troops were finally massacred because of a deception carried out by a retainer, Nobuhiro Takeda, who, soon afterwards, married into the Kakizakis and later founded the Matsumae clan.

At the end of the 16th century, Hideyoshi Toyotomi, the warlord of the Central Administration on Honshu, gave the Matsumae clan exclusive rights to conduct trade with the Ainu. In 1604 the Japanese occupation of Ezo was reasserted by Ieyasu Tokugawa, who gained supremacy over all the military lords of Honshu after the death of Hideyoshi in 1598 and the founding of the Tokugawa Shogunate in 1603. They set up a number of trading posts in Ezo and gave its vassals the right to trade with the Ainu. This trade caused discontent among the Ainu who, in 1669, again attacked the Japanese forts but once more were defeated and suffered heavy casualties.

In the 18th century, the vassals of the Matsumae clan leased the Ainu trading rights to Japanese merchants who later employed Ainu as cheap labour in their fisheries. This exploitative labour system forced the Ainu to live in poverty and gave tyrannical powers to the Japanese merchants in Ezo. A band of Ainu troops from the east of Ezo and the south of the Kuril islands rebelled against these merchants in 1789, but their forces were suppressed. Owing to the inability of the Matsumae clan to manage Ezo and defend the northern frontiers between Japan and Russia, the Tokugawa Shogunate took Ezo under their direct control from 1799 to 1821 and then from 1855 to 1869.

After the Meiji Restoration, the Meiji Regime established a Colonization Commission and in 1869 renamed the island of Yezo, Hokkaido. Japanese immigration to Hokkaido was again encouraged, Ainu land was given to settlers and Hokkaido's population soared to over one million people. The Ainu became a minority in their own land. After this long exploitation by the Japanese, which included a prohibition placed on traditional Ainu hunting and fishing, the Ainu were by this time in extreme poverty. In 1899 the Meiji Regime passed the *Act for Protection of Former Aborigines*, this Act attempted to force the Ainu to take up agriculture and also provided some welfare measures such as medical treatment and schooling. In actuality, this Act forced Ainu people to change their traditional livelihood and to assimilate into Japanese society.

AINU SELF-IDENTIFICATION

Through my analysis of the newsletters/journals/documents of the AAH (Ainu Association of Hokkaido) and its two predecessors I have identified four phases of changing attitudes and actions in the self-identity and political activism of the Ainu since 1930. Before this time there are no records of how the Ainu perceived themselves.

1930–1960

During this period, the Ainu expressed a desire to assimilate within mainstream Japanese in order to improve their living conditions. In the Preface of the first issue of *Ezo no hikari* (*Light in Ezo*) published in 1930, the journal of the Hokkai Ainu Association (one of the predecessors of the Ainu Association of Hokkaido), states that the 'Ainu people were completely assimilated into Japanese society and the Ainu even learned their own Ainu language from Japanese teachers' (Hokkai Ainu Kyokai, 1930: 23). The Ainu's positive attitude towards assimilation at this time appears to have been based on their desire to benefit from economic development and avoid subordination under the Japanese. The publication proudly recorded many success stories of Ainu members who adapted well to the Japanese customs. However, the contents of this publication also show that the Ainu certainly considered themselves to be the prior inhabitants of Hokkaido who had lived there for several hundred years (Hokkai Ainu Kyokai, 1930: 23).

1960–1980

In the 1960s, Ainu concerns gained wider attention within mainstream Japanese society. For example, the Ministry of Health and Welfare drew up a means of identifying Utari – an administrative term for Ainu that means 'compatriot' in the Ainu language. This term is also used by AAH. When AAH was founded in 1946, it was originally called Hokkaido Ainu Association but changed its name to Hokkaido Utari Association in 1961 because the term 'Ainu' was considered discriminative in those days. In 1997 the Executive Committee proposed a project to reclaim the Ainu name and call the association, Hokkaido Ainu Kyokai. However, at the debate on 16 May 1997 during the General Meeting many members rejected this proposal because they felt it would provoke discrimination against Ainu (Hokkaido Utari Kyokai, 1997). The Hokkaido authorities distinguish Ainu people as 'persons who are considered to have Ainu blood in local communities and their spouses and adopted children living together' (Hokkaido kankyo seikatsu bu, 2000).

In 1968, the Ainu criticized the Hokkaido local government's celebration of the 100th anniversary of the Hokkaido Development, which they considered the anniversary of Japanese invasion. In 1971 a statue of Ainu chief Shakushain (who had rebelled against the Japanese and was assassinated in 1660) was erected, and a museum of Ainu artefacts was constructed through the initiative of Ainu people in the Hidaka region (which has the largest Ainu population in Hokkaido).

1980s

Since the 1980s, the Ainu have been demanding that the Japanese government recognize their indigenous status. In 1988, the AAH, together with the Hokkaido prefectural government and the Hokkaido Assembly, released a Demand for the adoption of a new Ainu Act based on a 1984 Proposal to the national government for Legislation Concerning the Ainu People.

This Demand consisted of five basic themes, (1) a declaration of respect for the rights of the Ainu, (2) a consolidation of human rights movements, (3) the promotion of Ainu culture, (4) the establishment of a foundation to fund the Ainu people and end their dependence on welfare (37.2% of Ainu were dependent on welfare in 1999 – double the national average (Hokkaido kankyo seikatsu bu, 2000: 16)), and (5) the establishment of a new deliberation organization (Foundation for Research and Promotion of Ainu Culture, 2000). As well as demanding state recognition of the Ainu as the indigenous inhabitants of Hokkaido, the Northern territory and the southern four of the Kurile Islands. As stated at that time: 'indigenous rights are the basis for the enactment of the act' (Ainu Association of Hokkaido, 1998: 266).

In 1994 an Ainu, Shigeru Kayano, was elected as a member of the House of Councillors. He was the first Ainu to belong to the National Diet and his presence motivated the adoption of the *Act for Promotion of Ainu Culture*. Unfortunately, since his term of office ended in 1998 there has been no other Ainu representative elected to the Diet.

Through AAH delegations to various UN conferences, since 1987 the Ainu have demanded recognition of their indigenous status at an international level. In 1992, the Executive Director of the AAH, Giichi Nomura, was invited by the UN General Assembly to present the inauguration speech at the opening ceremony of the International Year of the World's Indigenous People. He asserted that the Ainu had inhabited Hokkaido, the Kurile Islands and southern Sakhalin 'from time immemorial' and proposed a society where Ainu people and the Japanese could coexist (Nomura, 1993).

1997 onwards

Since the adoption of the *Act for Promotion of Ainu Culture*, Ainu research and cultural events increasingly have been organized by the Foundation for Research and Promotion of Ainu Culture, an organization created in accordance with the Act. The foundation 'was established in June 1997 as an organization that implements nationwide projects to promote Ainu culture and facilitate understanding of the history and culture of Ainu in accordance with the new law ... This Foundation conducts projects according to the following four policies; 1) Promotion of comprehensive and practical research on the Ainu, 2) Promotion of the Ainu Language, 3) Promotion of Ainu Culture, 4) Dissemination of Knowledge on Ainu Traditions' (Foundation for Research and Promotion of Ainu Culture, 2000: 28–29).

However, some Ainu individuals criticized the AAH for accepting the Act, because it addresses only cultural aspects of Ainu society while ignoring social, political and economic issues. Many Ainu were particularly critical that its recognition of Ainu identity was too vague. At the General Meeting of AAH on 15 May 1998, some Ainu members expressed their dissatisfaction with the Act, which did not recognize the Rights of Indigenous Peoples, and expressed their intention of requesting revision to the 1997 Act to address the original demands made in 1984 (Hokkaido shinbun, 15 May 1998). Shigeru Kayano expressed the opinion that 'the occasion of the revision of this Act will be when the draft United Nations Declaration on the Rights of Indigenous Peoples would be adopted' (Hokkaido shinbun, 10 May 1998. See United Nations Draft Declaration on the Rights of Indigenous People 1994/45 E/CN.4/1995/2, E/CN.4/Sub.2/1994/56: 103–115). Further concerns were expressed about the real beneficiaries of the Foundation. '[T]he Foundation subsidizes scientific research and publication. As the scientific and academic projects do not concern most Ainu, who themselves have dramatically less access to the education system in Japan, the benefits of the Foundation are mostly destined for Japanese scholars' (Ainu Association of Sapporo, 2002: 1).

IDENTIFICATION OF AINU PEOPLE BY JAPANESE ACADEMICS

Japanese academics have played a principal role in defining Ainu identity but, apart from the linguist Mashiho Chiri (1909–1961), none have identified themselves as Ainu. Ainu studies were originally motivated by physical anthropology and investigations into the origin of the Japanese. Because the Meiji government engaged occidental scholars to introduce Western science to the Japanese, Ainu studies and the fields of archaeology and anthropology in general were (and remain) greatly influenced by Western thought.

The debate on Ainu racial origins was started by Philipp Franz von Siebold (1796–1866) and Erwin von Baelz (1849–1913). Siebold ([1854] 1979) argued that the Ainu were the first inhabitants of the Japanese archipelago, and were direct descendants of European Stone Age people. His son, Heinrich (1852–1908) supported this theory and maintained that the Ainu were Europeans living in miserable circumstances (Siebold, 1881). Baelz also insisted that the Ainu belonged to the Caucasian race. This theory was adopted by his students and was prevalent among Japanese scholars for a long time. In the 1870s, Morse argued that Ainu people had replaced a pre-Ainu population that had lived in the New Stone Age. In 1877, he conducted an excavation at Omori Shell Midden, the first scientific excavation to take place in Japan (Morse, 1983).

Anthropology was first established at Tokyo Imperial University in 1884, headed by Professor Shogoro Tsuboi. Influenced by John Milne, the English geologist and seismologist, Tsuboi argued that the inhabitants of the Stone Age in Japan were the Korpokkur (which means 'dwarf living under butterbur leaves'), a legendary group of people regarded by the Ainu as pit dwellers who made stone tools and pottery and who traded with the Ainu (Yoshioka and Hasebe, 1993). Yoshikiyo Koganei, an anatomist, developed a theory that the Ainu were isolates who could not be related to other races. Nonetheless, the typical view, held by subsequent Japanese academics, was exemplified by that of Shin'ichiro Takakura (e.g. 1966) who considered the Ainu people to be a Caucasoid race. At present, anthropologists who express an opinion on this debate consider the Ainu to be 'Mongoloids' (e.g. Omoto, 1995) or East Asian peoples, but most academics are now cautious of attributing racial identifications.

A recent position on the identity of Ainu people can be seen in the 1996 Report of the Experts Meeting Concerning Ainu Affairs (EMCAA, 1998). At the request of the Chief Secretary of the Japanese Cabinet, this Experts Meeting sought the opinion of academics from the fields of physical anthropology, historical science, ethnology and international law. The EMCAA consisted of seven experts, including three anthropologists and two jurists. The Report concluded that: 'according to historical facts it is indisputable that since the latter part of the medieval era the Ainu people were living indigenously in the northern part of the Islands of Japan, especially in Hokkaido which was a part of Japanese territory' (EMCAA, 1998: 238). This claim faced many critics, who pointed out that it is a retrospective logic, based on the present condition of the Ainu people as Japanese nationals and of Hokkaido belonging to Japan, without mentioning the earlier colonization and annexation of Hokkaido (Yamauchi, 1996). The EMCAA report continues, 'the Ainu people in our state should be expected to retain their individuality as an ethnic group, and it is unlikely that they will lose it in the near future' (EMCAA, 1998: 238). Concerning the Right of Self-determination and the Land Rights that remain a primary concern for indigenous peoples rights, 'it is impossible to put the right of self-determination, which relates to the decision of political status like separation/independence from our country, and to the compensation/restoration of resources and land of Hokkaido, into the basis of the implementation of new measures for the Ainu people' (EMCAA, 1998: 244).

Today, archaeologists and anthropologists are trying to clarify when and how Ainu culture began. The period in which the material culture identified and described by archaeologists as 'Ainu' flourished is distinguished from the previous 'Satsumon' culture (9th century to the 13th/14th century) that takes its name from a distinctive type of pottery decoration.

It is said that the period of the formation of Ainu culture can be defined materially by the replacement of earthenware by lacquerware, and spiritually by the appearance of Iyomante, the ceremony of the bear or the ritual killing of the cub (see Watanabe, 1972: 72–77). This ritual was observed only among Ainu people in Hokkaido and Sakhalin, and is therefore believed to characterize Ainu culture. On the other hand, AAH clearly considers Satsumon culture as 'the basis of Ainu culture' (Ainu Association of Hokkaido, n.d.).

However, there is also a tendency among archaeologists in Hokkaido to classify the period of the formation of Ainu culture as a 'Medieval Era'. Two recent archaeological exhibitions have adopted this classification: 'Ainu Culture Unearthed; Recreating Medieval and Modern Ages in the North', an exhibition sponsored by the government-funded Foundation for Research and Promotion of Ainu Culture in 2001, and 'The Unknown Medieval Era of Hokkaido', which was exhibited in Hokkaido and then in Osaka by the Hokkaido Historical Museum. The purpose of these exhibitions is clearly to represent the period of Ainu culture as a Medieval Era on Hokkaido. This use of the term 'Medieval Era' remains unclear because, in general, the Middle Ages in Japan date from the end of the 12th century to the beginning of the 17th century.

The former exhibition includes a feature on excavations at Katsuyama fort in Kaminokuni, (southern Hokkaido), calling the display, 'the Mixed World of Wajin [non-Ainu Japanese] and the Ainu Living Together' (Foundation for Research and Promotion of Ainu Culture, 2001: 44–86). The hypothesis that the Ainu and the Japanese cohabitated in the fort evoked enthusiasm among some Ainu and Japanese visitors. At this site, daily necessities, ritual materials and tombs of Ainu people are found in association with those of the Japanese. However, it may be that the archaeologists in charge of this excavation have been somewhat hasty in coming to this conclusion and that it would be better to undertake more detailed dating and further research before confirming this cohabitation of Ainu and Japanese. It should be remembered that Katsuyama fort was constructed in the 15th century by the feudal warrior, Nobuhiro Takeda, who slaughtered Koshamain and his troop.

IDENTIFICATION OF AINU PEOPLE BY THE JAPANESE AUTHORITIES

Until 1997, the method the Japanese authorities used to identify the Ainu remained that of the Meiji government that had officially classified the Ainu as former aborigines after the Colonization of Hokkaido Island in 1869. In 1997, the *Act for Promotion of Ainu Culture* replaced the earlier *Act for the Protection of Former Aborigines*, and only discussed the Ainu people's 'indigenous nature' as one of its Supplementary Decisions.

Three years before the adoption of the Act, and in spite of definitions by the United Nations Specialized Agencies, the ILO and the World Bank, the Japanese Minister for State said that, 'examining the status of the Ainu as Indigenous People is very difficult because the term of Indigenous Peoples has not yet been defined at the international level because of concerns over the Right of the Indigenous Peoples' (Igarashi, 1997: 202).

The Japanese government's position on Ainu people can be seen from its various references to Article 27 in the Reports submitted by Japanese delegations to the Human Rights Committee in accordance with the International Covenant on Civil and Political Rights, which Japan ratified in 1979. Article 27 states that 'In those States in which ethnic, religious or linguistic minorities exist, persons belonging to such minorities shall not be denied the right, in community with the other members of their group, to enjoy their own culture, to profess and practice their own religion, or to use their own language (United Nations, 1966, Article 27). In their initial report of 1980, the Japanese Government submission stated, 'minorities of the kind mentioned in the Covenant do not exist in Japan' (United Nations, 1980: Article 27). In response to remarks by the Committee on Japan's omission of Ainu people in its report, Japan said in its Second Periodic Report (United Nations, 1987) that, 'as for the question of the people of Ainu ... they are not denied enjoyment of the right mentioned' and, 'as Japanese nationals ... are guaranteed equality under the Japanese Constitution' (United Nations, 1987: Article 27).

In its Third Periodic Report submitted in 1991, the Japanese government distinguished between Japanese and Ainu for the first time by acknowledging that 'they may be called the minorities of that Article' although maintaining that they are still 'Japanese nationals' (United Nations, 1992: Article 27). In its First and Second Reports of 1996 submitted to the Committee on the Elimination of Racial Discrimination, Japan referred to 'the Ainu people, who have lived in Hokkaido, Japan's inherent territory' (United Nations, 2000: 18) and referred to the Report of 1996 by the EMCAA.

At the juridical level, Japan indicated its recognition of the Ainu people as a result of the passage of the Decision of Nibutani Dam in 1997. The Decision held that,

> The Ainu people have lived in Hokkaido and its adjacent areas, and constructed a distinct population before Japan extended jurisdiction over their land ... Their land was incorporated by the Japanese government and they suffered from economic and social dispossession under the policies imposed by the majority, Japanese. Even under these circumstances, the Ainu still maintain their distinct identity as an ethnic group. Thus, they should be regarded as an indigenous people. (Sapporo chiho saiban sho, 1999: 529).

However, despite this apparent recognition of the Ainu as an indigenous people, on 2 July 2001 the Minister of Economy and Industry, and the former Minister of Hokkaido Development Agency, stated, 'Japan is an ethnically homogenous nation'. Furthermore, the latter continued, 'Japan has one nation, one language and one ethnicity' and, 'at present, the Ainu are completely assimilated'. These words provoked disgust among Ainu people and demonstrated that the myth of a homogenous nation was still adhered to by a large proportion of Japanese politicians.

CONCLUSION

The actual identification of Ainu people by Japanese authorities refers to the Experts Meeting Concerning Ainu Affairs (EMCAA) 1996 Report, which states that Ainu people are the prior inhabitants of Hokkaido, which is 'Japan's inherent territory'. According to this EMCAA logic, the term 'indigenous' means just a population who had formerly possessed land but now has no right to it or its natural resources. In other words, there is no real difference between the terms 'indigenous people' and 'ethnic minority'. This logic fits well with the interest of Japanese authorities that have no intention of conceding any further rights to Ainu people, such as restoring or compensating for the land and resources that the Ainu formally owned on Hokkaido. This issue, which has been raised by academics, is a cause of concern among Ainu people. As Shigeru Kayano said, 'We do not say to give us back our land, but to set up a fund to assure the livelihood of Ainu people' (Hokkaido shinbun, 10 May 1998) because as the result of Japanese colonization of Hokkaido, the 'Japanese forbade Ainu to cut trees and catch fishes' and 'still now, Ainu people stay in poverty' (ibid.). To be officially acknowledged as an indigenous people, rather than the more limited designation of ethnic minority, would further the just demands of the Ainu for compensation for the loss of their traditional territory, Hokkaido.

Kaori Tahara is an Ainu from Sapporo. She participated in the first Indigenous Fellowship Programme at the Office for the UN High Commissioner for Human Rights in 1997, and has undertaken graduate studies at the École des Hautes Études en Sciences Sociales in Paris.

Contact address: Grand Rue 55, 2035 Corcelles, Switzerland. Email: tkaori@bluewin.ch

REFERENCES

Ainu Association of Hokkaido *Brochure on the Ainu People*. Ainu Association of Hokkaido, Sapporo (No date).

Ainu Association of Hokkaido *Statement Submitted to the Second Session the Working Group on Right of the Indigenous People*. In Ainu Association of Hokkaido (ed.) *Kokusaikaigi shiryoshu 1987nen–1997nen [Materials of International Conferences 1987–1997]* Ainu Association of Hokkaido, Sapporo (1998) 227–270.

Ainu Association of Sapporo. Statement submitted to the first session of the Permanent Forum on Indigenous Issues. New York (2002) (Unpublished).

Experts Meeting Concerning Ainu Affairs (EMCAA) Utaritaisaku no arikata nikansuru yushikishakaigi. 'Hokokusho: The Report' 1996. Reproduced in Ainu Association of Hokkaido (ed.) *Kokusaikaigi shiryoshu 1987nen–1997nen [Materials of International Conferences: 1987–1997]*. Ainu Association of Hokkaido, Sapporo (1998) 229–262.

Foundation for Research and Promotion of Ainu Culture. *To Understand the Ainu*. Foundation for Research and Promotion of Ainu Culture, Sapporo (2000).

Foundation for Research and Promotion of Ainu Culture. *Ainu Culture Unearthed; Recreating Medieval and Modern Ages in the North*. Foundation for Research and Promotion of Ainu Culture, Sapporo (2001).

Hokkai Ainu Kyokai [Ainu Association of Hokkai]. Ezo no hikari: Sokan go [Light in Ezo: the first number published in 1930]. In Hokkaido Utari Kyokai (ed.) *Ainu shi: Hokkaido Ainu Kyokai/Hokkaido Utari Kyokai katsudo shi hen [Ainu History: activities of the Hokkaido Ainu/Utari Association]* Hokkaido Utari Kyokai, Sapporo ([1930] 1994) 19–61.

Hokkaido kankyo seikatsu bu [Department of living environment, Hokkaido government]. *Heiseijuichinen hokkaidoutariseikatsujittaichosa hokokusho [1999 Report on Actual Conditions of the Ainu People in Hokkaido]*. Hokkaido kankyo seikatsu bu somuka ainuseisakusuishinsitsu, Sapporo (2000).

Hokkaido Utari Kyokai [Ainu Association of Hokkaido]. *Senkusha no tsudoi*. Hokkaido Utari Kyokai, Sapporo (1997) 74–75.

Igarashi, K. Speech at the 7th Record of the 131st House of Councilors on 24 November 1994. In Emori, S., Otsuka, K., Omoto, K., Kato, K., Kayano, S., Sasaki, K., Tsunemoto, T., Nomura, G. and Yoshizaki, M. *Kayano Shigeru no Ainu bunka koza: Ainu go ga kokkaini hibiku [Course of Ainu Culture by Shigeru Kayano: Ainu Language Sounds at the Diet]*. Sofukan, Tokyo (1997) 192–206.

Law for the *Promotion of the Ainu Culture and for the Dissemination and Advocacy for the Traditions of the Ainu and the Ainu Culture*. Law No. 52, 14 May (1997), Amendment: Law No. 160, 22 December (1999) http://www.frpac.or.jp/eng/e_prf/profile06.html

Morse, E. *Omori Kaizuka [Omori Shell Mound]*. Iwanami shoten, Tokyo (1983).

Nomura, G. Inaugural speech on 10 December 1992. In Ainu Association of Hokkaido *Brochure on the Ainu People*. Ainu Association of Hokkaido, Sapporo (1993).

Omoto, K. Genetic diversity and the origins of the 'Mongoloid'. In Brenner, S. and Hanihara, K. (eds) *The Origin and Past of Modern Humans as Viewed from DNA*. World Scientific Publishing, Singapore (1995) 92–109.

Sapporo chiho saiban sho [Sapporo District Court]. Hanketsu [Verdict] In Kayano, S. and Tanaka, H. (eds) *Nibutanidam saiban no kiroku [Records of the Nibutani Dam Case]*. Sanseido, Tokyo (1999) 509–548.

Siebold, H. *Studien über die Aino auf der Insel Yesso*. Verlag von Paul Parey, Berlin (1881).

Siebold, P.F. *Nihon [Japan]*. Translated by K. Kato. Yumatsudo syoten, Tokyo ([1854] translation republished 1979).

Tahara, K. Nibutani Dam Case. *Indigenous Law Bulletin* 4 (1999) 18–20.

Takakura, S. Vanishing Ainu of North Japan. *Natural History* 8 (1966) 16–25.

United Nations office for the High Commission of Human Rights. *International Covenant on Civil and Political Rights*. Adopted 16th December 1966. http://www.unhchr.ch/html/menu3/b/a_ccpr.htm

United Nations. *Japan Initial Report.* CCPR/C/10/Add.1. (1980).

United Nations. *Consideration of Reports Submitted by States Parties under Article 40 of the Covenant.* CCPR/C/SR (1981) 319–320, 324.

United Nations. *Japan Second Periodic Report.* CCPR/C/42/Add.4. (1987).

United Nations. *Consideration of Reports Submitted by the States Parties in Accordance with Article 40 of the Covenant: Third Periodic Reports of States Parties due in 1991: Addendum: Japan.* CCPR/C/70/Add.1. (1992).

United Nations. *Consideration of Reports Submitted by the States Parties in Accordance with Article 40 of the Covenant: Fourth Periodic Reports of States Parties due in 1996: Addendum: Japan.* CCPR/C/115/Add.3. (1997).

United Nations. *Reports Submitted by States Parties under Article 9 of the Convention: Second Periodic Reports of States Parties due in 1999: Addendum: Japan.* CERD/C/350/Add.2. (2000).

Watanabe, H. *The Ainu Ecosystem: Environment and Group Structure.* University of Washington Press, Washington DC (1972).

Yamauchi, M. Ainushinpo o do kangaeruka [Understanding the legislation concerning the Ainu people]. *Sekai* **623** (1996) 153–162.

Yoshioka, I. and Hasebe, M. *Milne no jinshuron* [*The Racial Theory of Milne*]. Yuzankaku, Tokyo (1993).

Archaeology and the study of indigenous peoples in Siberia

Ole Grøn

ABSTRACT

This paper provides a brief outline of the inter-relationship between changes in the Russian state's policy of control in Siberia and academic study of the indigenous cultures in the area. Although the indigenous hunter-gatherers of Siberia were classified according to some of the same stereotypes that were (and are) applied in other parts of the world (representing them as remnants of the evolutionary process, noble savages or ecological guardians) these frameworks emerged in distinctive political, ideological and economic contexts during Russia's turbulent history.[1]

THE RUSSIAN STATE'S ATTITUDE TO THE INDIGENOUS POPULATIONS OF SIBERIA

In 1581, the Russian army crossed over the Ural mountains for the first time, and Russia engaged in a rapid, brutal and bloody occupation of a region that corresponds approximately to today's Siberia (including the 'Far East'). In the century that followed, Siberia's indigenous populations were forced to pay a tax in fur pelts (*iasak*) to the tsar, and hostages were taken to secure regular payment. During this period the Russian state's interest in the indigenous population of Siberia was centred on the extraction of fur and minerals (Forsyth, 1992: 1–47).

A change in attitude appeared during the reigns of Peter the Great (1672–1725) and Catherine the Great (1729–1796). Peter founded the Russian Science Academy and thus created an important vehicle for a systematic survey of the vast Siberian areas. Many of the leading scientists of the time served him as advisors and researchers (for example, G.W. Leibnitz) and played an important role in the rapid development of Russia from a medieval to a modern state (Crownhart-Vaughan, 1972).

Catherine the Great developed a more humanitarian, rational and profitable interaction with the Siberian indigenous populations. She also saw the consequences of the unsuccessful and often brutal Christian missionary work that was practised, and implemented a greater degree of religious tolerance. This led to an improvement in relations between not only the Russians and the indigenous populations, but also *among* the different indigenous groups, who had previously been played off against each other by the Russians in the course of conflict (Forsyth, 1992: 143–151).

Under the new rational Russian policy, the existing institutions of the indigenous societies were used to facilitate communication and exchange. Russian agents in trade and transportation frequently married aboriginal women and adopted pagan religion (Forsyth, 1992: 154–158). The development of a large 'buffer-group' between the Russians and the indigenous groups (Cruikshank and Argounova, 2000), as well as the absence of government-supported Christian morality condemning non-Christian behaviour, seems to have promoted a relatively balanced relationship between the many different ethnic groups (Fig. 1).

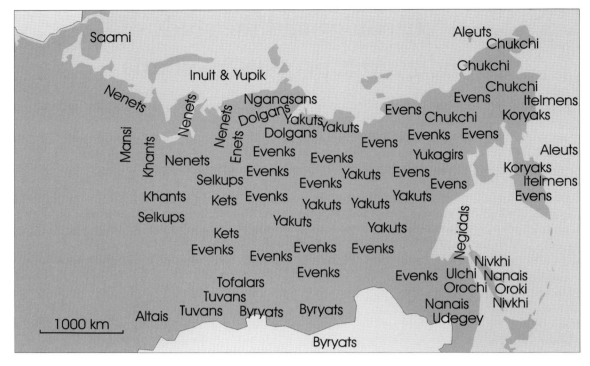

Figure 1. Map illustrating the distribution of indigenous groups in Siberia.

THE DEVELOPMENT OF ARCHAEOLOGY AND ETHNOGRAPHY IN SIBERIA BEFORE THE MID-1930s

In order to support colonization of the 'uninhabited' Siberian areas, from the beginning the Russian government supplemented the influx of soldiers, trappers and farmers with various forms of punitive exile for criminals, prisoners-of-war and political prisoners. In the late 19th and the early 20th centuries, highly educated exiles belonging to the last category, such as Bogoras, Jochelson, Seroshevskiey, Pekarsky and Petri, played an important role in the development of burgeoning research into indigenous culture and archaeology, as well as in the foundation of a number of professional museums in Siberia (Forsyth, 1992: 42–47; Krupnik, 1993: 14–17; Mielnikova, 1994: 3–20; Cruikshank and Argounova, 2000).

Early nationalistic and romantic archaeology focused on fortifications and gold-laden Scythian barrows, which fostered ideas of a glorious past (Soffer, 1985: 7–15). A large part of the Russian intellectual elite from the 1850s onwards formed a romantic, nationalistic and idealistic opposition to the tsarist government, and were organized in a manner similar to medieval guilds. For many members of this group the central purpose of life was to conduct pure research, especially in the field of the natural sciences (Weiner, 1988: 1–40, 1999: 1–35).

The emerging Siberian nationalism regarded Siberia's indigenous groups as an integral part of this region's history and culture. A close relationship between ethnography and hunter-gatherer archaeology is apparent in the fact that Palaeolithic archaeology was termed 'palaeoethnology' and was linked to the natural sciences (similar to placing hunter-gatherers and human evolution together in European museums of natural history), whereas the archaeology of the Bronze Age and later periods were linked to history (Soffer, 1985: 7–15). Several Siberian researchers, such as Petri, for example, were active in ethnography as well as in archaeology (Petri, 1923; Mielnikova, 1994: 3–20).

By the beginning of the 20th century, several high-quality economic surveys had already been carried out about native subsistence patterns, including detailed statistics of local fishing, hunting and reindeer breeding, as well as the status and welfare of indigenous people (Krupnik, 1993: 14–17). These surveys should be seen against the late 19th-century backdrop of developing notions of ecological concepts amongst the Russian intelligentsia; this led to the emergence of a strong nature conservation movement at the beginning of the 20th century (Weiner, 1988: 1–40, 1999: 1–35).

Multiethnic nationalism as an aspect of state ideology seems to have been useful as a means of justifying the Russian presence in a large and sparsely populated region that shared a problematic border with China. This nationalism also appears to have been useful as a cover for criticism of the pre-revolutionary government by some of the revolutionary ethnographers. For instance, Bogoras' criticism of the sloppy administration under which these native groups lived seems to have had a wider objective (e.g. Bogoras, [1909] 1975: 711–730).

During the early period of Communism the Russian State demonstrated a philanthropic spirit towards the 'small peoples'.[2] As members of the so-called 'Committee of the North', a central body for the administration of the indigenous peoples, the ethnographers Bogoras and Shternberg were quite influential. The hunters' debts to traders were cancelled, they were absolved from all state taxes and labour obligations, the sale of alcohol was prohibited and the development of a school system began, which taught the local indigenous language as well as Russian (Forsyth, 1992: 283–287).

Interdisciplinary research into the economy, health, cultural traditions and prehistory of the Siberian indigenous populations continued and reached a scientific level unparalleled in the West until the 1970s. One of the aims of these studies was to find out how indigenous peoples could be integrated into the new economic system in a way that would not undermine their cultural identity (Krupnik, 1993: 14–17; Mielnikova, 1994: 3–20).

The antagonism that existed between those who wanted to leave the indigenous cultures to their traditional ways and the powerful functionaries of the Communist Party who wanted them fully integrated into the communist economy was, perhaps inevitably, resolved in favour of the latter. The idealistic intelligentsia became opposed to the political changes it had itself supported. The introduction during the 1930s of a hard Stalinist line brought the excellent research into Siberian indigenous people to a complete halt (Forsyth, 1992: 241–248). The main researchers either left the country or were shot, and in some cases their archives were deliberately destroyed (Mielnikova, 1994: 3–20).

DEVELOPMENTS FROM THE MID-1930s ONWARDS

By about 1935, nearly all non-Marxist and pre-revolutionary elements had been removed from academic institutions. From being a nationalistic discipline based on studies of indigenous peoples, archaeology became dogmatically Marxist, with close links to history and to the ethnographic theories presented by Engels ([1884] 1972) in *The Origin of the Family, Private Property, and the State*, as well as in Morgan and Tylor's evolutionary schemes (e.g. Morgan, 1877). The purpose of archaeology was to 'illustrate' such development (Soffer, 1985: 8–15).

Archaeology was now linked formally to ethnographic theory based on Cultural Darwinism, and it is only in recent years that research into indigenous culture has begun to recover (Krupnik, 1993: 11–17). It can be noted that, since Palaeolithic cultures *and* modern hunter-gatherers were ascribed to the lowest, most unimportant and least well-defined category in the system – namely, primitive society – it seems that this field was less bound by the rigid theoretical framework that constrained the archaeology of 'higher' cultural stages (Soffer, 1985: 8–15).

After Stalin, two factors seem to have been important for Siberian archaeology's further development in the direction of what one might call regular ethno-archaeology. First, the close relationship between archaeology and the rather advanced and interdisciplinary research into indigenous populations that took place before Stalin seems to have survived as an indirect source of inspiration. Second, the nature conservation movement that survived through the 1930s and 1940s appears to have served as a vehicle for the transfer of *romantic* attitudes towards indigenous peoples and their history and prehistory to the post-Stalin era. The survival into the milder climate of the Khruschev period of this movement that, among other things, had served as a cover for parts of the oppositional intelligentsia, can only be explained by the fact that the authorities regarded its members as a group of politically harmless, nationalistic and idealistic nature cranks (Weiner, 1999: 1–35).

When the All-Russian Society for Conservation (VOOP) was established in 1924, a central member was S.A. Buturlin, an ornithologist who, as a member of the Committee of the North, had championed the cause of the small hunting and trapping peoples. Many local societies for the preservation of local lore were linked to VOOP. Its journal, *Okhrana Prirody*, in addition to articles on the status of endangered species, dealt with such controversial subjects as the positive role of shamanism in ensuring a sustained yield-based exploitation of game among the peoples of Siberia (Weiner, 1988: 45–50).

As the situation relaxed after Stalin's death, data contradicting the idea of a strict and general development in stages appeared in print. Rogachev's discovery at the Kostienki I-1 site of an Aurignacian layer sandwiched between two Solutrean layers is one example, as he interpreted the phenomenon to be the result of two distinct but contemporary ethnic groups (Rogachev, 1957). This discussion parallels the debate about multilinial evolutionism in Western archaeology (Steward, 1955; Sahlins and Service, 1960; Klein, 1970).

In order to be able to deal with synchronic as well as diachronic archaeological cultures, an increasing focus on typology emerged within Soviet archaeology (Soffer, 1985: 8–15). From the early 1950s onwards an increasing polarization between the 'typologists', who believe that it is improper to use ethnographic information in the interpretation of material from archaeological cultures, and those who adopt a regular ethno-archaeological approach can be observed.

Exemplary of the ethno-archaeological approach are Chernetsov and Moszynska, who, in their introduction to a collection of papers published between 1953 and 1961, state, '... data cannot be understood nor brought to life to a sufficient degree without recourse to ethnography and folklore, which often can acquaint us, albeit in vestigial form, with phenomena that appeared and developed in the remote past' (Chernetsov and Moszynska, 1974: 5).

Further examples of detailed archaeological use of ethnographic information is Okladnikov's argument for a connection between the Evenks and the Bronze Age, or possibly even Neolithic, culture in the Baikal area, based both on similarities in, among other things, clothing, ornamentation and dwelling types, as well as the use of ethnographic information in his interpretations of rock art (Okladnikov, 1955: 123–165, 1964: 1972).

CONCLUSION

Today the importance of interdisciplinary research in the fields of archaeology, social anthropology and ecology in Siberia is increasing, facilitated by the improving economic situation. This is not so much the result of new ideas being imported from the West as of the existence of a Russian research tradition that has survived from the 19th century. In spite of the radical political changes the country has experienced, there seems to have been a remarkable continuity in the existence of an influential intellectual opposition based ideologically on its faith in 'pure science', and possessing a multiethnic, nationalistic and romantic perspective on indigenous life.

The interest and engagement in the protection of local indigenous cultures, as well as in research into 'their prehistory' that one surprisingly often encounters today within the Siberian administration, must be seen both as a result of this research tradition, and as a result of the fact that many of the administrators themselves have roots in the indigenous cultures. Today the economy continues to be dominated by extraction of raw materials (mainly oil, gas and minerals) and the Russian state has delimited specific territories within which indigenous groups can continue their hunting way of life. With an improvement in the Russian economy and a return of National pride it would not be surprising to see the emergence of new, radical and interdisciplinary approaches to the protection of the indigenous cultures and cultural heritage in Siberia.

ENDNOTES

1. This paper was originally submitted in January 2002.
2. The term 'small peoples' refers to the numerically small populations of indigenous groups. Today over 40 of these groups are officially recognized by the governments of the Russian Federation as: living in their historical territory; preserving traditional way of life, occupations

and trades; with less than 50,000 members within Russia; and claiming self-recognition as a separate ethnic group.

Ole Grøn was an archaeologist at the Langelands Museum, Rudkøbing, Denmark, from 1986 to 1993. In 1993 he completed his PhD on the spatial organization of Mesolithic dwellings at the Institute of Archaeology, Copenhagen University. From 1994 to 1996 he was a researcher at the Danish National Museums Centre for Maritime Archaeology, Roskilde and from 1996 to 2004 he undertook research into ethnoarchaeology, remote-sensing and maritime archaeology at the Norwegian Institute for Cultural Heritage in Oslo. Since 2004 he has been a research fellow and visiting professor at the Institute of Archaeology, University College London.

Contact address: Institute of Archaeology, University College London, 34 Gordon Square, London WC1H 0PY, UK.

REFERENCES

Bogoras, W. *The Chukchee – Part III – Social Organization*. AMS Press, New York [1909] (1975).
Chernetsov, V.N. and Moszynska, W. *Prehistory of Western Siberia*. Translated and edited by H.N. Michael. Arctic Institute of North America, Montreal (1974).
Crownhart-Vaughan, E.A.P. Introduction to S.P. Krasheninnikov: *Explorations of Kamchatka: North Pacific Scimitar*. [Opisanie Zemli Kamchatki. Report of a journey made to explore eastern Siberia in 1735–1741, by order of the Russian Imperial Government.] Translated by E.A.P. Crownhart-Vaughan. Oregon Historical Society, Portland OR (1972).
Cruikshank, J. and Argounova, T. Reinscribing meaning: memory and indigenous identity in Sakah Republic (Yakutia). *Arctic Anthropology* 37 (2000) 96–119.
Engels F. *The Origin of the Family, Private Property, and the State*. New York: Pathfinder Press [1884] (1972).
Forsyth, J. *A History of the peoples of Siberia. Russia's North Asian Colony 1581–1990*. Cambridge, Cambridge University Press (1992).
Klein, L.S. Archaeology in Britain: a Marxist view. *Antiquity* 44 (1970) 296–303.
Krupnik, I. *Arctic Adaptations. Native Whalers and Reindeer Herders of Northern Eurasia*. Hanover NH: University Press of New England (1993).
Mielnikova, L.V. *Torfi. Istorisko-etnograficheskii atcherk*. Irkutsk (1994).
Morgan, L.W. *Ancient Society, or Researches in the Lines of Human Progress from Savagery through Barbarism to Civilization*. New York: H. Holt and Company (1877).
Okladnikov, A.P. *Neolit I bronzovii vek Pribaikaliar*. Akademia Nauk. Moscow (1955).
Okladnikov, A.P. Ancient population of Siberia and its culture. In Levin, M.G. and Potapov, L.P. (eds) *The Peoples of Siberia*. University of Chicago Press, Chicago IL (1964) 13–98.
Okladnikov, A.P. *Der Hirsch mit dem Goldenen Geweih*. Übers. aus dem Russ. v. I. Filter, Wiesbaden (1972).
Petri, B.E. Sibirski paleolit. *Sbornik trudov professorov i prepodavateley Gos. Irkutskovo universiteta* 5 (1923) 209–213.
Rogachev A.N. Mnogoslioniye stoyanki Kostenkovsko-Borschevskovo raiona na Donu I problema razvit'ya kul'tury v epokhy vernego Paleolita na Russkoi ravinie. *Materialy i issledovaniia po arkheologii SSSR* 59 (1957) 9–134.
Sahlins, M.D. and Service, E.R. (eds) *Evolution and Culture*. University of Michigan Press, Ann Arbor MI (1960).
Soffer, O. *The Upper Paleolithic of the Central Russian Plain*. Academic Press, Orlando FL (1985).
Steward, J. *Theory of Culture Change*. University of Illinois Press, Urbana IL (1955).
Weiner, D.R. *Models of Nature Ecology, Conservation, and Cultural Revolution in Soviet Russia*. Indiana University Press, Bloomington IN (1988).
Weiner, D.R. *A Little Corner of Freedom. Russian Nature Protection from Stalin to Gorbachëv*. University of California Press, Berkeley CA (1999).

Of grizzlies and landslides: the use of archaeological and anthropological evidence in Canadian aboriginal rights cases

Jean Leclair

ABSTRACT

This paper discusses some of the most contentious problems raised by the use of archaeological and anthropological evidence in aboriginal rights litigation in Canada. The first part of the paper deals with the general impact of archaeological and anthropological theories on law. The more specific problems related to the use of archaeological and anthropological evidence in aboriginal rights litigation are the subject of the second part. The final section deals with the reverse problem, that is, the question of the law's impact on the disciplines of archaeology and anthropology.[1]

THE IMPACT OF ARCHAEOLOGICAL AND ANTHROPOLOGICAL THEORIES ON LAW

Law, as much as history, archaeology and all other social sciences, is not a neutral, value-free discipline. Changes in the values and beliefs of society at large will generally result in political and, consequently, in legal changes, and those popular beliefs are often fuelled by what science tells us about our world. More specifically, law is influenced by the generally accepted scientific conclusions of contemporary archaeology and anthropology (Ragsdale, 2001). Legal and ethical debates, in their turn, often influence our beliefs and sometimes science itself.

When one looks at aboriginal legal issues, archaeological and anthropological theories have undeniably influenced, and still influence, developments in law. For instance, the scientific paradigm of the 'vanishing Indian' in 19th-century North America claimed that 'Indians' were:

> racially, culturally and religiously inferior, vulnerable to disease and alcohol, prone to violence and warfare, and low in resistance or adaptability when faced with the loss of land or the diminishment of natural resources [and it]
> led [anthropologists] to the conclusion that tribes were destined, inexorably, to be displaced, if not destroyed, by evolutionary principles. (Ragsdale, 2001: 7–8).

These theories formed the basis of laws whose object was to assimilate, as fast as possible, the Indian population into the general population. On the explicit or implicit basis of these theories, courts felt justified in their conclusions that aboriginal sovereignty was either non-existent or extinguished by the 'higher' culture of the Euro-Americans. It also justified the dominant cultures' policy of dispossession.

At the end of the 19th and the beginning of the 20th centuries, the abandonment of such extreme beliefs in social evolution also influenced new developments in the legislation. Assimilation was discarded and legal reformers sought to preserve and restore tribal cultures. Some even thought that indigenous societies could provide possible models for the majority. In the USA, the result was the adoption of the *Indian Reorganization Act* (1934) that focused, as its title indicates, on restoration rather than assimilation.

Still today, much depends on archaeology and anthropology because, for example, according to the Supreme Court of Canada, the unique status that aboriginal people enjoy in Canadian law is premised on the fact that, 'when Europeans arrived in North America, aboriginal peoples were already here' (*R. v. Van der Peet*, 1996: 30). It is also based on the idea that they were, and still are, culturally different from non-indigenes. Archaeological and anthropological discoveries have the potential of either defeating or upholding, in the public's mind, the idea that aboriginal peoples' difference is deserving of constitutional protection. They are viewed as 'different' because they are perceived as ecologists, communitarians and, most importantly, as the first inhabitants of the continent. If, by any chance, archaeology and anthropology came to demonstrate the contrary, i.e. that aboriginal peoples have not always been respectful of the environment, that they were not governed under egalitarian principles or that they were not the first inhabitants, then, in the public's mind, the basis of their special status might be questioned and, in consequence, this might lead to demands for legal change.

> If the current tribes can be scientifically described as relatively recent immigrants or as themselves the unjustified displacers of predecessor tribes, then post-discovery dispossession by the European invaders may be revisioned as somewhat less egregious or unprecedented, and thereby less supportive of continuing sovereignty and political distinctiveness for the contemporary tribal remnants. (Ragdale, 2001: 42)

In other words, archaeologists, anthropologists and historians are now right in the middle of the battlefield. Their knowledge will either contribute to the justification of the special collective rights legally recognized to the aboriginal peoples, or it will provide ammunition for those who claim that the principle of equality calls for the abolition of special group rights. These changes in archaeological and anthropological doctrines might also impact on how the courts define legal concepts such as aboriginal rights and the Crown's fiduciary duty owed to aboriginal peoples. It might lead to a reassessment of the liberal rules of interpretation applicable to the treaties signed by the Crown with the Indians.

The impacts just described are of a rather indirect nature. Archaeology, anthropology and history have a much more direct impact on law when they are used as tools of evidence in aboriginal rights litigation.

EVIDENTIARY PROBLEMS IN ABORIGINAL RIGHTS CASES

A court's duty is to render decisions on the basis of the best evidence possible, and this duty does not change where aboriginal and treaty rights are concerned. In Canada, those rights are now constitutionalized under subsection 35(1) of the *Constitution Act 1982*, which states that '[t]he existing aboriginal and treaty rights of the aboriginal peoples of Canada are hereby recognized and affirmed'.

Cases dealing with aboriginal rights are 'highly site-specific' (Macaulay, 2000: ch.9, p.4). The tests developed by the Courts put the emphasis on specific historical facts. Aboriginal rights cases can rarely serve as precedents in other cases because the factual situation of each tribe is so different from another. Justice Dickson's statement, although made prior to 1982, still rings true today:

> [c]laims of aboriginal title are woven with history, legend, politics and moral obligations. If the claim of any Band in respect of any particular land is to be decided as a justiciable issue, and not a political issue, it should be so considered on the facts pertinent to that Band and to that land, and not on any global basis. (*Kruger and Manuel v. R.*, 1978: 109).

In the 1996 *Van der Peet* decision, the Supreme Court of Canada defined, for the very first time, the meaning of the words 'aboriginal rights', in s. 35 of the Constitution. The Court stated that an aboriginal right is 'an element of a practice, custom or tradition integral to the distinctive culture of the aboriginal group claiming the right' (*R. v. Van der Peet*, 1996: 46). To establish such distinctiveness, the claimant must demonstrate, 'that the practice, custom or tradition was one of the things [...] that truly *made the society what it was*.' (*R. v. Van der Peet*, 1996: 55, original emphasis). The time period that a court must consider in identifying whether the practice, custom or tradition claimed meets the standard of being integral to the aboriginal community claiming the right was said to be, 'the period prior to contact between aboriginal and European societies' (*R. v. Van der Peet*, 1996: 60). This was so because what underlies the aboriginal rights protected by s. 35(1) is the fact that distinctive aboriginal societies lived on the land *prior* to the arrival of Europeans. Consequently, it is to that pre-contact period that the courts must look in identifying aboriginal rights. Antiquity and not Indian sovereignty thus forms the basis of aboriginal rights in Canada. As can be noticed, the test is extremely fact-specific.

A year later, in *Delgamuukw*, the Supreme Court established a similar test for proving a claim of aboriginal title. Whereas aboriginal rights are concerned with pre-contact *activities* and *practices* that were integral to the culture, aboriginal title confers a right to the territory itself: 'the right to exclusive use and occupation of the land held pursuant to that title for a variety of purposes, which need not be aspects of those aboriginal practices, customs and traditions which are integral to distinctive aboriginal cultures' (*Delgamuukw v. British Columbia*, 1997: 111). Proof of aboriginal title requires that an aboriginal group satisfy the following criteria, which are, again, very fact-specific:

> (i) the land must have been occupied prior to sovereignty, (ii) if present occupation is relied on as proof of occupation pre-sovereignty, there must be a continuity between present and pre-sovereignty occupation, and (iii) at sovereignty, that occupation must have been exclusive. (*Delgamuukw v. British Columbia*, 1997: 143)

In treaty rights cases, evidence must also be adduced to understand the meaning to be given to the covenant. Sometimes this requires proof of specific facts surrounding the signing of the treaty or proof of the intentions, or of the understanding, of the parties involved.

The Supreme Court's approach to aboriginal rights, based as it is on 'cultural "distinctiveness"' (Asch, 2000: 120) rather than on a recognition of the survival of aboriginal sovereignty, has been the subject of extremely severe criticisms, not the least being that it fossilizes aboriginal identity (Borrows, 1997; Rotman, 1997; Barsh and Henderson, 1997; Lambert, 1998; McNeil, 1998; Asch, 2000). Those criticisms will not be addressed here except to say that there is some truth in the crude saying: 'people like their savages naked' (cf. Stohr, 1999: 701).

What I wish to underline is that, in view of the Court's approach, aboriginal rights claims necessarily depend on facts and events that occurred hundreds of years ago. And they involve claimants whose traditional culture was non-literate.

Notwithstanding these obstacles, '[c]laims must still be established on the basis of persuasive evidence demonstrating their validity on the balance of probabilities' (*Mitchell v. Minister of National Revenue*, 2001: 39). The Supreme Court nevertheless stated that some flexibility was needed and that, 'a court should approach the rules of evidence, and interpret the evidence that exists, with a consciousness of the special nature of aboriginal claims, and of the evidentiary difficulties in proving a right which originates in times where there were no written records of the practices, customs and traditions engaged in' (*R. v. Van der Peet*, 1996: 68). In the name of such flexibility, the Supreme Court allowed the admissibility of evidence of post-contact activities to prove continuity with pre-contact practices, customs and traditions. Nevertheless, even if aboriginal rights require 'a unique approach to the treatment of evidence which accords due weight to the perspective of aboriginal peoples', such an accommodation must be done in a manner, 'which does not strain "the Canadian legal and constitutional structure"' (*Delgamuukw v. British Columbia*, 1997: 82). Evidentiary principles must not be strained beyond reason (*Mitchell v. Minister of National Revenue*, 2001: 52). The Court is thus torn between equity and certainty.

Consequently, as we will see, in order to establish their claims, aboriginal peoples must resort to evidence unfamiliar to courts – most importantly, oral histories and ancient documentary records of a non-legal nature. Courts are also confronted with expert evidence based on a variety of unfamiliar sources, archaeological and anthropological findings being two of them. Accepting and evaluating these types of evidence poses great problems in the judicial arena.

Oral histories

Their traditional culture being non-literate, most aboriginal peoples will need to invoke oral histories to establish their claim to an aboriginal right (activity) or an aboriginal title (exclusive use of territory). Such histories are also used to prove that a particular person is a descendant of the signatories of a treaty or to establish the intent or the understanding of the aboriginal signatories.

The aboriginal historical tradition has been described in the *Report of the Royal Commission on Aboriginal Peoples* as:

> ... an oral one, involving legends, stories and accounts handed down through the generations in oral form. It is less focused on establishing objective truth and assumes that the teller of the story is so much a part of the event being described that it would be arrogant to presume to classify or categorize the event exactly or for all time. In the Aboriginal tradition the purpose of repeating oral accounts from the past is broader than the role of written history in western societies. It may be to educate the listener, to communicate aspects of culture, to socialize people into a cultural tradition, or to validate the claims of a particular family to authority and prestige. (Canadian Royal Commission, 1996: 33)

Oral histories are 'memories of memories' (Gernet, 1996: 8). Their non-literate nature clashes with the Western Judaeo-Christian reverence for the written word (Stohr, 1999). An oral history is the recounting of a story heard from someone else. In strict legal terms, these accounts should not be allowed in court because, technically, they qualify as hearsay. A witness is only allowed to relate facts that he/she has personally experienced. The truthfulness of the testimony can thus be ascertained immediately through cross-examination.

Courts have nonetheless concluded that oral histories are an acceptable exception to the hearsay rule. To conclude otherwise would have made it impossible for aboriginal peoples to make their case. In *Delgamuukw*, the Supreme Court went as far as saying that, not only were these histories admissible, but that they stood on an 'equal footing with the types of historical evidence that courts are familiar with' (*Delgamuukw v. British Columbia*, 1997: 87). Before *Delgamuukw*, oral history was held to be admissible, but little or no weight was given to it, unless corroborated by written or archaeological evidence.

For instance, the trial judge in *Delgamuukw* concluded that oral histories were not helpful except as confirmatory evidence (*Delgamuukw v. British Columbia*, 1991: 49, 66). He was of the opinion that such evidence could not be relied on, on its own, because it was not 'literally true' (ibid.: 41). He thought that the plaintiffs were 'recounting matters of faith which had become fact to them' (ibid.: 41). The stories qualified as mythology rather than history (ibid.: 37–38, 48); they were extremely vague and lacking in details (ibid.: 48). The trial judge also quoted extensively from anthropologist Bruce Trigger's *Time and Traditions, Essays in Archaeological Interpretation* in which the latter warns against using oral histories uncritically as a valuable source of information (ibid.: 39–40).

The Supreme Court eventually ordered a new trial in *Delgamuukw* precisely because the trial judge had refused to give independent weight to the oral histories of the Gitksan and Wet'suwet'en peoples. This, the Court concluded, did not conform to the sensitive approach to evidentiary issues enunciated in *Van der Peet* and dictated by the unique situation of the aboriginal peoples.

What did the trial courts make of the Supreme Court's admonition in *Delgamuukw* to give equal standing to oral and written evidence? When the case law is examined, a trend seems to emerge. Notwithstanding the Court's entreaty, trial judges have refused to give weight to oral history when important – that is *territorial* – issues were concerned, especially if the oral evidence was not corroborated or if the written record contradicted it. In cases involving *activities* such as a right to trade, oral histories were more successfully relied upon.

The trial courts' failure to give independent weight to oral history is not surprising. I said earlier that the Supreme Court, in *Delgamuukw*, ordered a new trial, so it did not have to assess and weigh the evidence. The Court essentially stated that oral history was admissible. But the problem with such evidence is not its admissibility but the weight it should be given. Unless corroborated, what is the probative value of such evidence? Respect for aboriginal difference is one thing, but judges are called upon to decide, and decide finally, an issue. They cannot live with uncertainty. They thus require the most conclusive evidence possible.

The trial case in *Delgamuukw* provides a very good example of the difficulties related to the use of oral history in litigation. In that case, two tribes were claiming an aboriginal title on a large part of British Columbia's territory. One of these tribes, the Gitksan tribe, made use of the following story to demonstrate that they were present since time immemorial near a place now called Seeley Lake. According to one elder's story, one day, a very long time ago, after the men had finished the day's fishing, young 'maidens' from the tribe made headdresses out of the backbones and tails of the fishes; delighted with their new ornaments, they started to dance and sing. Suddenly, their festivities were interrupted by a thunderous noise coming from the mountain beside the lake. A gigantic grizzly bear was coming down the side of the mountain 'tramping down the trees'. The warriors came out of the village to confront the animal. The grizzly went down to the lake, crossed it and trampled the warriors to death. Its gruesome task finished, it went back from where it had come. The elder summed up the morality of the story in the following way:

> That's why the wise elders told the young people not to play around with fish or meat or anything, [...] because the Sun God gave them food to eat [...] [T]hey should just take enough to eat and not to play [sic] with it, that's why this tragedy happens [sic] to them. (*Delgamuukw v. British Columbia*, 1991: 53).

What can a judge do with such evidence? 22,000 km² of territory were at stake in *Delgamuukw*. The elder in this case was undeniably sincere and honest. But, is this story, on its own, sufficient evidence to establish a claim of aboriginal title? How can the defendant cross-examine the elder to determine the veracity of her story? As Justice Lambert of the British Columbia Court of Appeal remarked:

> How can a defendant's counsel attack it by the traditional method of cross-examination? How dark was it? How good was the eyesight of the people there? How many fingers am I holding up? Could the bear have been only 80 feet tall? (Lambert, 1998: 264–265).

Nevertheless, such evidence can certainly be of great use if corroborated. Again, *Delgamuukw* provides an eloquent example. A geomorphologist testified at trial that a major landslide had occurred about 3500 years ago. A landslide of such magnitude that it would have produced a tremendous noise, a great cloud of smoke and debris, and that huge swathes of forests would have been cleared away. A great mass of debris would also have ended up at the bottom of the lake. A palaeobotanist confirmed these findings. He had taken a core-sample from the bed of Seeley Lake and analysed a layer of clay situated about 1.5m below the lakebed. He concluded that the clay layer was 3380 years old and the result of a rise in the lake's water level occasioned by a landslide blockage of the stream outlet. Scientific evidence together with the oral history constituted a much more convincing proof of the Gitksan presence on British Columbian territory prior to sovereignty, than just the oral history alone.

In the *Mitchell* case (2001), the Supreme Court reassessed, and backtracked, on what it had earlier said about oral histories in *Delgamuukw*. To be admissible, said the Court, evidence had to be both useful and reliable. Oral histories satisfied the usefulness test because they offered evidence of ancestral practices, and their significance, that would not otherwise be available, and because they provided the aboriginal perspective on the right claimed. The reliability test rests upon an inquiry into the witness's ability to know and testify to orally transmitted aboriginal traditions and history. On the issue of weight, the most contentious of all, although the Court repeated what it had earlier said in *Delgamuukw*, it underlined that:

> [p]lacing 'due weight' on the aboriginal perspective, or ensuring its supporting evidence an 'equal footing' with more familiar forms of evidence, means precisely what these phrases suggest: *equal* and *due* treatment. While the evidence presented by aboriginal claimants should not be undervalued [...] neither should it be artificially strained to carry more weight than it can reasonably support. (*Mitchell v. Minister of National Revenue*, 2001: 39)

More particularly, the Court indicated that the *Van der Peet* approach did 'not operate to amplify the cogency of evidence adduced in support of an aboriginal claim' (*Mitchell v. Minister of National Revenue*, 2001: 39).

In *Mitchell*, the Court had to determine whether the Mohawks of Akwesasne had an aboriginal right to bring goods across the St Lawrence River for the purposes of trade. Such an aboriginal right would have precluded the imposition of duty under the *Customs Act*. There was an undeniable geographical element to the claim (the establishment of a North–South axis of trade), since the Mohawks wanted the Court to recognize their 'right to convey goods across an international boundary for the purposes of trade' (*Mitchell v. Minister of National Revenue*, 2001: 57). The trial judge had found in favour of the claimants on the basis of oral history and archaeological evidence. Although there was ample evidence to demonstrate that trade was a central feature of Mohawk culture prior to contact, the Supreme Court nevertheless overruled the trial decision stating that there was 'no support in the evidentiary record' (*Mitchell v. Minister of National Revenue*, 2001: 42) to establish an ancestral Mohawk practice of transporting goods across the St Lawrence River for the purposes of trade. Although the oral histories were to the effect that there had been commercial exchanges between the Five Nations and their northern neighbours, archaeological evidence demonstrated the contrary. On the basis of D.K. Richter's (1992) book, *The Ordeal of the Longhouse: The Peoples of the Iroquois League in the Era of European Colonization*, the Supreme Court concluded that 'long-distance Mohawk trade, at least at the time of contact, fell along an east–west axis' (*Mitchell v. Minister of National Revenue*, 2001: 44).[2] Constant warfare between the Mohawks and the northern tribes precluded the possibility of trade on a North–South axis. The geographical element of the claim had thus not been proven.

In conclusion, even useful and reliable oral evidence cannot stand unless corroborated by other evidence. Some archaeologists agree with such an approach, stating that, even for the purposes of the anthropological discipline, oral history must be subjected to both internal and external tests in order to determine its reliability and validity (Gernet, 1996: 9).

Stohr (1999: 701) states that '[o]n the one hand, courts protect [aboriginal] practices only to the extent that they are "traditional" while disparaging oral history, the only evidence available to prove the tribal past'. There is some truth in this, but on the other hand, giving independent weight to oral history puts those denying the existence of the claim in a next to impossible position. As one judge said, 'They are unlikely to be able to persuade a member of the same First Nations community to give convincing evidence of a contradictory oral history. So they will have to rely on experts to try to disprove the oral history, or they will have to rely on cross-examination' (Lambert, 1998: 264). And who would dare cross-examine a respectable elder on the reliability of his/her testimony? Finally, by putting too much emphasis on oral history, courts run the risk of overevaluating oral histories. They seem to ignore that other types of evidence, some much more reliable, do exist (including archaeological and ethnographic sources).

For oral history to stand a chance in court, it will have to be adapted to the litigation environment. Firstly, courts should be reminded that the differences between oral and written narratives should not be overemphasized: '[b]oth ... are selective characterization of events, both are subject to bias, and both can easily perpetuate fictions' (Gernet, 1996: 5). Secondly, the main problem with oral histories is that they are generally offered in testimony during trial. Unable as they are to assess their validity, judges have a tendency to reject them. One way of avoiding such a result is to write down the stories so as to enable their analysis by expert witnesses better equipped than judges to assess them (Gernet, 1996:15–16).

Before moving on to the use of documentary records, I want to underline two other difficulties related to the use of archaeological evidence. Firstly, one problem faced by all claimants in an aboriginal rights case is that, very often, there is no archaeological evidence available because no research has been done. Secondly, judges often consider the identification and interpretation of archaeological evidence insufficiently precise, or detailed, to be of any help in establishing proof of occupation by a specific tribe. In *Delgamuukw*, for example, findings consisting in cache pits and house remains dating back 3000 years or more were introduced to establish the claimants presence on the claimed territory. They were dismissed by the trial judge, who concluded that, '[a]ny aboriginal people could have created these remains' (*Delgamuukw v. British Columbia*, 1991: 50).

Documentary records

Documentary records refer to historical documents, including reports of the Hudson Bay Company agents, the diaries of early clerics, traders and explorers. These documents are admissible if their authors are considered disinterested and if the document came about before the claim was contemplated.

The main problem with such written evidence is that, contrary to oral evidence, its reliability is generally not questioned. It can stand on its own without any need for corroboration. The fact that it was the product of Europeans, and that it expresses the prejudices and misconceptions of their time, does not seem to bother some judges. For instance, in *Delgamuukw*, although the trial judge was quite concerned about the reliability of oral history, he said that he had 'no hesitation accepting the information' (*Delgamuukw v. British Columbia*, 1991: 64) contained in the reports of William Brown, the first Hudson's Bay Company agent to have visited the Gitksan country in 1822. The judge's attitude as to what evidence should be admissible was undoubtedly culturally biased.

Expert evidence

Archaeologists and anthropologists have not always been seen as friendly by aboriginal peoples. The 'imperial archaeologists' and 19th century ideas of evolution and progress that they adopted, played an important role in justifying the adoption of laws aimed at assimilating the 'inferior races' (Ragsdale, 2001: 7–9). But now, whether they like it or not, aboriginal peoples have been forced to resort to archaeologists and anthropologists to collect evidence that is considered acceptable by the courts to corroborate their oral evidence.

There are various problems faced by social science experts in aboriginal litigation. Firstly, the archaeologist or anthropologist has to establish that they are qualified in their field of expertise and, more specifically, that they are qualified to testify about the tribe or territory involved in the litigation. Secondly, the opinion will only be reliable if the methodology of research and analysis is generally accepted in the discipline. This opens the door to the debates raging in the discipline itself.

FACTUAL BASIS OF THE OPINION

The biggest problem with expert evidence is that usually it is not based entirely on facts of which the expert has personal knowledge. As such, it offends the rule against hearsay. For example, an expert will usually ground his/her opinion on findings made by other scientists in the field. In view of the impossibility of proving every single fact that has gone into the formulation of the opinion the rule is that, 'in circumstances where the factual basis of an expert's opinion is a mixture of proven and unproven facts or hearsay, the weight given to the opinion will depend on the amount and quality of the admissible evidence' (Macaulay, 2000: ch.9, p.80). Learned treatises are also admissible in evidence (if they meet the test of trustworthiness), so that the opinion of the expert witnesses may be assessed during cross-examination. In a preliminary ruling in the *Delgamuukw* case, the trial judge said that, admitting other written work, the authors of which have not been called to testify, allows a court to assess the weight to be attached to expert evidence (*Delgamuukw v. British Columbia*, 1990: 37–38).

The other problem with expert opinion, especially that of cultural anthropologists, is that it is often based on oral histories, the testimony of others. We have already seen what kind of problems such evidence poses.

BIAS OF THE EXPERTS

An expert witness, although paid a fee by the party who hired him, must nevertheless be as impartial as possible. Bias will undermine the credibility of a witness – including an expert witness – and sometimes completely discredit him/her. The problem is that, very often, expert witnesses have developed strong emotional ties with the aboriginal people involved in the claim. This has unfortunate consequences, as illustrated by the following excerpt from the 1985 *Bear Island* case:

> While [Mr Macdonald] is very familiar with the Temagami area in general, it was obvious from his comments that he viewed the court process as being rigged against the Indians and that, from his two references to 'we' in the context of being part of the defendants' team, he was biased in favour of the defendants. He [...is] typical of persons who have worked closely with Indians for so many

years that they have lost their objectivity when giving opinion evidence. (*Attorney General for Ontario v. Bear Island Foundation et al.*, 1985: 37)

Cultural anthropologists engaged in participatory research have great difficulties establishing that they are not biased in favour of the aboriginal group they studied: 'For anthropologists to understand a culture, they must learn about it. However, once anthropologists engage in field study, a recognized technique of their profession, their objectivity is called into question' (Asch and Bell, 1993: 545–546). At trial, in *Delgamuukw*, the evidence of two cultural anthropologists who had both lived for more than two years with the Gitksan was rejected. The trial judge said of one of them that he was 'more an advocate [that is, a lawyer] than a witness', while the other's testimony was rejected in the following manner: 'I place little reliance on Dr Daly's report or evidence. This is unfortunate because he is clearly a well-qualified, highly intelligent anthropologist. It is always unfortunate when experts become too close to their clients, especially during litigation (*Delgamuukw v. British Columbia*, 1991: 41 and 43).

THE IMPACT OF LAW ON THE ARCHAEOLOGICAL AND ANTHROPOLOGICAL DISCIPLINES

Law engenders moral and ethical problems for the historian, the archaeologist and the anthropologist. It also creates epistemological problems, at least for the historians in Canada.

Moral and ethical problems

The duty of a court is to settle an issue once and for all. Such certainty is anathema in the social sciences. In the academic world, no one has the pretence to settle an issue once and for all. What happens, then, when an expert is asked, in exchange for a fee, to furnish information for one of the party to a legal claim? Firstly, this might go against the explicit rules of ethics of his/her profession. For instance, in *Delgamuukw*, one of the disqualified cultural anthropologists had quoted in his report the following passage taken from the Statement of Ethics of the American Anthropological Association: 'In research, an anthropologist's paramount responsibility is to those he studies. When there is a conflict of interest, these individuals must come first. The anthropologist must do everything within his power to protect their physical, social and psychological welfare and to honour their dignity and privacy' (*Delgamuukw v. British Columbia*, 1991: 41).

The expert's dilemma is great if we remember that, in participating in the litigation process, social scientists somehow give legitimacy to the legal tests that fossilize aboriginal identity to what it was prior to contact with the Europeans. Secondly, because litigation necessarily involves a winner and a loser, the danger is real that the historical analysis will not be as dispassionate, or as balanced, as it should be, so that a black-and-white portrait of history will be drawn (Beaulieu, 2000: 542–543). Furthermore, in Canada, litigation has created two classes of social scientists. The noble ones, defending aboriginal groups, and the not-so-noble ones, working for government. The problem is that such Manichean division is not the ideal context for a truly scientific study of aboriginal issues (Beaulieu, 2000: 543–545). Furthermore, it seems that sometimes the nobility of the aboriginal cause serves as an excuse for methodological deficiencies and lack of rigor. In the words of a leading historian in Quebec, 'La noblesse de la cause suffit-elle à garantir la rigueur de la démarche et à immuniser les chercheurs contre tout biais idéologique?' (Beaulieu, 2000: 546).

If they wish to act as expert witnesses social scientists must resist the temptation to take sides in a way that would jeopardize their professional integrity. The credibility of the discipline and of the experts themselves is at stake.

Epistemological problems

Another intriguing consequence of litigation in Canada is that some of the Supreme Court's 'historical' findings have had repercussions in the historical discipline itself. Some historical questions are now 'taboo'.

For example, in the *R. v. Sioui* case (1990), at issue was the legal nature of a document of 1760 signed by General Murray a few days prior to New France's capitulation. The document guaranteed the Hurons, in exchange for their surrender, British protection and the free exercise of their religion, customs and trade with the English. The Court had to decide whether or not this document was a treaty within the meaning of s. 35(1) of the *Constitution Act, 1982*. In a controversial decision, the Court said it was, whereas many historians believed the document to be simply a safe conduct. What is of interest for the purposes of our discussion is that, since then, historians who persist in referring to it as a safe conduct stand a chance of being held out as racists by other historians in highly credible social science reviews (for an example of such an accusation, see Savard, 1996: 80).

The solution, it seems, would be for historians and other social scientists to criticize, not one another, but the courts for having developed such discriminatory tests for establishing a claim of aboriginal rights (Beaulieu, 2000: 549–550).

CONCLUSION

In conclusion, social science expert witnesses are often disconcerted by the 'all or nothing' methods of the courts, particularly when interpretations that they have presented within academic debate are treated as decisive facts within a courtroom ruling. Courts are not unaware of the problem. In the words of the Supreme Court of Canada:

> The law sees a finality of interpretation of historical events where finality, according to the professional historian, is not possible. The reality, of course, is that the courts are handed disputes that require for their resolution the finding of certain historical facts. The litigating parties cannot await the possibility of a stable academic consensus. The judicial process must do as best it can. (*R. v Marshall*, 1999: 37)

One should remember that to abandon precedents and the internal logic of the legal discipline to improve the situation of aboriginal peoples might be at the cost of the courts' own legitimacy. The better solution might be to put in place an administrative tribunal staffed with lawyers, social scientists and aboriginals. This appears to be the only solution that would at once enable an accurate assessment of all the pertinent facts and avoid some of the pitfalls described in this article.

ENDNOTES

1. This paper was first read at the Institute of Archaeology in March 2002 and is based on Canadian case law up to that date.
2. *Mitchell v. Minister of National Revenue* (2001: par. 43–47) states:

The archaeological evidence consisted of two works, submitted by expert witnesses, purportedly documenting an historical north–south trade in copper and ceremonial knives, respectively. Sexton, J.A., writing for the majority of the Federal Court of Appeal in upholding the trial judge's finding of a cross-border trading right, placed significant emphasis on the former. He concluded at para. 50 that D.K. Richter's book, *The Ordeal of the Longhouse: The Peoples of the Iroquois League in the Era of European Colonization* (1992), demonstrated that the Iroquois living in what is now the State of New York traded in copper which originated from the north shore of Lake Superior. Justice McKeown recognized that this was clear archaeological evidence of North–South trade across what is now the Canada–United States border.

This is, with respect, an overly generous interpretation of both the book and the trial judgment. The book merely states that plates of worked copper originating in the Great Lakes region were particularly prized as gifts by the members of the Five Nations Confederacy (Richter, *supra*, at p. 28). It indicates that this copper *originated* to the north of the Mohawk Valley, not that the Mohawks obtained this copper through direct trading with their northern neighbours. Indeed, Richter's book confirms that long-distance Mohawk trade, at least at the time of contact, fell along an east–west axis. The Mohawks traded with the Wenros and Neutrals to the west (in the Niagra Region, south of the Great Lakes) and the Mohicans in the east, but not with their enemies in the disputed territory to the north. Richter contends that warfare between the Five Nations and their northern neighbours precluded the possibility of trade (at pp. 28–29):

The lack of any need for large-scale trade helps explain not just the isolationism of Five Nations villages from each other and outsiders but their <u>wars with such sixteenth-century neighbours as the Hurons, the Susquehannocks, the Algonquins, and the St. Lawrence Iroquoians.</u> Because relationships among people rested on the alliances of spiritual power that came from reciprocity, a *lack* of reciprocity, <u>as epitomized by the absence of trading</u>

relationships, could easily lead to a presumption of hostility. Just as a shaman or an other-than-human person could be expected to wreak havoc when denied respect and reciprocity, so too could people of another village with whom no exchange relationships existed. [Underlining added; italics in original].

Richter then proceeds to note that the opposite dynamic prevailed where trading occurred between nations: reciprocal trade facilitated and signified peaceful relations between communities. In a passage not quoted by McKeown, J., Richter concludes that the copper plates, originating in the Great Lakes region and prized by the Confederacy for their spiritual power, were obtained indirectly along the east–west trade axis, not directly from the north as implied by the trial judge and asserted by the Court of Appeal (at p. 29):

[A]mong the few neighboring peoples with whom all of the autonomous villages of the Five Nations seem to have been regularly at peace during the period when Europeans first arrived on the Turtle's Back were the Neutrals and Wenros to the west and the Mahicans and River Indians to the east. Each sat astride routes to the sources of exotic commodities associated with spiritual power that were not available in the homelands of the Five Nations: Great Lakes copper and other minerals linked with spiritual power came from beyond the country of the Neutrals and Wenros, and shell beads arrived from the coast of Long Island Sound presumably by way of the Mahicans and River Indians. [Emphasis added].

Consequently, while Richter's book may support the pre-contact existence of north–south trade routes, it refutes the direct involvement of the Mohawks in this trade. This is a significant fact, given the reliance by the trial judge on this evidence in concluding the aboriginal right was established, and in rejecting the testimony of the appellant's expert witness, Dr von Gernet, to the effect that he had 'yet to find a single archaeological site anywhere in Ontario dating to the prehistoric, the protohistoric or the early historical period which has in any way ever been associated with the Mohawks' (p. 30).

The second item of archaeological evidence relates to an alleged trade in chalcedony ceremonial knives, raised by the claimant's expert witness, Dr Venables, on the basis of W.A. Ritchie's *The Archaeology of New York State* (1980). Again, Ritchie describes the Iroquois trade networks as falling "chiefly westward toward the Upper Great Lakes, where also the strongest cultural ties are found" (p. 196, emphasis added). The only evidence of northerly trade is found in a single 'smoky chalcedony ceremonial (?) knife', from which Ritchie postulates a potential trade route 'evidently to the north in Quebec' (p. 196) established somewhere between 3000 BC and 300 BC. This evidence, standing alone, can hardly be called compelling.

Jean Leclair is a Professor in the Faculty of Law, Université de Montréal. He gained a LL. B. Montréal 1985; and a LL. M. Montréal 1990 (Duff-Rinfret scholar). He has been a Professor at the Université de Montréal, since 1991 and was a Lecturer at the Université de Montréal from 1989 to 1991. He was a Law clerk, Federal Court (Appeal Division), 1986–1988; Member of the Québec Bar Association since 1987. His fields of research and teaching include Canadian Legal History, Constitutional Law and Aboriginal Legal Issues.

Contact address: Université de Montréal, Faculty of Law, C.P. 6128; Succursale Centre-ville, Montréal, Québec, Canada H3C 3J7. Email: Jean.leclair@umontreal.ca

REFERENCES

Asch, M. The judicial conceptualization of culture after Delgamuukw and Van der Peet. *Review of Constitutional Studies* 5 (2000) 119–137.

Asch, M. and Bell, C. Definition and interpretation of fact in Canadian aboriginal title litigation: an analysis of Delgamuukw. *Queen's Law Journal* 19 (1993) 503–550.

Barsh, R.L. and Henderson, J.Y. The Supreme Court's Van der Peet trilogy: naive imperialism and ropes of sand. *McGill Law Journal* 42 (1997) 993–1009.

Beaulieu, A. Les pièges de la judiciarisation de l'histoire autochtone. *Revue d'histoire de l'Amérique française* 53 (2000) 541–551.

Borrows, J. The trickster: integral to a distinctive culture. *Constitutional Forum* 8 (1997) 27–32.

Canadian Royal Commission. *Report of the Royal Commission on Aboriginal Peoples. Vol. 1: Looking Forward, Looking Back*. Supply and Services, Ottawa (1996).

Gernet, A. *Oral Narratives and Aboriginal Pasts: An Interdisciplinary Review of the Literatures on Oral Traditions and Oral Histories*. A Report submitted to the Department of Indian Affairs and Northern Development. (1996) http://www.ainc-inac.gc.ca/pr/pub/orl/index_e.html

Lambert, D. Van der Peet and Delgamuukw: ten unresolved issues. *University of British Columbia Law Review* 32 (1998) 249–270.

Macaulay, M.L. *Aboriginal and Treaty Rights Practice*. Carswell, Scarborough (2000).

McNeil, K. Aboriginal rights in Canada: from title to land to territorial sovereignty. *Tulsa Journal of Comparative & International Law* 5 (1998) 253–298.

Ragsdale, J.W. Some philosophical, political and legal implications of American archaeological and anthropological theory. *University of Missouri-Kansas City School of Law* 70 (2001) 1–53.

Richter, D.K. *The Ordeal of the Longhouse: The Peoples of the Iroquois League in the Era of European Colonization*. University of North Carolina Press, Chapel Hill NC (1992).

Ritchie, W.A. *Archaeology of New York State* (second edition, revised). Harbor Hill Books, Harrison NY (1980).

Rotman, L.I. Creating a still-life out of dynamic objects: rights reductionism at the Supreme Court of Canada. *Alberta Law Review* 36 (1997) 1–8.

Savard, R. Commentaire sur La fin des alliances franco-indiennes: enquêtes sur un sauf-conduit de 1760 devenu un traité en 1990. *Recherches amérindiennes* 26 (1996) 78–80.

Stohr, G. The repercussions of orality in Federal Indian Law. *Arizona State Law Journal* 31 (1999) 680–704.

Trigger, B. Time and traditions: essays in archaeological interpretation. Edinburgh University Press, Edinburgh (c1978) 273.

Case laws

Attorney General for Ontario v. Bear Island Foundation et al. [1985] 1 Canadian Native Law Reports 1.

Delgamuukw v. British Columbia [1990] 1 Canadian Native Law Reports 29.

Delgamuukw v. British Columbia [1991] 5 Canadian Native Law Reports 1.

Delgamuukw v. British Columbia [1997] 3 Supreme Court Reports 1010; http://www.lexum.umontreal.ca/csc-scc/en/pub/1997/vol3/html/1997scr3_1010.html

Kruger and Manuel v. R. [1978] 1 Supreme Court Reports 104.

Mitchell v. Minister of National Revenue [2001] 1 Supreme Court Reports 911; http://www.lexum.umontreal.ca/csc-scc/en/pub/2001/vol1/html/2001scr1_0911.html

R. v. Marshall [1999] 3 Supreme Court Reports 456; http://www.lexum.umontreal.ca/csc-scc/en/pub/1999/vol3/html/1999scr3_0456.html

R. v. Sioui [1990] 1 Supreme Court Reports 1025; http://www.lexum.umontreal.ca/csc-scc/en/pub/1990/vol1/html/1990scr1_1025.html

R. v. Van der Peet [1996] 2 Supreme Court Reports 507; http://www.lexum.umontreal.ca/csc-scc/en/pub/1996/vol2/html/1996scr2_0507.html)

Social scientists and native title cases in Australia

Peter Sutton

ABSTRACT

Recent legal developments in Australia have led the courts to reject the doctrine of *terra nullius*, which denied pre-existing Aboriginal rights to land ownership, and Aboriginal prior occupation and ownership of land are now acknowledged. However, in the absence of consent determinations the courts have to evaluate the justification for legally recognizing native title based on specific local evidence for continuities in the traditional customs and laws of Aboriginal claimants since British sovereignty. Much of the evidence for such continuities can come from the Aboriginal claimants themselves. However, proving the time, depth and relevance of these continuities and presenting them in a form that is considered acceptable by the courts has drawn upon the 'expertise' of academics. This paper considers the types of evidence that anthropologists, linguists, historians and archaeologists are able to present and makes some suggestions as to how this could be improved in the future.

THE LEGISLATIVE BACKGROUND

In 1969 and 1970 members of land-holding groups in northeast Arnhem Land, in the Northern Territory of Australia, brought action against the mining company Nabalco and the Commonwealth of Australia in an attempt to gain recognition of their own traditional rights over the land of the Gove Peninsula. This led to the famous 'Gove case' of 1971, which resulted in a reaffirmation of the doctrine of *terra nullius* that had long been the basis for official non-recognition of customary and pre-existing indigenous rights to land and waters in Australia.

However, a form of statutory Aboriginal titles was introduced by the Commonwealth government for the Northern Territory in the *Aboriginal Land Rights (Northern Territory) Act* (Commonwealth) (1976), section 3(1) of which reads:

> 'traditional Aboriginal owners', in relation to land, means a local descent group of Aboriginals who
>
> (a) have common spiritual affiliations to a site on the land, being affiliations that place the group under a primary spiritual responsibility for that site and for the land; and
>
> (b) are entitled by Aboriginal tradition to forage as of right over that land;

This definition, which rested on anthropological ideas and advice of the time, inevitably drew many anthropologists into researching and providing evidence in the many claims heard under this Act, claims that by the end of the 1990s were coming to a close. The State land rights scheme created for Queensland in 1991 has similarly drawn many anthropologists into the application of the legislation to the claims process, which recognizes three bases of claim: traditional affiliation, historical association and economic viability. Other state legislative schemes that deal with Aboriginal land interests (other than native title, see below) have not required the same kind of anthropological involvement.

In 1982 three Murray Islanders, Eddie Mabo, David Passi and James Rice, on their own behalf and on behalf of their families, commenced proceedings in the High Court of Australia seeking, *inter alia*, a declaration that they were the holders of traditional native title and that the Crown's sovereignty over the Murray Islands was subject to their rights according to local custom and traditional native title. In 1992 the High Court delivered its historic *Mabo* judgement, in which a majority (6:1) held that native title could be recognized by the common law of Australia. By the end of 1993 the Australian government had passed the *Native Title Act*, which created a statutory scheme for the recognition and protection of native title and, among other things, provided (i) a mechanism for determining claims to native title, (ii) ways of dealing with future acts affecting native title and (iii) in certain circumstances, compensation for its extinguishment. Although the Act was subject to far-reaching amendments in 1998, attaining a complexity found daunting even by lawyers, it retained its essential definition of what constitutes 'native title' or 'native title rights and interests'. Section 223(1), reads in part:

> The expression *native title* or *native title rights and interests* means the communal, group or individual rights and interests of Aboriginal peoples or Torres Strait Islanders in relation to land or waters, where:
>
> (a) the rights and interests are possessed under the traditional laws acknowledged, and the traditional customs observed, by the Aboriginal peoples or Torres Strait Islanders; and
> (b) the Aboriginal peoples or Torres Strait Islanders, by those laws and customs, have a connection with the land or waters; and
> (c) the rights and interests are recognized by the common law of Australia.

A series of High Court decisions have gradually refined the construction and meaning of these words, although there will undoubtedly be more decisions to come. It is now clear that claimants need to establish that the traditional laws they acknowledge, and the traditional customs they observe and on which their rights in land and waters are based, are substantially the same as those of their predecessors in the same area prior to the acquisition of British sovereignty. Those laws and customs must have normative content. The chain of transmission of these traditions also must be shown to be substantially unbroken, and traditions reconstituted in recent times will be of no avail. Many are of the view that this decision effectively removes the possibility of succeeding in achieving recognition of native title, except in remote regions where classical traditions have persisted most appreciably. It is also clear now that the High Court has rejected broad traditional claims of an essentially proprietary kind, preferring instead the 'bundle of rights' approach. These decisions have pushed the emphasis of social science research on native title cases into greater historical depth of detail and into a greater focus on particular rights or traditional 'activities'.

ANTHROPOLOGISTS

It is conceivable that a native title scheme that did not encourage or require work to be done by anthropologists might have been created, and it is notable that the definition of native title rights and interests in the *Native Title Act* (1993), unlike the Northern Territory Land Rights Act and similar legislation, owes little of a direct nature to anthropological models. There is variable opinion on the extent to which anthropologists are necessary even in the evidentiary testing process, given that claimants are typically called, in contested cases, to give evidence about themselves. But, there are good reasons why expert evidence is normally called as well, and may be relied upon by a court (see Fingleton and Finlayson, 1995; Finlayson and Jackson-Nakano, 1996; Peterson and Rigsby, 1998; Finlayson et al., 1999).

Anthropologists working on native title cases record claimants' and other informants' statements about how one may rightfully belong to a place, what rights flow from one's traditional connection to a place, how one should behave according to customary rules to do with interests in sites and areas of country, and so on. These statements are highly important guides as to how people consciously formulate relevant principles. However, those statements do not alone account for or predict how people relate systematically to places or how they in practice allocate rights and interests in them.

They are 'folk models' – and usually only fragments of them – that contribute important subjective knowledge to the record. An anthropological model, on the other hand, has to take into account what we can learn from people's actual behaviours, including other statements, as well. A senior man may say, for example, that strong interests in a country can only come from having a birthplace there or a father from that place, but it may become fully apparent that there are many cases that do not conform to this 'rule', yet which are so patterned as to clearly be manifestations of a regular customary system. Bagshaw (2003) presents an excellent example of the kind of ethnography that is submitted for legal purposes in such cases. Furthermore, a scholar who has good archival or other older historical records of the relevant ethnographic area can reach longer-term conclusions spanning as much as a couple of centuries, well beyond living memory or even oral history. Do patterns that people do not recognize, or do not wish to recognize, fall outside the normative?

In non-legal and anthropological terms the 'normative' covers not only explicit rules but may also include the behavioural reflection of the *assumption* of a norm, and *average* or *typical behaviour* as well as ideal norms. In classical Aboriginal cultural traditions it would be abnormal, perhaps even inconceivable, that people would produce explicit, full and objective articulations of how their social order works, comparing ideals with action, and extracting underlying patterns of typical behaviour. Anthropologists rely on combined informant verbal and behavioural evidence, together with documentary evidence, in order to gradually form a systematic picture of topics such as customary ways of recognizing rights in country and how they might have changed over time. For these reasons it would be both unsophisticated and counterproductive to reduce the category of evidence for traditional 'laws and customs', for example, entirely to verbal formulations that might be elicited from particular Aboriginal informants or witnesses, although this position is argued by some lawyers. One cannot put the weight of responsibility for such central probative matters on brief statements given in what is often a culturally alien context, and sometimes in a person's third or fourth language. Furthermore, some Aboriginal people objectify and intellectualize their customary behaviours more than others. There is a significant contrast – and one that has classical, pre-colonial roots – between the people of northeast Arnhem Land, for example, who can articulate their culture to a high degree, and those of the Western Desert who largely do not. An insistence that courts rely solely on indigenous witness evidence for adequate explication of their normative systems would thus disadvantage those from the Western Desert compared with those from the more complex society of northeast Arnhem Land, for example.

If one takes a narrow view of how traditional rights are 'acknowledged' by claimants, restricting it merely to their verbalizations and omitting what may be abundant other evidence for their possession of a complexly patterned cultural logic, an ingrained system, of recognizing rights, one may miss important evidence. Patterned behaviour is not merely a statistical norm when it comes to human social behaviour. Such behaviour is informed by often deeply submerged cultural presuppositions, of which the people concerned may be only partly aware. There may also be presuppositions and rules of which people are aware but which they may be constrained, by customary law, sometimes by political self-interest, from articulating, especially in public. Without the analysis of an external observer they may not be able to do justice to their cases, in a context where a negotiation or court hearing simply can never offer claimants and their assessors the kind of direct exposure to significant periods of everyday life and to multiple sources of evidence that an anthropologist necessarily engages with during field work. Further, contemporary statements by claimants may be of little assistance in articulating the normative content of relevant laws and customs that applied before sovereignty was established, or in articulating transformative and other relationships between past and present.

For further information: Mantziaris and Martin (2000) provide an anthropologically and legally informed approach to native title corporations, and Sutton (2003) discusses the main ethnographic issues concerned with proof of native title under the Australian legal regime.

LINGUISTS

Linguistic evidence has played a role in Australian indigenous land claims for some decades, but in native title cases this type of evidence seems to be assuming a more prominent role than ever, and it may be destined to play an even greater part in the future (Henderson and Nash, 2002; also McKeown, 1996). It has now become quite common for there to be a separate linguistic report alongside the main anthropological, archaeological and historical reports lodged on behalf of claimant groups prior to determinations of native title. This is partly a reflection of the raised standard of evidence that flows from the possibility of native title litigation, by contrast with the more limited degree of detail required of administrative inquiries such as those of the Aboriginal Land Commissioner (Northern Territory) or the Land Tribunal (Queensland). It is also a consequence of the peculiar demands of native title law itself, especially its emphasis on evidence for continuity of native titles since the establishment of British sovereignty.

Linguists and others have for some decades provided expert evidence or have published writings that deal with the problems of cultural difference, communicative style, translation and transcription that may arise where indigenous witnesses give evidence in English-dominated and culturally very European legal hearings. Such issues were first given an airing in the early 19th century when colonists debated among themselves the question of whether or not native witnesses should be able to give evidence in criminal trials. Later the anthropologists T.G.H. Strehlow and A.P. Elkin published on the linguistic and other cultural problems of indigenous court evidence, and Strehlow played a significant, if thwarted, historic role when providing expert linguistic evidence to the Stuart Royal Commission in 1959.

In the native title field, one particular contribution of linguistics remains rather under-utilized, and that is the field of the contemporary semantics of indigenous languages and of indigenous varieties of English. Of course, in any kind of land claim it is to be expected that words and phrases that carry key meanings relevant to understanding the principles of land tenure, kinship and genealogical relationships, the character of country groups, and forms of spiritual and other connections between people and country will at least be mentioned in passing and may be explored in some depth.

Land claims have also long required skilful interpretation of earlier literature sources, with their often bewildering array of spellings and their frequent lack of clarity as to what the recorded names of various kinds of groupings or speech varieties referred to. In the earlier colonized areas of the east and southwest of Australia the problems of establishing exactly what classical group nomenclatures referred to can be very great.

Native title as a special jurisdiction can place heavy evidentiary weight on at least two other main areas with which linguists are concerned. These are:

1 the nature of contemporary relationships between linguistic varieties, indigenous groups that identify with those linguistic varieties, and the rights such groups assert over countries held to be intrinsically connected with those varieties, and
2 the reconstructible or documented history of those relationships in the past, including prehistory.

It has been the first of these that has had the greater exposure in land claims since the early 1980s but, even so, much localized and detailed case work still needs to be done on topics such as how and why it is that language groupings have risen to such prominence as marking the territorial identity of groups in the post-colonial era in certain regions.

Importantly, a linguist can tell a court hearing what relationship exists between, for example, fragmentary but localized colonial-era linguistic records and those varieties that have been better recorded and mapped by linguists more recently. Even where the record contains no name for the variety represented in a colonial police sergeant's wordlist, for example, its degree of closeness to known and usually named and locatable varieties can establish which one it is likely to have been drawn from. At a deeper level, linguists can often provide expert evidence as to the nature of the relationship between language and country as understood by the native title applicant groups themselves.

HISTORIANS

Historians are quite often engaged to provide a social history of the region in which a claim is located (Choo and Hollbach, 2003). They typically recount a document-based history of colonial exploration, conquest and non-indigenous settlement, provide a sketch of the changes in the legislative contexts through which indigenous people have lived and look at specific themes such as the trend of race relations and the redistribution of power, or employment and economic patterns, over time.

In many cases, though not all, these reports tend to take a broad brush to the subject. They sometimes privilege broad processes, principles and trends, using local specifics only by way of exemplification. They also tend to concentrate on non-indigenous people and leave many references to indigenous characters to broad descriptions such as 'local Aborigines' or 'several families', for example. As evidence for relevant occupation by knowable forebears of claimants this is not particularly useful or highly relevant. It also puts the cart before the horse, in a litigation context. The court is not there to understand history, but to know whether there is reliable and probative evidence as to the history of *these* particular people in relation to *these* specific forms of occupation over *these* particular lands and waters.

For historical reports to be much more frequently useful in litigation contexts would require them to contain far more local detail. For example, one essential would be a detailed chronology of which relevant non-indigenous settlements were created and by whom and where and when, and which indigenous settlements came into existence, when, where and under whose control. This requires the careful assembly of lists of, for example, all relevant pastoral (ranch) holdings, their starting and finishing lease dates, and the names of their lessees and managers; and all mission settlements, dates when they were founded or closed, who were their superintendents and responsible churches, and so on. The keyboarding of employee lists, blanket distributions and registers of births, baptisms, deaths and marriages, for example, is very labour-intensive, but to have a searchable database of such material can be vital to tracing efficiently the whereabouts of pertinent individuals over time. Cross-referenced to genealogies and ethnographic maps, such lists also can be powerful research engines about long-term trends and processes. For example, they would

enable us to answer questions such as to what degree the present claimants in a case are the descendants of immigrants, versus descendants of those who were in occupation at sovereignty in 1788 or 1825 or whenever (depending on the region), or at least from the earliest records following the relevant sovereignty date?

Unglamorous as detailed lists may be, they are very important to understanding claimants' oral evidence and the historical strands of the ethnographic evidence assembled by anthropologists. Aboriginal people in remote areas, especially, may sometimes have little or no skill in the use of calendar years when discussing the past, but can often recall the names of key people and past settlements when recalling events. Knowing when these historical figures were on the scene enables the Court to ascertain roughly during what years the events took place. Knowing the names and locations of the many, often ephemeral, non-indigenous settlements of the past is also important to knowing if evidence about events occurring there falls within the geographical purview of the case or not.

Like some anthropologists, some historians have been criticized in court, from time to time, for wearing their hearts on their sleeves. Even where this counterproductive tendency is not evident, courts and native title parties often show some reluctance to consider historical reports in any detail. This may be principally because it is the lawyers' chronologies of official tenure changes, and the anthropologists' diachronic accounts of indigenous laws and customs giving rise to customary rights and interests in land and waters, that form the crucial historical evidence. Were the historical reports more consistently localized, detailed and personalized, they would more often yield a better return on the investment of effort involved. They would also, for the same reason, be more likely to attract the attention of judges and non-party lawyers, because they would contain more material that went to the specific evidentiary issues of the cases.

ARCHAEOLOGISTS

Archaeologists have provided research reports for a number of native title cases (Lilley, 2000). It is often said that such field surveys and reports can do nothing more than establish that some unidentified indigenous people physically occupied the relevant area for varying lengths of time in the past. This is usually the case, but there are some exceptions in the sense that archaeological trait distribution can be tested against the recent material culture of a regional population to see how far they constitute a match (Veth and McDonald, 2002).

Archaeology can also provide past occupational evidence regarding sites said to be of cultural or economic significance to claimants. It may be that a ritual site is, or is not, found to have flat rocks on which red ochre has been ground in the past. A place said to have been a camping area for members of a seed-grinding culture may be checked for evidence of millstones, nether stones or grinding platforms on rocky outcrops. If this kind of use of archaeology is to have weight in Court, the field surveys should be conducted after the ethnographic ones, not before.

As far as I am aware there has been no use of physical anthropology in native title claims. In particular, use of DNA testing has not become an issue. It would not be surprising if it entered the picture in the future, especially where indigenous people are contesting assertions of shared descent and relatedness among themselves. At least one Native American internecine contest of this kind, where handsome casino profits are at stake, has led to DNA testing (Tanner, 2005). It is less likely, perhaps, that DNA testing could also be used to establish a connection of biological descent between living claimants and the remains of the deceased found in archaeological sites on or near the claimed land, although one cannot rule out this possibility.

Peter Sutton is a linguist and an anthropologist, and is currently ARC Professorial Fellow at the University of Adelaide and the South Australian Museum, and Honorary Research Fellow at the Institute of Archaeology, UCL. He was Senior Anthropologist at the Northern Land Council of the Northern Territory 1979–1981 and Head of the Division of Anthropology, South Australian Museum 1984–1990. Professor Sutton has assisted in various capacities with over fifty indigenous land claim cases in the Northern Territory, Queensland, New South Wales, Western Australia and South Australia since 1979. He has published a wide range of books and academic papers including *Native Title in Australia: an Ethnographic Perspective* (2003).

Contact address: School of Social Sciences, University of Adelaide, North Terrace, Adelaide SA 5000, Australia. Email: sutton.peter@saugov.sa.gov.au

REFERENCES

Bagshaw, G. *The Karajarri Claim: a Case-study in Native Title Anthropology*. Oceania Publications, Sydney (2003).

Choo, C. and Hollbach, S. (eds) *History and Native Title*. University of Western Australia, Perth (2003).

Fingleton, J. and Finlayson, J. (eds) *Anthropology in the Native Title Era: Proceedings of a Workshop*. Australian Institute of Aboriginal and Torres Strait Islander Studies, Canberra (1995).

Finlayson, J. and Jackson-Nakano, A. (eds) *Heritage and Native Title: Anthropological and Legal Perspectives*. Australian Institute of Aboriginal and Torres Strait Islander Studies, Canberra (1996).

Finlayson, J.D., Rigsby, B. and Bek, H.J. (eds) *Connections in Native Title: Genealogies, Kinship and Groups*. Centre for Aboriginal Economic Policy Research, Australian National University, Canberra (1999).

Henderson, J. and Nash, D. (eds) *Language in Native Title*. Aboriginal Studies Press, Canberra (2002).

Lilley, I. (ed.) *Native Title and the Transformation of Archaeology in the Postcolonial World*. Oceania Publications, Sydney (2000).

Mantziaris, C. and Martin, D. *Native Title Corporations, a Legal and Anthropological Analysis*. The Federation Press, Sydney (2000).

McKeown, F. (ed.) *Native Title: An Opportunity for Understanding*. National Native Title Tribunal, Perth (1996).

Peterson, N. and Rigsby, B. (eds) *Customary Marine Tenure in Australia*. Oceania Publications. Sydney (1998).

Sutton, P. *Native Title in Australia: an Ethnographic Perspective*. Cambridge University Press, Cambridge (2003).

Tanner, A. American Indians look to DNA tests to prove heritage. *Dawn* (Internet edition) 29 March (2005) http://DAWN.com.

Veth, P. and McDonald, J. Can archaeology be used to address the principle of exclusive possession in native title? In Harrison, R. and Williamson, C. (eds) *After Captain Cook. The Archaeology of the Recent Indigenous Past in Australia*. AltaMira Press, Walnut Creek CA (2002).

Indigenous peoples' rights to their cultural heritage

Lyndon Ormond Parker

ABSTRACT

This paper discusses indigenous peoples' rights to their cultural heritage, using the example of rights to indigenous human remains, held by institutions, universities, scientific centres and museums. It addresses international developments in indigenous cultural policy at the United Nations and the European Union, with specific reference to Australia and the United Kingdom. It also outlines issues relating to indigenous peoples' collective rights, free, prior and informed consent, ownership of indigenous human remains and the issue of benefit sharing and sustainable justice. There are now several international declarations, conventions and policies in place to assist indigenous people in gaining some form of control and protection over their heritage, however, these international instruments are often unco-ordinated and lacking in any enforcement mechanisms and they hold little sway with those who retain indigenous human remains against the wishes of descendant communities.

INTRODUCTION

In this paper I argue that international instruments, polices and statements are of great relevance to indigenous people in the development of cultural policies favourable to indigenous peoples around the world. However, the legal and moral basis for ownership of indigenous human remains collected by institutions is currently unclear.

CULTURAL AND INTELLECTUAL PROPERTY

While much is written about the indigenous perspective on protecting indigenous cultural and intellectual property rights, in defining this subject I use the definition set down in the Aboriginal and Torres Strait Islander Studies report *Our Culture, Our Future*:

> Indigenous Cultural and Intellectual Property Rights refers to Indigenous Australians rights to their heritage. Such rights are also known as Indigenous Heritage Rights. Heritage consists of the intangible and tangible aspects of the whole body of cultural practices, resources and knowledge systems developed, nurtured and refined by Indigenous people and passed on by them as part of expressing their cultural identity. (Janke, 1998: 19)

For the purposes of this paper

> Heritage includes, all items of moveable cultural property including burial artefacts, Indigenous ancestral remains ... Indigenous human genetic material (including DNA and tissues) ... Immovable cultural property (including Indigenous sites of significance, sacred sites and burials) ... Documentation of Indigenous people's heritage in all forms of media (including scientific, ethnographic research reports, papers and books, films, sound recordings). (Janke, 1998: 20)

Furthermore, Janke (1998) suggests that any definition of indigenous cultural and intellectual property rights should be flexible.

A global effort will ensure that there is respect for Indigenous heritage and culture; however this does not mean that

Indigenous communities agree to operate within western paradigms of cultural and intellectual property rights. (Battiste and Henderson, 2000).

Background

At the outset it is important to point out that progress has been made in many countries and in the international arena with respect to the recognition of indigenous rights to their heritage, and with the development of cultural policies and international instruments that reflect indigenous peoples' interests. Although some indigenous people may criticize a museum or scientific institution when it makes a decision that appears to fall short of the international standards of human rights protection, museums, academic institutions and national legislation have made important and positive contributions towards the recognition of indigenous cultural rights, particularly in Australia, New Zealand and North America.

In a debate in the *Science and Public Affairs Journal* of the British Association, Dr Robert Foley, Director of the Leverhulme Centre for Human Evolutionary Studies at the University of Cambridge, argues that there are two key justifications for keeping collections of human remains in museums. Firstly 'the role of museums and research collections – preserving irreplaceable scientific material for future generations – remains at the core of a rational society, even if at the margins it is questioned'. Secondly, 'skeletal collections are kept as part of a global human heritage, not the preserve of any one culture' (Foley, in Morris and Foley, 2002: 4)

Most indigenous peoples do not share these views. Indigenous people have historically asserted their rights to their own cultural heritage both tangible and intangible; this is based both on traditional laws within indigenous communities and has been reinforced more recently through the 'euro-centric world view' of cultural and intellectual property rights (Battiste and Henderson, 2000)

Most recently, at the International Indigenous Peoples' World Summit on Sustainable Development, in Kimberly South Africa, the Khoi-San peoples reaffirmed their wishes in respect to their ancestors' human remains:

> We are the original peoples tied to the land by our umbilical cords and the dust of our ancestors ... Disturbing the remains of our families and elders is desecration of the greatest magnitude and constitutes a grave violation of our human rights. We call for the full and immediate repatriation of all Khoi-San human remains currently held in museums and other institutions throughout the world, as well as all the human remains of all other Indigenous Peoples. We maintain the rights to our sacred and ceremonial sites and ancestral remains, including access to burial, archaeological and historic sites. (Kimberley Declaration, 2002)

The return of indigenous human remains has been in debate for many years and it is not only indigenous people who are concerned about the fate of the remains of their kin. There are currently many projects where archaeologists are excavating and trying to identify the remains of the disappeared, such as those in Bosnia, Cambodia, Vietnam, Guatemala, Chile and Peru, so individuals can be identified and returned to their community of origin (Fforde, 2002).

In September 2002, in an address to the United Nations General Assembly in New York President George W. Bush stated:

> If the Iraqi regime wishes peace, it will release or account for all Gulf War personnel whose fate is still unknown. It will return the remains of any who are deceased, return stolen property, accept liability for losses resulting from the invasion of Kuwait, and fully cooperate with the international efforts to resolve these issues, as required by Security Council resolutions. (Bush, 2002)

One challenge for many indigenous peoples has been the re-education of scientists and academics in European and colonial powers to appreciate indigenous views and wishes in relation to the acquisition, curation and return of human remains. In some countries this challenge has been met, but in others the debate is only just beginning. The assertion by indigenous peoples to intellectual and cultural property rights has played a key role raising public awareness of these issues.

UNITED NATIONS, EUROPEAN UNION AND THE COMMONWEALTH

I will now detail recent significant developments in cultural and intellectual policy and law through the United Nations, European Union and the Commonwealth on indigenous rights and its implications for the protection and return of indigenous cultural property and human remains.

United Nations

ECOSOC – PERMANENT FORUM FOR INDIGENOUS PEOPLE

One of the most significant developments in the international arena has been the establishment under the Economic and Social Council (ECOSOC) of the United Nations of a Permanent Forum for Indigenous Issues (UNPFII), which held its first meeting in New York in May 2002. The Permanent Forum is made up of 16 members, eight nominated by governments and elected by the Council, and eight indigenous people appointed by the President of the Economic and Social Council (UNPFII, 2005).

Indigenous members of the Permanent Forum were elected on the basis of broad distribution of the indigenous peoples of the world, with all members serving in their personal capacity as independent experts on indigenous issues for a period of three years. Governments based on the United Nations regions of the world, nominated government representatives (UNPFII, 2005).

The Permanent Forum serves with a mandate to discuss and make recommendations to the ECOSOC regarding indigenous issues relating to economic and social development, culture, the environment, education, health and human rights (UNPFII, 2005).

In May 2002, the United Nations Permanent Forum on Indigenous Issues during its inaugural meeting discussed a broad range of topics including a recommendation in relation to indigenous cultural and intellectual property issues and made the following recommendation to ECOSOC:

> Requests Governments [to] include in their programs and plans and in their educational and cultural policies the contents of indigenous knowledge, indigenous spiritual and religious traditions, indigenous customs and ceremonies as well as indigenous history, vision of the cosmos, philosophy and values. The rights of indigenous peoples to their sacred sites and ceremonial objects and to the distribution of their ancestral remains should be respected. They wish to have their cultural properties returned to them, particularly if these properties were taken without their permission. (United Nations Economic and Social Council (ECOSOC), 2002a)

As ECOSOC reports directly to the General Assembly, the main decision-making body of the United Nations, the Permanent Forum has the potential to greatly strengthen the indigenous voice in the United Nations (UNPFII, 2005). The recommendations from the first Permanent Forum held in New York were tabled and accepted by the Third Committee of the General Assembly (ECOSOC, 2002a (Part I);-E/CN.19/2002/3 (Part I). What action the General Assembly may take in assisting with the implementation of these recommendations is yet to be seen.

COMMITTEE ON ECONOMIC, SOCIAL AND CULTURAL RIGHTS

The Economic and Social Council has established committees that monitor and report on state signatories to conventions within their jurisdiction. The Committee on Economic, Social and Cultural Rights (CESCR) hears country compliance with the International Convention on Economic, Social and Cultural Rights (1966). In August 2000 CESCR heard the Aboriginal and Torres Strait Islander Commission (ATSIC) raise concerns about Australia's compliance with the convention. ATSIC was concerned that recent developments in respect of legislation protecting indigenous cultural heritage, i.e. the proposed amendments to the Aboriginal and Torres Strait Islander Heritage Protection Act, were contrary to the right to the enjoyment of culture (ATSIC, 2000). In their concluding observations the CESCR Committee expressed 'its deep concern that, despite the efforts and achievements of the State party, the indigenous populations of Australia continue to be at a comparative disadvantage in the enjoyment of economic, social and cultural rights' (ECOSOC, 2000a). So while Australia is a signatory to the convention, domestically the principles contained in the convention are not being fully implemented with Australian domestic policy or legislation.

PRINCIPLES AND GUIDELINES FOR THE PROTECTION FOR THE HERITAGE OF INDIGENOUS PEOPLES

Links between cultural and intellectual property rights and human rights are being made at the international level and are now seen by many international experts as interdependent. However, 'the cultural aspect of human rights is relatively underdeveloped compared with political, economic and social aspects' (O'Keefe, 1999: 182). Two key international instruments addressing the protection of indigenous heritage are currently being developed under the United Nations Office of the High Commissioner for Human Rights, these are the Principles and Guidelines for the Protection of the Heritage of Indigenous People and the Draft Declaration on the Rights of Indigenous People.

In 2000 a seminar held at the United Nations, Geneva, further developed the Principles and Guidelines for the Protection of the Heritage of Indigenous People based on a UN Report and Study undertaken by Mrs Erica-Irene A. Daes, in 1993 and elaborated in 1995 (E/CN.4/Sub.2/1995/26). In relation to the return of indigenous human remains to their community, the new article reads:

> Article 19
> Human Remains and associated funerary objects and documentation must be returned to their descendants in a culturally appropriate manner, as determined by the indigenous peoples concerned. Documentation may be retained, or otherwise used only in such form and manner as may be agreed upon with the peoples concerned. (ECOSOC, 2000b)

The current draft of these principles and guidelines (ECOSOC, 2000b) is yet to be approved by the Commission on Human Rights and referred to the United Nations General Assembly for final approval. If approved, the Principles and Guidelines are not legally enforceable, such as conventions, and are only a set of principles that governments and organizations may choose to abide by; this will also be the case with the United Nations Declaration on the Rights of Indigenous Peoples (ECOSOC, 2002b: Annex II). Even if not legally binding on countries, these instruments are important for indigenous peoples, because they establish principles derived from consultations with indigenous peoples at an international level and can provide a framework for institutions and nation states in drafting and developing their policies.

United Nations Draft Declaration on the Rights of Indigenous People

The United Nations Draft Declaration on the Rights of Indigenous Peoples (ECOSOC, 1994) has been in deliberation in the United Nations system for many years. In February 2002, discussion on articles 12 and 13 occurred; these are the most relevant articles for those working in the heritage and museum sector.

> Article 12
> Indigenous peoples have the right to practise and revitalize their cultural traditions and customs. This includes the right to maintain, protect and develop the past, present and future manifestations of their cultures, such as archaeological and historical sites, artefacts, designs, ceremonies, technologies and visual and performing arts and literature, as well as the right to the restitution of cultural, intellectual, religious and spiritual property taken without their free and informed consent or in violation of their laws, traditions and customs.

> Article 13
> Indigenous peoples have the right to manifest, practice, develop and teach their spiritual and religious traditions, customs and ceremonies; the right to maintain, protect, and have access in privacy to their religious and cultural sites; the right to the use and control of ceremonial objects; and the right to the repatriation of human remains.
> States shall take effective measures, in conjunction with the indigenous peoples concerned, to ensure that indigenous sacred places, including burial sites, be preserved, respected and protected (ECOSOC, 1994)

During discussions at United Nations Working Group on the Draft Declaration on Article 13, indigenous representatives stressed the importance of access to sacred sites, the use and control of cultural and ceremonial objects, as well as the right to the repatriation of human remains. (ECOSOC, 2002b)

Representation was made by non-governmental institutions in discussion on articles 12 and 13. For example, the World Archaeological Congress (at the World Archaeological Congress 4 meeting in Cape Town, January 1999), deliberated on the Draft Declaration; the General conference of the Congress showed strong support for the principles in articles 12–14 of the Draft Declaration and passed the following resolution:

> In recognition of the International Decade of Indigenous Peoples and in the year of the 50th anniversary of the Universal Declaration of Human Rights, WAC supports the established text in Part III, Articles 12, 13 and 14 of the United Nations Draft Declaration on the Rights of Indigenous People. (ECOSOC, 2002b: Annex II)

The support for these articles by the World Archaeological Congress was announced during the debate at the UN meeting noted in Annex II of the official report (ECOSOC, 2002b).

The UN Draft Declaration is still in draft form and changes continue to be suggested by governments, therefore there is currently no agreed revision of the final declaration and meetings continue. Encouragingly for indigenous peoples, the overriding principle of repatriation was upheld by the majority of governments and indigenous people involved in the deliberation on these articles (personal observations, 2001) (ECOSOC, 2002b).

The principle of *Free Prior and Informed Consent* in article 12, the principle of indigenous peoples' *collective rights* as implied in the term 'peoples', and the issue of ownership. and *control* are the principles some governments found most problematic and difficult to accept within the Draft Declaration.

(i) Collective rights

The issue of indigenous peoples' collective intellectual, cultural and human rights is constantly in debate. However, the establishment of indigenous collective rights as a matter of international law has already been implied in the International Labour Organisation Indigenous and Tribal Peoples Convention No. 169, more recently this has been upheld with the Awas Tinigi case, brought by the Mayagna People against the Nicaraguan government, in which the Inter-American Court of Human Rights affirmed that indigenous peoples within their jurisdiction have, as a matter of international law, collective rights to the lands and natural resources that they have traditionally used and occupied. The court further stated that governments violate the human rights of indigenous peoples when they fail to take affirmative measures to protect and enforce these property rights (Indian Law Resource Centre, 2002).

> The AWAS TINGNI CASE represents the first occasion in modern times in which an international court with binding authority has heard a case that directly addressed the property rights of Indigenous Peoples. This seminal decision provides a unique opportunity to inform and advance the dialogue concerning indigenous collective property rights. (Indian Law Resource Centre, 2002: 1)

It was pointed out during debate on collective rights that it is 'erroneous, invalid and self-serving for States to argue' to the Working Group on the Draft Declaration on the Rights of Indigenous People that international law does not recognize collective rights (ECOSOC, 2002b: Annex II). Indigenous participants suggested that the following international instruments, among others, affirm collective or group rights in International law:

- International Covenant on Civil and Political Rights;
- International Covenant on Economic, Social and Cultural Rights;
- International Convention on the Elimination of All Forms of Racial Discrimination;
- UNESCO Declaration on Race and Racial Prejudice (1978);
- African Charter on Human and Peoples' Rights;
- Indigenous and Tribal Peoples Convention, 1989, No. 169;
- Convention on Biological Diversity;
- The Universal Declaration on Cultural Diversity (2001); and
- The Declaration on the Granting of Independence to Colonial Countries and Peoples (ECOSOC, 2002b: Annex II).

Indigenous peoples' collective cultural and intellectual property rights will continue to be debated at the international level. In Australia, however, the law has recognized indigenous collective rights in several cases, most notably in the area of Native Title, where 'it may be possessed by a community, group or individual depending on the content of the traditional laws and customs' (*Native Title Act*, 1998: http://www.austlii.edu.au/au/legis/cth/consol_act/nta1993147/; see also Sutton, this volume).

A further development in the area of recognition of the term 'Indigenous Peoples' came in paragraph 25 of the final declaration at the World Summit on Sustainable Development (WSSD), held in Johannesburg, South Africa, 26 August–4 September 2002, which reads 'We affirm the vital role of Indigenous Peoples in sustainable development' (WSSD, 2002). It has been argued that this represented an acceptance by the United Nations of the unqualified term 'Indigenous Peoples' (Whall, 2002).

(ii) Free, Prior and Informed Consent
Governments were reluctant to agree to the principle of free and informed consent as outlined in article 12 of the Draft Declaration on the Rights of Indigenous People. This reluctance was an issue of concern to the United Nations Permanent Forum members who recommended in the first report to ECOSOC:

> the establishment of a Working Group on Free and Prior Informed Consent and Participatory Research Guidelines [(PRG)] broaden and deepen the dialogue on prior informed consent by: (i) defining what prior informed consent and PRG mean in substantive terms; (ii) recommending criterion and guidelines for consideration when Indigenous Peoples and others address issues of prior informed consent and PRG, to ensure that IPs [Indigenous Peoples] and their communities are fully informed, meaningfully participate in decision making and benefit sharing processes and that their interests are protected. (E/2002/43. 2002)

A workshop was held on the issue of free, prior and informed consent in January 2005, following concerns raised in the second and third meetings of the Permanent Forum. The workshop went some way to defining these principles and recommended further discussion on the issue (E/C.19/2005/3, 2005).

The issue of free prior and informed consent as it relates to research standards, is not new. The question arises: to what extent are institutions retaining collections of human remains and biological material aware of relevant international declarations and principles in this area, are these being taken notice of and what can indigenous peoples do to use these instruments to protect their interests?

The UNESCO's *Universal Declaration on the Human Genome and Human Rights* (1997) contains article 5(b), which relates to the collection of human genome samples:

> Article 5b
> In all cases, the prior, free and informed consent of the person concerned shall be obtained. If the latter is not in a position to consent, consent or authorization shall be obtained in the manner prescribed by law, guided by the person's best interest.

The Declaration also states that:

> Article 10
> No research or its applications concerning the human genome, in particular in the fields of biology, genetics and medicine, should prevail over respect for the human rights, fundamental freedoms and human dignity of individuals or, where applicable, of groups of people.

Principles as set down in international law are an important tool that indigenous peoples can use in their negotiations with institutions over the use of their human remains for scientific purposes and to assert their right to free prior and informed consent, not only in terms of past or current scientific research but also as it applies to the curation of human remains. While the Universal Declaration is not legally binding on states, and applies mainly to living subjects and specifically to the human genome, it contains widely accepted important principles, such as free and informed consent and benefit sharing, which can be asserted and used by indigenous peoples in their dealings with scientific institutions researching indigenous remains. Article 24 of the Universal Declaration on the Human Genome and Human Rights requests:

> Article 24
> The International Bioethics Committee of UNESCO should contribute to the dissemination of the principles set out in this Declaration and to the further examination of issues raised by their applications and by the evolution of the technologies in question. It should organize appropriate consultations with parties concerned, such as vulnerable groups.

There is currently no indication that the International Bioethics Committee has yet undertaken wide consultations with Indigenous Peoples, especially in light of the announcement by the National Geographic Society's new 'Genographic Project', which targets indigenous communities (https://www5.nationalgeographic.com/genographic/ 13 April 2005) and has seen the Indigenous Peoples Council on Biocolonialism (IPCB) (http://www.ipcb.org/issues/human_genetics/htmls/geno_pr.html) call for a boycott of this project.

In a press release of 13 April 2005 by the Indigenous Peoples Council on Biocolonialism (IPCB)

> Le'a Kanehe, a Native Hawaiian who serves as the IPCB's Legal Analyst, gives the example of the Havasupai Tribe, who filed a lawsuit in 2004 against Arizona State University for taking and subsequently misusing their genetic samples. 'Indigenous peoples are holding scientists accountable for use of their genetic material without prior informed consent, which is the accepted legal standard.' The tribe authorized diabetes research, but later discovered their samples were used for schizophrenia, inbreeding and migration theories.

While indigenous peoples assert their rights in terms of free prior and informed consent this can also be very problematic. This was highlighted in Sweden where interviews were conducted with people who had participated in a genetic research project. They were asked about the consent they had given. The study was astonished to find that 'many of them did not know what they had consented to, and that the majority refuse to assume responsibility for all the difficult ethical dilemmas involved' (Gibson, 2002: 30).

In other words, research institutions should not delegate their ethical responsibilities back to the individuals or communities who gave their consent. Those taking part in the trial did so in the belief that ethical, political and regulatory frameworks had been worked out and safeguarded before their consent was given (Gibson, 2002: 31).

In a symposium on 'Ethics, Intellectual Property and Genetics', recommendations made included the promotion by UNESCO of the establishment of national and regional bioethical bodies to encourage the participation of peoples generally, including indigenous peoples in an informed debate on these issues (Kirby, 2002).

It is important that indigenous peoples become fully informed and involved in the ethical debate surrounding current and potential research being undertaken on their own genes and those of their ancestral human remains held in scientific institutions.

However, the question remains, have scientific research institutions using indigenous human remains for scientific purposes put regulatory frameworks and policies in place to deal with ethical dilemmas that arise from such research? Few of these institutions have gained free, prior and informed consent from indigenous communities for such research purposes but, even where such consent exists, a moratorium should be placed on controversial research until such time as ethical, political and regulatory frameworks are in place with the agreement of the indigenous peoples concerned.

(iii) Ownership of indigenous human remains/genes

Although current museum policies in Australia allow for the return of human remains, and outline protocols for research, 'the risk of physical anthropologists and other scientists obtaining samples of DNA from the muscles, bones, teeth or hair of these remains to analyse the genetic disposition of these people before colonisation is highly likely' (Janke, 1998). In the current era of human genetic research, indigenous peoples are the subjects of 'evolutionary genetic research, pharmaco-genetic research, the search for single nucleotide polymorphisms (SNPs), or genes associated with behavioural or health-related conditions' (Harry, 2002: 2). This makes the legal status over the ownership of indigenous human remains and what Aboriginal people can do to protect their ancestors of vital concern.

The issue of ownership of human remains and related research was discussed by the Australian Law Reform Commission (ALRC) and Australian Health Ethics Committee (AHEC) Inquiry into the Protection of Human Genetic Information (ALRC/AHEC Inquiry Report 66, 2002). The traditional position has been that a human corpse could not be an object of property; however, a recent shift away from this position has seen recognition of ownership interests where body parts and sections of tissue have been accorded property status:

The 1998 case of *R v. Kelly* held that preserved body parts taken from the Royal College of Surgeons [London] were the property of the Royal College. The Court found that the exception to the rule was now accepted at law and that preservation for study and retention, as well as dissection, were enough to meet the criterion of work or skill. Whoever undertakes that work or skill becomes the owner of the tissue sample, as long as they have performed it with lawful authority. (ALRC/AHEC Inquiry Report 66, 2002)

The ALRC/AHEC inquiry report went on to state that:

> The present state of the law suggests that preserved samples of tissue are the property of the hospital that holds them where its staff has exercised the work or skill required for preservation. This has implications for access, storage and use of such samples.

The courts have not produced any clear ruling on the particular property rights that may be held over tissue samples, beyond a right to possess. It is not clear how far other property rights could be said to exist in relation to tissue samples (ALRC/AHEC Inquiry Report 66, 2002).

Should museums and research institutions have a right to the income from the use or sale of indigenous samples? Would such a right prevent others from accessing the genetic information contained within the sample such as other community members? And could it also be used to discriminate against individuals or communities from where the material was collected? (ALRC/AHEC Inquiry Report 66, 2002).

Museums and institutional policy should involve communities in relation to standards that may develop as an outcome of this inquiry and develop principles of benefit sharing and sustainable justice and incorporate the wishes of communities in relation to research guidelines.

(iv) Benefit sharing and sustainable justice

Despite the moral question as to whether genetic material can be 'owned', indigenous people usually do not receive a share in the benefits, even though their biological resources have been essential to the development of new medicines (Janke, 1998: 81).

The benefits that may flow from research are often very slow to filter down to indigenous communities, for example a recent report by the Australian Bureau of Statistics shows that the average life expectancy for Aboriginal men in the northern territory is only 45 years and for females 51 years (*Sydney Morning Herald* 11 December, 2002). Although there have been huge advances in science and medical treatments, indigenous peoples still have an average life expectancy of some 20 years less than the rest of the Australian population, arguments that scientific study of Aboriginal peoples' human remains will benefit communities must become more convincing given the current health status of communities.

As indigenous peoples are at the forefront of a 'new wave of scientific investigation, that is the search for genetic resources that can be used in new commercial products. Through the application of intellectual property rights law, namely patents, corporations can claim monopoly ownership over genes, products, and data derived from genetic resources' (Harry, 2002: 1). It is also important that these issues are discussed in terms of benefit sharing and sustainable justice.

The ALRC/AHEC Inquiry Report (2002) considers that the benefits of regarding genetic samples as property are outweighed by the drawbacks, and the current status of genetic material should be maintained. That is, property ownership remains with the institutions that hold this material (ALRC/AHEC Inquiry Report 66, 2002). This suggestion may alarm some indigenous people.

On 9 February 2005 in Paris, UNESCO's International Bioethics Committee (IBC) produced the 'Preliminary Draft Declaration on Universal Norms on Bioethics', which applies the principle of free, prior and informed consent and sets out ways in which benefit sharing could occur. However, it fails to take into consideration the unique situation of indigenous peoples.

Owing to the commercial nature of much research in the area of genetics, institutional arguments that indigenous human remains should be retained 'as part of global human heritage, not the preserve of any one culture' (Foley, in Morris and Foley, 2002: 4) do not reflect the commercial reality of such research.

The World Intellectual Property Organisation (WIPO), Intergovernmental Committee on Intellectual Property and Genetic Resources, Traditional Knowledge and Folklore is currently looking into the 'practices, guidelines, and model intellectual property clauses for contractual agreements on access to genetic resources and benefit-sharing, taking into account the specific nature and needs of different stakeholders, different genetic resources, and different transfers within different sectors of genetic resource policy' (WIPO, 2002).

It is hoped this WIPO Intergovernmental Committee will develop international guidelines for protection of indigenous peoples' traditional knowledge and intellectual and cultural property rights based on current best practice in this area. This intergovernmental committee has given a commitment to the involvement of indigenous peoples and may also provide an opportunity for institutions to raise concerns about the practical implementation of such guidelines (WIPO, 2002).

Indigenous people are concerned by the fact that institutions within Europe reveal little about those institutions holdings and research undertaken, therefore guidelines developed by the WIPO may assist indigenous people in gaining some form of control over research by insisting on the application of best practice in global research ethics, which will hopefully include clauses about the disclosure of collections, gaining informed consent for research and providing some form of benefit sharing.

European Union

While there is an increase in demands for the return of indigenous human remains and cultural heritage held in Europe, the European Union has yet to develop policies or legislation on a European-wide basis with respect to such claims. The European Union does have an indigenous peoples policy, but only in relation to the field of development co-operation.

There is a European Union Directive on the Return of Cultural Objects, but this seeks the return of national treasures of artistic, historic or archaeological value that have been unlawfully removed by a European member state from the territory of another member state (O'Keefe, 1999). There is nothing that regulates other material taken unlawfully from a non-EU member state and then housed within the European Union.

There is currently, therefore, potential for the European Union to strengthen its work with indigenous peoples, which may provide an opportunity for the EU to facilitate the return of indigenous human remains and cultural property from within the EU to external countries. Nonetheless, indigenous groups may have recourse to the European Convention of Human Rights to assist repatriation claims. Unlike the UN instruments mentioned above, the European Court of Human Rights has legally enforceable mechanisms implemented in the law of all European states except Ireland (European Court of Human Rights, 2002: http://www.echr.coe.int).

Legal opinion suggests that a case could also be brought before the courts in the United Kingdom, under the *Human Rights Act* 1998. English courts would be able to consider 'claims based on rights conferred to individuals by the articles of the European Convention, which expressly guarantees the freedom of religion and belief (Article 9) and the prohibition on discrimination (Article 14)' (Shek, 2000).

Indigenous claimants have yet to take their grievances before the European Court. Instead, as elsewhere, strategies for return have focused on negotiation, media exposure and political pressure, often at an intergovernmental level, rather than the more costly and unpredictable route of a legal challenge. It is usually preferable to persuade institutions with moral and ethical arguments.

In France, the remains of Saartjie Baartman, a Khoi-Khoi woman, displayed during her life as the 'Hottentot Venus', whose skeleton, preserved genitalia and brain were held by the Musée de l'homme in Paris, were handed over to the South African embassy in May 2002. This was the culmination of years of requests by South Africans, including Nelson Mandela, who wanted to bring her home. The French senate was required to pass legislation in order for Saartjie to return home, however, the legislation was very specific and was not intended to allow for the return of other indigenous remains held in France (Tetrel, 2002).

On Saartje Baartman's return to South Africa, Matty Cairncross, a member of the Khoisan community said, 'The return of Saartje Baartman to South Africa is a victory for all South Africans and Indigenous Peoples of the world. It's an historic moment for everyone, especially for women in South Africa. She can be a unifying symbol for us' (Tetrel, 2002).

In October 2000, after many years of campaigning, the remains of an African man from Botswana were returned. A Christian ceremony took place in a public park in the capital, Gaborone, attended by more than 1000 mourners, including government leaders and foreign diplomats (Parsons and Segobye, 2002). The Botswana Foreign Minister said: 'We are prepared to forgive, but we cannot forget the crimes of the past, lest they are repeated' (*Associated Press*, 2000). The Botswana government was quoted as saying, 'the reburial is intended to cleanse Africa of the humiliation of colonialism' (*Associated Press*, 2000).

These cases show that the repatriation of remains can attract intense media coverage. These highly publicized returns are seen as part of a reconciliation process and have played a role in shaping national and indigenous identity.

European Union support for indigenous issues has grown and these developments have been reflected in a recent report from the Commission of the European Communities to the Council of Europe (Commission of the European Communities, 2002). The Commission argues that the European Union believes that 'building partnerships with Indigenous Peoples is essential to fulfil the objectives of poverty elimination, sustainable development, and the strengthening of respect for human rights and democracy' (Commission of the European Communities, 2002: 291).

Furthermore, the report from the Commission stated that the EU has been one of the 'most active promoters of the development of the Draft Bonn Guidelines on Access to Genetic Resources and Fair and Equitable Sharing of the Benefits Arising out of their Utilisation'. These guidelines are aimed at 'ensuring that the principles of "free informed consent" and "mutually agreed terms" are duly respected when access to genetic resources or to traditional knowledge of Indigenous Peoples or local communities are sought' (Commission of the European Communities, 2002: 291).

If the European Union is serious about dialogue and implementation of principles in relation to research, the EU should incorporate the concerns of indigenous peoples into policy on a European Union-wide basis in respect to the research, curation and return of the cultural property of indigenous peoples within the European Union.

The United Kingdom

In the United Kingdom, Australian indigenous peoples have made numerous requests for the return of remains from British museums. In response, important steps towards the recognition of indigenous peoples' rights in relation to their human remains, both on a national level and with individual institutions, have been made. For example, after many years of lobbying by organizations such as Foundation for Aboriginal Islander Research Action (FAIRA) and the Tasmanian Aboriginal Center (TAC), institutions such as The Horniman Museum, Manchester Museum, London's Royal College of Surgeons of England have all allowed for the recent repatriation of Aboriginal remains to Australia.

This change in policy follows a series of developments over the past ten years in the United Kingdom. In 1999, the British government announced that the House of Commons Select Committee on Culture Media and Sport was to consider issues relating to *Cultural Property: Return and Illicit Trade*. In 2000 the Committee accepted written and oral evidence from a range of interest groups, including museums, governments and indigenous peoples (Fforde and Ormond-Parker, 2001). The author presented evidence to the Committee in May 2000 on behalf of FAIRA. Having considered all evidence presented, the committee made certain recommendations in relation to human remains, noting that:

> Our approach to the return of cultural property during this inquiry has been based on a broad consideration of the many types of cultural property concerned. However, as the inquiry progressed, we became convinced that a category of return claims deserves separate analysis – that of human remains. (Commons Committee, Seventh Report, 2000a)

The Committee considered that the guidelines developed and published in 2000 by a group of UK museum organizations, *Restitution and Repatriation*, did not give sufficient weight to the particular issues relating to requests for the return of human remains. It recommended that:

> the Department for Culture, Media and Sport initiate discussions with appropriate representatives of museums,

of claimant communities and of appropriate Governments to prepare a statement of principles and accompanying guidance relating to the care and safe-keeping of human remains and to the handling of requests for return of human remains. (Commons Committee, Seventh Report, 2000)

The Committee recognized that, as in the USA and Australia, identification of human remains in collections and the provision of such information to all interested parties should be the first step towards such discussions and sought commitments from all holding institutions in the United Kingdom to facilitate access to information on holdings of indigenous human remains for all interested parties, including potential claimants, as part of these discussions.

In March 2001, the UK government published a response to the Committee's report of July 2000 and appointed Professor Norman Palmer to chair a 'Working Group on Human Remains'. The working group was to examine the current legal status of human remains within the collections of publicly funded museums and galleries in the United Kingdom, to examine the powers of museums and galleries to de-accession human remains and to consider proposed legislative change in respect of human remains.

The UK government's commitment to facilitating the repatriation of human remains, voiced in its response to the Committee, came after the British and Australia 'Prime Ministerial Joint statement on Aboriginal Remains' (July, 2000) announced during Australian Prime Minister John Howard's visit to the UK in July 2000 (Fforde and Ormond-Parker, 2001).

Although efforts to comply with indigenous peoples' wishes for the return of human remains and cultural artefacts continue, some museums are resisting this change. In a public statement signed by some of the Western world's leading museums, the *Declaration on the Importance and Value of Universal Museums* stated that museums 'serve not just the citizens of one nation but the people of every nation' (Declaration, 2002). They also argue that to narrow the focus of museums would be a 'disservice to all visitors' (Declaration, 2002). However, not everyone shares these views. In an article published by *The Spectator* in London, Dr Tom Flynn, an expert on the illegal trade in artefacts and art states:

> The question of deaccessioning, and indeed of restituting objects, should be at the top of any reforming agenda. If it is true that we live in a 'global' world, in which decentralisation and the return of power to the periphery are the catchwords of future cultural progress, then why do we balk at the idea of selected objects being dispersed to more relevant locations? This might mean dispersing parts of London or metropolitan collections to other regions in the UK, but it could also mean returning objects to their countries of origin. Liberated from the oblivion of a darkened store room, their greater cultural significance to local communities could ensure a better future for both the objects and their new custodians. (Flynn, 2002)

In November 2003, the Working Group on Human Remains (HRWG) published their report and recommendations (Department of Culture Media and Sport (DCMS), 2003). In July 2004, the DCMS released the *Care of Historic Human Remains* (DCMS, 2004), which summarized the HRWG report and invited comments on it.

Key recommendations from the HRWG that have been implemented to date include the development of a 'Code of Practice', as well as legislative changes to allow national museums to deaccession human remains (the *Human Tissue Act*, 2004; http://www.opsi.gov.uk/acts/acts2004/20040030.htm). In March 2005, The Department for Culture Media and Sport established a 'Human Remains Code of Practice Drafting Group' (DCMS, 2005), to draw up the Code of Practice, setting out 'guidance on the keeping of human remains in museums ... The Code should address the handling of requests for the return of human remains' (DCMS, 2005: 1). A draft of this Code of Practice is currently being circulated for comment. The Code of Practice only applies to England and Wales, while Scotland will have a separate code of practice.

In November 2004, the *Human Tissue Act* 2004 received Royal Assent. Section 47 of the Act will come into force when the Code of Practice is in place; this should allow nine institutions, including London's Natural History Museum and The British Museum, the power to deaccession human remains in their collections.

(2) Any body to which this section applies may transfer from their collection any human remains which they reasonably believe to be remains of a person who died less than one thousand years before the day on which this section comes into force if it appears to them to be appropriate to do so for any reason, whether or not relating to their other functions. (*Human Tissue Act*, 2004, Section 47 (2))

This may be welcome news for indigenous peoples who have sought the return of human remains from The British Museum or the Natural History Museum. However, what indigenous Australians may find distressing is that the *Human Tissue Act* also removes (from institutions such as the Natural History Museum and the Duckworth Collection at the University of Cambridge, holding some of the largest collections of Aboriginal human remains in Britain) any legal impediment from 'engaging in research projects using their collections of human remains and involving the analysis of DNA' (DCMS, 2004: 21). Consent is only required where the remains are of a known individual who died less than 100 years prior to the Act coming into effect (DCMS, 2004). The Duckworth collection has still failed to fully disclose the extent of their collection of Australian indigenous remains, let alone allow the necessary research to provenance this collection or identify any named and known individuals that may be within it.

While the legal impediments to returning human remains from English institutions are being reduced, this does not mean that institutions are more likely to return human remains to communities of origin when requested to do so.

FURTHER CONSIDERATIONS

In an era of globalization the indigenous voice is becoming louder. Indigenous peoples need to capitalize on the development of international laws and guidelines by placing increasing pressure on governments and institutions to treat requests for curation and return of indigenous cultural property seriously. Globally, indigenous peoples need to work with museum practitioners to develop research ethics that are respectful of indigenous cultures. Positive developments in New Zealand, USA, Canada and Australia can be used as a basis for negotiating and developing mutually beneficial relationships in other countries.

Non-enforcement of international mechanisms

The international declarations and guidelines I have described, with the exception of the European Convention of Human Rights, suffer from enforcement difficulties. International rules often remain unimplemented in national legal systems and therefore cannot be enforced by the courts. However, in practical terms this problem may have been overstated as more indigenous people work in museums and become involved in the day-to-day running of museum policy. Indeed in the USA, Australia, New Zealand and Canada, indigenous people are also involved in drafting and implementing national policies and legislation.

Freedom of information

Another issue of concern for many indigenous peoples is access to information about museum holdings of their cultural property. Museums and other publicly funded institutions have an obligation to provide full access to information about their collections. This remains an issue of significance. Many European institutions have displayed a great reluctance to disclose information about their holdings, especially of indigenous human remains (Ormond-Parker, 1998). National laws in many countries have provisions in relation to freedom of information. After much pressure, some institutions in Europe have now undertaken programmes to document their indigenous human remains collections.

CONCLUSIONS

Indigenous peoples need to reflect on the way forward in the development of international declarations, conventions and cultural policy.

Firstly, implementation of agreed international principles will only be effective if they occur in law, policy and practice at local, national and international levels.

Secondly, international bodies such as UNESCO's Bioethics Committee need to work more closely with indigenous peoples and draw up concrete Action Plans for securing the principle discussed in the work of institutions around the world and in the protection of indigenous peoples' cultural and intellectual property rights.

Thirdly, indigenous peoples need to engage in the debate on research ethics, in particular in the area of biomedics and genetics research.

Finally, the development of meaningful cultural policies and law at an international level, which take into account indigenous wishes in terms of acquisition, curation, study, research and repatriation of indigenous human remains and cultural property, can be of mutual benefit to both institutions and indigenous peoples alike. Unless institutions obtain indigenous peoples' informed consent, accept indigenous peoples' collective rights and provide for benefit sharing and sustainable justice in relation to decisions concerning the study, curation and return of human remains and cultural property, they are merely continuing old colonial practices.

Lyndon Ormond-Parker is an Australian indigenous researcher and consultant. He has worked for ten years in documenting and cataloguing Australian indigenous human remains in Australian and European institutions and has assisted communities and institutions with the repatriation process.

Contact address: C/-Aboriginal and Torres Strait Islander Unit, RMIT University, GPO Box 2476V Melbourne VIC 3001, Australia. Email: ormond_parker@hotmail.com

REFERENCES

Aboriginal and Torres Strait Islander Commission (ATSIC). *Aboriginal and Torres Strait Islander Peoples and Australia's Obligations under the United Nations International Covenant on Economic, Social and Cultural Rights*. A report submitted by the Aboriginal and Torres Strait Islander Commission to the United Nations Committee on Economic, Social and Cultural Rights. August (2000). http://www.atsic.gov.au/issues/indigenous_rights/international/cescr/ICESCR%20Report.doc

Associated Press. Stuffed man buried in Botswana *Associated Press*, 14.25 GMT Friday 6 October (2000).

Australian Law Reform Commission and Australian Health Ethics Committee (ALRC/AHEC). *Australian Law Reform Commission and Australian Health Ethics Committee Inquiry into the Protection of Human Genetic Information Report*. Inquiry Report 66 (2002).

Battiste, M. and Henderson, J. *Protecting Indigenous Knowledge and Heritage: A Global Challenge*. Purich Publishing Ltd, Saskatoon (2000).

Bush, G.W. President Bush's Remarks at the United Nations General Assembly, New York, 12 September 2002.US Department of State (2002). http://www.state.gov/p/nea/rls/rm/13434.htm

Commission of the European Communities. *Report from the Commission to the Council: Review of progress of working with indigenous peoples*. 11.6.2002 COM (2002) 291. Commission of the European Communities, Brussels (2002).

Commons Committee.-*Seventh Report of the House of Commons Culture, Media and Sport Committee: Cultural Property: Return and Illicit Trade*. Session 1999–2000. 18 July (2000a). http://www.parliament.the-stationery-office.co.uk/pa/cm199900/cmselect/cmcumeds/cmcumeds.htm

Declaration on the Importance and Value of Universal Museums, Signed by the Directors of 18 Museums. Media Release by British Museum. December (2002). http://www.thebritishmuseum.ac.uk/newsroom/current2003/universalmuseums.html

Department of Culture Media and Sport. *Cultural Property Unit: Report of the Working Group on Human Remains: November 2003*. (2003) http://www.culture.gov.uk/NR/rdonlyres/D3CBB6E0-255D-42F8-A728-067CE53062EA/0/Humanremainsreportsmall.pdf

Department of Culture Media and Sport, Cultural Property Unit. *Care of Historic Human Remains: A Consultation Report of the Working Group on Human Remains*. July (2004) http://www.culture.gov.uk/NR/rdonlyres/0E977E00-9465-4A42-9C1D-4D860A6E9339/0/HistoricHuman.pdf

Department of Culture Media and Sport. *Human Remains Code of Practice Drafting Group – Terms of Reference*. 6 March (2005) http://www.culture.gov.uk/cultural_property/hr_uk_institutions/ http://www.culture.gov.uk/NR/rdonlyres/F9E51025-4785-4A15-B405-11C7930ED117/0/tof_hr_cpdg.pdf

Fforde, C. Introduction. In Fforde, C., Hubert, J. and Turnbull, P. (eds) *The Dead and their Possessions: Repatriation in Principle, Policy and Practice*. One World Archaeology, Routledge, London (2002).

Fforde, C. and Ormond-Parker, L. Repatriation developments in the UK. *Indigenous Law Bulletin* **5** (2001) 9–13.

Flynn, T. Who dares speak its name? *The Spectator*. 23 November (2002). http://www.tomflynn.co.uk/Deaccessioning.html

Gibson, I. Biobank UK: time to talk. *Science & Public Affairs* **December** (2002) 30.

Harry, D. *BIOPIRACY – Ten Years Post Post-Rio*. Human Genetic Research and Indigenous People Seminar. Johannesburg, South Africa, 22–23 August (2002).

Indian Law Resource Centre. *The Mayagna (Sumo) Indigenous Community of Awas Tingni v The Republic of Nicaragua 2001*. Judgement of the Inter-American Court of Human Rights, 31 August 2001. Briefing Paper February (2002).

Janke, T. *Our Culture, Our Future – Report on Australian Indigenous Cultural and Intellectual Property Rights*. ATSIC (Aboriginal and Torres Strait Islander Commission) Canberra. AIATSIS (Australian Institute of Aboriginal and Torres Strait Islander Studies) (1998).

Kimberley Declaration. *International Indigenous Peoples Summit on Sustainable Development Khoi-San Territory, Kimberley, South Africa, 20–23 August*. (2002). http://www.iwgia.org/sw217.asp

Kirby M. Report of the Rapporteur Kirby, M. UNESCO *Report of the International Bioethics Committee (IBC) on Ethics, Intellectual Property and Genomics*. SHS-503/01/CIB-8/2Rev. Paris, 10 January (2002).

Morris, J. and Foley, R. Should British museums repatriate human remains? *Science Public Affairs* **December** (2002) 4–5.

O'Keefe, P.J. Archaeology and human rights. *Public Archaeology* 1 (1999) 181–194.

Ormond Parker, L. Access to museum archives – whose information is it anyway? *Museum National* 7 (1998) 9.

Parsons, N. and Segobye, A.K. Missing persons and stolen bodies: the repatriation of 'El Negro' to Botswana. In Fforde, C., Hubert, J. and Turnbull, P. (eds) *The Dead and their Possessions: Repatriation in Principle, Policy and Practice*. One World Archaeology. Routledge, London (2002) 245–255.

Prime Ministerial Joint Statement on Aboriginal Remains, 4 July (2000). http://www.number-10.gov.uk/output/page2829.asp

Shek, T. Can dust remain dust? English law and indigenous human remains. *Art, Antiquity and Law* 5 (2000). 265–293.

Tetrel, S. African woman going home after 200 years. April 30, 2002. *Associated Press*, 6 May (2002).

United Nations Economic and Social Council. *Draft United Nations Declaration on the Rights of Indigenous Peoples*. E/CN.4/Sub.2/1994/2/Add.1 (1994). http://www.unhchr.ch/huridocda/huridoca.nsf/(Symbol)/E.CN.4.Sub.2.1994.2.Add.1.En?Opendocument

United Nations Economic and Social Council. Protection of the heritage of indigenous people. Final report of the Special Rapporteur, Mrs Erica-Irene Daes, 21 June 1995 E/CN.4/Sub.2/1995/26.

United Nations Economic and Social Council. *Concluding Observations of the Committee on Economic, Social and Cultural Rights*. E/C.12/1/Add.50, 2000 Australia. September (2000a) http://www.unhchr.ch/tbs/doc.nsf/(Symbol)/E.C.12.1.Add.50.En?Opendocument

United Nations Economic and Social Council. *Report of the Seminar on Draft Principles and Guidelines for the Protection of the Heritage of Indigenous People*. E/CN.4/Sub.2/2000/26, held at the United Nations Office held Geneva 28 February to 1 March (2000b). http://www.unhchr.ch/Huridocda/Huridoca.nsf/0/42263fd3915c047ec1256929004f1ffc?Opendocument

United Nations Economic and Social Council. *Permanent Forum on Indigenous Issues First Session, New York 13–24 May 2002*. E/2002/43. 2002, Economic and Social Council Supplement No. 43 June (2002a).

United Nations Economic and Social Council. *Report on the 7th Session of the Working Group on the Elaboration of a Draft United Nations Declaration on the Rights of Indigenous People, March 2002*. E/CN.4/2002/98 2002. United Nations Office of the High Commissioner for Human Rights (2002b). http://www.unhchr.ch/huridocda/huridoca.nsf/(Symbol)/E.CN.4.2002.98.En?Opendocument

United Nations Economic and Social Council. *Report of the International Workshop on Methodologies regarding Free, Prior and Informed Consent and Indigenous People*. E/C.19/2005/3. New York 17–19 January (2005).

United Nations Educational Scientific and Cultural Organisation. *Universal Declaration on the Human Genome and Human Rights Adopted* (1997).

United Nations Permanent Forum on Indigenous Issues (2005) http://www.un.org/esa/socdev/unpfii/index.html

Whall, H. *Indigenous Self-Determination in the Commonwealth*. Occasional Papers Commonwealth Policy Studies Unit, Institute of Commonwealth Studies, University of London, November (2002).

World Intellectual Property Organisation (WIPO), Intergovernmental Committee on Intellectual Property and Genetic Resources. *Traditional Knowledge and Folklore Report*. 3rd Session. 13–22 June. WIPO/GRTKF/1C/3/17 (2002). http://www.wipo.org/

World Summit on Sustainable Development (2002) http://www.johannesburgsummit.org/

Strands of indigenism in the Bolivian Andes:

competing juridical claims for the ownership and management of indigenous heritage sites in an emerging context of legal pluralism[1]

Denise Y. Arnold and Juan de Dios Yapita

ABSTRACT

The diverse linguistic, cultural and ethnic identities within Bolivia have given rise to different strands of indigenism and a wide variety of groups who claim indigenous status and rights. These groups assert their identities in different ways (through subsistence methods, clothing and textiles, festivals and music, and documentary evidence). Indigenous groups currently use both long-standing institutions within their communities and state juridical structures to compete with Bolivian elites and assert their linguistic and territorial rights, within an emerging context of legal pluralism. Crucial differences have emerged between these elites and the indigenous groups in the legal criteria they recognize: the forms of legal codification they practice (writing or weaving), their methods of appointing and recognizing authorities, and their rights of jurisdiction. Competing claims to the national archaeological site of Tiwanaku, are used as a case study. A general ignorance by external funders and policy-makers of prior forms of indigenous control and communal inheritance are alienating some indigenous groups, and are in danger of destroying the very cultural practices that gave rise to such heritage sites in the first place.

INTRODUCTION: WHOSE FACTS AND FIGURES?

Of the indigenous population of South America 80% live in the Andean highlands, which stretch from the south of Columbia down through Ecuador, Peru and Bolivia, to the north of Chile and Argentina. There are two dominant language groups, Quechua with around 12 million speakers (in Ecuador, Peru, Bolivia and northern Argentina) and Aymara with around 3 million speakers (in Bolivia, Peru, northern Chile and Argentina). In the case of Bolivia, official estimates based on the 2001 census data give an indigenous population comprising 49.9% of the total population (Huarcacho et al., 2003) while more generous estimates based on the same data give a figure of 65% and over (Xavier Albó, personal communication). These differences in interpretation are currently in debate. Similarly, in a question concerning self-identity, the 2001 census identifies 1.28 million Aymara speakers over 15 years old (25.23% of the total population of this age), and 1.55 million Quechua speakers of the same age (30.7 of the total population). The rest of the population is a combination of Guarani and other lowland groups (6% of the total), while *mestizo-criollo* (more middle-class) groups located in the urban centre make up just 38% of the population (Huarcacho ibid., 2003).

Bolivian Aymaras, the focus of this article, inhabit the Titicaca basin, the highlands and valleys of La Paz (and parts of Oruro and Potosí), the Yungas of La Paz and other Andean eastern slopes, and increasingly the major cities. Present-day Aymara linguistic territories spill over modern national boundaries into Chile and Peru, the regional variants of this language often following the boundaries of past and present Andean territories (ayllus, communities, nations, federations) rather than modern Republican ones. Even so, official attempts to document these Aymara linguistic territories, and cite the numbers of speakers, refer almost exclusively to maps where Bolivian Republican political divisions predominate (Albó, 1995), a technique that also tends to promote the labelling of 'dominant' and 'subordinate' languages within an economic conceptualization more oriented to the market and political ends (Silverstein, 1998: 414).

Although Aymara was granted the condition of 'official language' of the Nation in 1983 and later of the city of La Paz, which implies its use and development in the public contexts of the territories where it is spoken, in practice Bolivian elites have been able to limit the application of these norms. In spite of its predominantly indigenous population, only 2% of those who manage Bolivia come from this 'powerless majority', who have little real representation in the national politics of division and exclusion.

Whose indigenism?

The diverse linguistic, cultural and ethnic setting of Bolivia has given rise to many different overlapping and competing strands of indigenism. This blurring of categories as to who is 'indigenous' and what this denomination might imply juridically, probably has contributed to the lack of co-ordination amongst indigenous groups in their demands for change. Each indigenous group uses its distinct historical traditions, ideological demands, recruitment methods, policy-making and alliances of convenience, to vie for dominance and external funding.

For example, the specific localized pasts of each of the 12,000 or so rural highland communities has affected their sense of self-identification, formulation of political alliances and views of the modern State. With Inka expansion from Cusco, Aymara-speaking Collasuyo formed the southernmost of the four *suyo* divisions of the Inka state, of which there are still faint memories in many of the free ayllu communities. (Ayllu, a Quechua term for a territorial unit based originally on localized kindred groups, has gradually disseminated into the Aymara region, the equivalent Aymara term being *jatha*.) Later, during the colonial and republican periods, many tracts of land appropriated from local communities were taken by Spanish and then *criollo* landlords into large holdings called *haciendas*, especially in the highlands around La Paz. Finally, in the modern period, with the Bolivian revolution of 1952 and the Agrarian reform in the following year, both under the National Revolutionary Party (MNR), there was an attempt to return some of these hacienda lands to peasant ownership, amid wider political changes that included the replacement of some older communal authority systems by a newly formed state-directed union movement.

In the ex-hacienda communities, the overall result was an untenable smallholding system, but the recent memory of these political changes tends to dominate any older memories of the Inka state and former Andean systems of land ownership. By contrast, in those communities whose lands were never appropriated, an ayllu-led politics grounded in historical memories of past Andean States, above all the Inka state, survives (see, for example, Crespo, 2000 and Platt, 1999). (Curiously enough, another Andean state, Tiwanaku, hardly figures in these memories.) The direct representatives of some 3000 ayllu communities until 1994 were indigenous authorities (ayllu leaders, and so on), and in some places perhaps the last generation of *caciques apoderados* or land title-bearers, indigenous leaders empowered by the communities to defend their lands against the *hacienda* appropriations of past centuries.

In both the ex-haciendas and traditional ayllus, the constant political struggles to defend (or free) their communities from land appropriations meant that, far from being isolated from the rest of the country, rather a close engagement between community representatives, such as the title-bearers, and the state juridical apparatus was an on-going reality. In this way, a complex form of regional organization (economic and political networks, language norms, forms of dress, bodily, textual and ritual communication), transmitted through institutional settings little-known to outsiders, has interacted for centuries with directives from more central institutions of power.

Another distinctive strand of intellectual indigenism (and more overt 'indianism') characterizes urban centres such as the city of La Paz. Rooted in a Bolivian intellectual tradition dominated by Aymara (and Quechua) speakers in tandem with radical *mestizos*, this movement has important links with the international indigenist movement, through organizations such as Consejo Indio de Sud América (CISA) that seek representation in the newly formed United Nations Forum for Indigenous Peoples. Its principal intellectuals, who are mainly from ex-hacienda communities around La Paz, ground their ideas in the specific local experience of more recent history (particularly the 1884 indigenous land confiscations, and the resistance movement of the empowered title-bearers who sought to reclaim these lands), and their vision of a modernist future tends to derive from the US community development programme of the 1960s. There is less interest in the *longue durée* of Andean history, members having little identification with the Inka State, and much more with regional culture heroes such as Tupaq Katari, whose Liberation Army against Spanish occupation surrounded the city of La Paz for several months in 1781.

A lesser-known provincial indigenism in cities such as Oruro, Potosí, Llallagua, Cochabamba, and Sucre, is led by intellectuals working in universities, NGOs and indigenist institutions who privilege regional interests and perhaps have closer contacts with the grass roots. These are more likely to play musical instruments, speak fluent Aymara (or Quechua) and have a longer social memory than their La Paz counterparts. Both groups, however, have more in common with one another than with another strand, the *mestizo-criollo* researchers and experts, who run indigenist NGOs working *for* indigenous peoples rather than *with* them.

At the heart of the current struggle between 'ayllu' and 'union'-centred views of indigenism, is an emerging group of leaders from both traditions. Some have risen through the ranks of ayllu authorities to enter the newly conformed regional supra-ayllu political organizations, or their national counterparts. The 'Mallku' Felipe Quispe, who led the September 2000 Aymara uprising (information concerning which was largely held from the international press), bridges both traditions (Bigio, 2002). Present leader of a faction of the main peasant union (CSUTCB), and elected MP in the 2002 elections in his own Movimiento Indio Pachakuti party (MIP), Quispe's training in the 1990s was in the Tupaq Katari Guerrilla Army (called EGTK), and he claims his ancestor Diego Quispe was a colonel in Tupaq Katari's Liberation Army. His politics are supported by the Comuna group of urban *mestizo-criollo* intellectuals.

Yet another tendency is 'official indigenism', centred in the official policies of the MNR (the Nationalist Revolutionary Movement, a mainstream political party), which has sought since the Revolution of 1952 to attract indigenous votes within a consensus programme of national identity. This strand was revitalized in the 1994–1998 alliance between President Sánchez de Losada and his Katarist Aymara Vice-president (Víctor-Hugo Cárdenas), when outside demands for lowering the levels of illiteracy and bettering the conditions of indigenous populations (within the framework of internationally applied structural adjustments) were instrumental in their passing a series of neoliberal laws that would attract international backing (see, for example, Velasco Reckling, 1994). The main thrust of their programme was an Educational Reform Law (to modernize the public schooling system) and the Law of Popular Participation (to decentralize the benefits of a head-count taxation by transferring its control to newly formed municipalities).

These new laws engaged with Constitutional changes that introduced a first article recognizing Bolivia as a 'multiethnic' and 'pluricultural' Nation (although no mention was made of its being 'multilingual'). These and other related buzz words now permeate national discourses about education, health and other matters, in relation to indigenous peoples. In reality, the new reforms, far from influencing the widespread racism in Bolivian society, concentrate more on broadening the outlook of indigenous rural communities through a modernist and urbanizing development programme. In this context, many commentators interpret the reforms as barely disguised replays of previous attempts to integrate indigenous groups into national society at the expense of their own notions of self-identity (see, for example, the arguments in Yapu, 1999 and Medina, 2000).

Competing discourses and textual practices

These indigenous and indigenist groups compete with Bolivian elites in a dynamic juridical field of contesting discourses and institutional frameworks, where indigenous and linguistic rights, the recognition of indigenous authorities and institutions and, above all, problems of defining land and territory, are being reframed within an emerging context of legal pluralism. As a part of the struggle to have their nations and territories recognized, Aymara leaders often appeal to the body of international 'soft laws' that support indigenous peoples, drawing on the collective nature of the rights to which they refer. Bolivia ratified Convention 169 of the International Labour Organisation in 1991, and it has been translated since into many native languages, including Aymara.

In these debates, Aymara intellectuals and their lawyers argue that their own legal criteria are distinct from dominant national ones, as are their forms of inscription. They reject the dual colonial categorization of 'Spanish law' versus 'uses and customs', arguing for the formal recognition of 'indigenous law', even 'ayllu law' (Fernández, 2000). They criticize 'rights-based development', grounded in European notions of citizenship and individual human rights, in favour of an Andean form of commons, and the alternative cosmovision that sustains it.

Unlike conventional *criollo* politics based on representation by individuals, ayllu political structure is dependent on wider kin structures and a system of community service through the gradual accession to higher offices, This is achieved by means of a 'pathway' of minor posts, the rotation of office between community groups and a gendered system of leadership, whereby male leaders represent the male elements of the universe, including the highest mountains as primary symbols of power, while their wives or other female kin represent the female elements, including the earth.

In addition, male authorities were traditionally empowered by lightning and by the powerful stones called *wak'a* (Astvaldsson, 2000; Arnold and Yapita, 2000: 282). The Law of Popular Participation, drawn up by MNR intellectuals as a concession to indigenous land claims and other tensions, is generally held to ignore these Andean institutions, forms and gendering of authorities and decision-making, and notions of territory and jurisdiction (Pacheco Balanza, 2001).

In the so-called 'War of the Ayllus' (during 2000), fierce disputes between neighbouring ayllus on the modern boundary between the departments of Oruro and Potosí resulted in an armed confrontation that was only brought under control when several hundred troops from the Bolivian army, directed by the Southern Command of the USA, entered the zone. Underlying the conflict was the problem of 'double frontiers' where indigenous traditions and *criollo* or republican authorities had developed alternative means of designating the limits of ayllu territories. These differences in practice of how to mark out ayllu boundaries, and the lack of a common consensus as to which authority should supervise them (the army, the President or ayllu authorities), led to all maps of Bolivia being withdrawn, apart from the republican map of 1826, in a highly volatile situation that might re-erupt at any time.

As alternative forms of legal codification, Fernández (2000) cites the oral practices of ayllu assemblies and councils of elders, and Andean forms of oratory and libation-making that still draw on the braided structures of the knotted cords called *chinu* in Aymara, and *kipu* in Quechua (see also Arnold and Yapita, 2004). Loza (1998) shows how such *kipus* served as juridical documents in defence of communal patrimony throughout the colonial and into the Republican and modern periods. And Bubba (1997) documents the recent use of Andean textiles as 'maps' to defend community lands, in the case of Coroma (Oruro). A common language of knotting and unknotting threads in key moments still announces impending peace (or war) in conflicts between ayllus, just as it did when Tupaq Katari besieged La Paz in 1781. Similarly, the coding of designs on the knitted pullovers of the indigenous leader, 'Mallku' Felipe Quispe's, seem to announce his status as leader (a cosmic axis between llamas, see Fig. 1), or figurehead of an imminent Civil War

Figure 1. The 'Mallku' Felipe Quispe, whose knitted pullover's coded design announces his status as Aymara leader (from *el juguete rabioso*, Año 2, No. 36, La Paz, del 15 al 28 de julio de 2001, 8–9. Photo by Anzo De Lucca).

(with 'Inka' war designs), when Aymaras 'sowed the roads into La Paz with stones' in September 2000, cutting off supplies for weeks on end, just as Tupaq Katari had done in 1781.

This alternative textualization of rights (supported in Part III of the 1994/5 UN Draft Declaration of Rights of Indigenous Peoples) implies that current efforts to translate national Bolivian laws into native languages do not go far enough, and this is further undermined by current attempts to subjugate native Andean legal practices to national jurisdiction in a new normative proposal for community law. Other possibilities might include regional initiatives to define inheritance rights, or draw up regional constitutions, with a view to a gradual standardization of such practices. For example, the small Chipaya Nation (of some 2000 speakers) in the heart of Aymara territory, has already elected a President and published its own Political Constitution (Nación Originaria Uru (NOU), 2000).

Who is indigenous: memory and transmission

The ways in which different social groups (*criollo* elites, *mestizos*, indigenous groups) have appealed to distinctly formulated inscriptions (whether written or woven) in order to validate their claims to identity or land, have generated a superimposition of categories concerning group adscription. At an official level, Aymara (and Quechua) speakers tend to accept the colonial definition of themselves as 'original peoples' (*pueblos originarios*), a fiscal category used to define tributary payments in relation to socio-economic status and land (the key issue here), and inscribed in vital title documents dating to the colonial period that are preserved in community archives. During the same period, 'Aymara' and 'Quechua' were also fiscal categories of this kind (Bouysse-Cassagne, 1975). For Aymaras then and now, the term 'indigenous' when used in popular parlance refers to lowland Amazonian groups (and frequently implies a pejorative sense of superiority on the part of the speaker), who were considered savages by the colonial authorities and whose land rights were not documented. On the other hand 'Andean', as a general term of affiliation used by outsiders (anthropologists and so on), comes surprisingly close to the territorial limits of Inka expansion (Harris, 1994).

Regional terms of affiliation appeal more to the rural community or ayllu to which a person belongs, and often allude to toponyms in native languages. This local sense of affiliation is reinforced through the practices of *thakhi*, 'custom' or 'law', an overriding regional institution that embraces the body of juridical norms, language interactions, styles of dress, body language, ritual, political, economic, social and textual practices that we call 'culture'. *Thakhi* also describes the difficult 'pathway' of practices men and women must pass through on their way to becoming full ayllu leaders (see Abercrombie, 1998).

As a consequence of the 1952 Revolution, the new *mestizo-criollo* MNR apparatus, ignoring these former differences, imposed a unifying model of 'Bolivianness' upon the Nation. In response to this globalizing concept, other levels of society subsumed a variety of new identities. With the massive rural outpouring to cities, a new generation of migrants began to consider themselves as Aymara (or Quechua), using language, dress and cultural expression in *barrio* feasts and dances to create a common identity, and differentiate themselves from the *mestizo-criollo* populations already established there (Abercrombie, 1991). The gradual emergence of a city-wide manifestation of Aymara presence in the La Paz festival of *Gran Poder*, when Aymaras dance their history and cultural identity, their spectacular music, costumes and choreographic forms (*morenada, caporal, tinku*) taking over the streets, has become a powerful cultural nexus for renewing annually a pan-Andean sense of Aymara identity for groups living as far away as Peru, Chile and Argentina.

When *mestizo-criollo* social groups have sought to re-appropriate these same socio-cultural spaces they have done so through legal battles, for example the claims for Bolivian ownership of the *morenada* dance during the 1980s, against rival groups in Chile or Peru. This concern is not shared by Aymara-speakers, who view this cultural expression as theirs, no matter what present-day political borders are surpassed.

Whose past, whose tongue, whose territory? The case of Tiwanaku

These competing claims to ownership of cultural and symbolic capital by indigenous and indigenist organizations also apply to claims of ownership over vestiges of the more distant past. For example, the recent Aymara uprisings under the 'Mallku' Felipe Quispe demanded recognition of their autonomous territory and incipient Aymara Nation. According to the *Manifesto of Jach'ak'achi* (2001) drawn up with the help of the international indianist organization CISA, this territory is centred in the colonial town of Achakachi (re-aymarized as *Jach'ak'achi*), a claim supported by citing the Middle Horizon archaeological site of Tiwanaku (c.200 BC–AD 1000) as a key symbol of Aymara longevity in this region. A related aspect of this affirming of Aymara identity is the recent forging of a unified Aymara New Year, based around the ceremonies of the June solstice at this site, resulting in part from the influence of local shamans (*yatiri*) in the MNR politics of Sánchez de Losada's government, whose populist stance generated many folkloric ceremonies of this kind.

The Mallku's claim was probably quite spontaneous, part of a generalized recognition that his forebears had something to do with the construction and ceremonial apparatus of the Tiwanaku culture complex, much as the Aymara claim the *morenada* dance. The claim that Tiwanaku is an ancestral site for the Aymara is generally shared among locals (see Astvaldsson, 2000), regional shamans and those who come from as far away as the north of Potosí to copy weaving designs from the monoliths standing there. Even young urban musicians of Aymara descent like to flaunt themselves in front of Tiwanaku's 'Gate of the Sun' in their digital videos.

However, the reality is more problematic. While the site has been known and revered by locals for centuries and it is said by many chroniclers of the colonial period ('El Inka' Garcilaso and others) to have been visited by Inka chieftains, nevertheless a wider Aymara identity with the site, let alone a Bolivian nationalist one, is much more recent (see Kolata, 1993: 1–37). Although Tiwanaku was described in travellers accounts from the 19th century onwards (Squier in 1878; Rivero and Von Tschudi in 1853), it was only with the 1952 Revolution that nationalist interests turned to this site as a symbol of identity. At this point, archaeological visions of the Tiwanaku State, and of *Taypiqala* (the 'Stone at the centre' of the site) as a world cosmological axis, especially those of the Bolivian archaeologist and MNR-member, Carlos Ponce Sanginés, were instrumental in forging these nationalist claims.

Modern tensions between Peru and Bolivia, with their emphasis in recent frontiers, also contributed to this nationalist reworking of the past. So, while Tiwanaku became a national symbol for Bolivians, Inka Cusco and, to a lesser degree another Middle Horizon site, Wari, became equivalent national symbols for Peru. In this context, Peru's current head of state, Alejandro Toledo, staged his 2000 presidential inauguration in the Inka site of Machhu Pichu, while Bolivia's then President Quiroga, chewed coca leaves in Cochabamba, at a site held to be miraculous.

Faced with this appropriation by outsiders of indigenous cultural capital, Carlos Mamani Condori (of the indianist Workshop of Oral History, THOA), in an essay of 1992, reclaimed Tiwanaku as a pre-existing ancestral Aymara site from what he describes as the *mestizo-criollo* dual project of 1952: of forging the Nation by encountering there its prehispanic cultural roots, while integrating the 'Indian' population into its new civilizing programme (Mamani Condori 1992: 2; see also 1989). He similarly derides the Portugals (father-and-son archaeologists who were members of the Ponce Sanginés school) for claiming to have 'discovered' Tiwanaku, and then comparing it with Old World points of reference (Ninevah, Babylon) rather than appreciating its proper cultural context.

Similarly, the indianist Internet bulletin, *Aymara Today*, demanded the return to Tiwanaku, as the 'Religious Centre of the Aymara Nation', of the so-called 'Bennett Monolith', a 20 ton carved stone named after the North American archaeologist Wendell C. Bennett who excavated at Tiwanaku in the 1930s. The 7.3m high statue, decorated with calendrical carvings, was originally taken from Tiwanaku in 1933 and lodged in the capital La Paz for 'safe-keeping' (by the Polish-born Bolivian archaeologist Posnansky), first in El Prado and then, in 1940, at a major road junction in the Plaza Tejada Zorzano, in front of the Football Stadium. There, what Aymaras call *jach'a wak'a*, or 'great sacred-one', was renamed by Posnansky the Pachamama or 'Earth Mother' Stele, and was adopted by local civic watchdogs who allowed it to be used for decades as a 'urinal, a rubbish dump and a site for graffiti'. This kind of desecration might explain the current distrust shown by indigenous peoples when asked to part with cultural objects for exhibitions: for example, in 1992 Aymara groups prevented a Tiwanaku sculpture from being loaned to an exhibition in the USA to celebrate the centenary of the 1492 Spanish invasion.

Equally problematic is the skewing of Tiwanaku's linguistic origins by the vested interests of nationalist movements, and strong regional sympathies (Cook, 1994: 62). For example, the former inductive *mestizo-criollo* claims that Tiwanaku's founders were Aymara or Quechua (in the old arguments of Max Uhle, Middendorf, Ibarra Grasso, Markham, Riva Agüero, etc.) are now regarded as untenable, modern linguistic and ethnohistorical studies showing that they were more probably Pukina-Urukilla (Cerrón-Palomino, 1998; Torero, 1998 and see also Gonzalez de la Rosa, 1910). The extension of Pukina territories gradually diminished in the colonial period as the Pukinas mixed with more dominant Andean language groups, and they then all but disappeared (Torero, 1987: 352). Aymara speakers arrived there around the 13th century, followed by Quechua speakers in the 15th century.

These kinds of nationalist claims to ancient patrimony still prevailed in 2001. For example, an interactive educational CD of Bolivian history that won a major university prize speaks of the 'Bolivian' Inka Empire, illustrating only Bolivian Inka sites (the Island of the Sun, etc.) with no mention at all of Cusco (in present-day Peru) – a curious categorization considering that Bolivia only came into existence in 1825.

However, the stakes at issue, and the parties in conflict, are gradually becoming more clear-cut. In December 2001, a particularly damaging attack on the Bennett Monolith with indelible marker paint by a gang of 'pretty boys' (young white boys from downtown La Paz, rumoured to be expressing their rejection of recent Aymara political claims), led to new pleas from indigenous groups, led by the mayor of Tiwanaku, for the return of this 'millenary Aymara monument' to its original site, despite the many technical difficulties of doing so. It was finally returned on 16 March 2002, accompanied by lavish Aymara ceremonies, the waving of *wiphala* indigenous flags, and 'readings' of its remarkable powers, its imminent removal being associated with the tremendous hailstorm that had raged through La Paz a month earlier, and memories of a similar storm that had raged when it was first taken there in the 1930s.

These new claims, led by the Tiwanaku mayor, insisted that present *criollo* institutions (e.g., the Vice-ministry of Culture, the National Institute of Archaeology, and cultural groups in La Paz), had been more bent on seeking funds than representing Aymara interests, and proposed instead the conformation of new Aymara cultural watchdogs to do so in future. The question now is, who will finance them?

CONCLUSION

These collages of distinct social groups with differing interests and textual practices, competing for different forms of capital (cultural, economic, symbolic) in a common territory, are just as evident in the latest claims for patrimony generated by UNESCO's World Heritage programme. *Criollos* and *mestizos* have tended to seek official written UNESCO and municipally backed ownership of and protection for major feasts (Carnival in Oruro), whole cities (Potosí), national archaeological and colonial sites (Tiwanaku and the Chiriguano churches) and extraordinary national landscapes (the Salt Flats of Uyuni). However, Aymara and Quechua ownership, at least until recently, has tended to be traced out in many-layered ritual performances (sung, spoken, danced, woven) of memory and continuity in familiar landscapes (Rowe, 2000), less easily adapted to the legal and financing criteria of outsiders.

A danger now is that the current trends towards external funding, and the general ignorance by funders and policy-makers of prior indigenous practices and institutional controls of communal inheritance, are gradually alienating important social actors from participating fully in the new heritage sites, and even prohibiting some of those practices (for example the traditional offerings made there by indigenous ritual specialists) that gave rise to such sites in the first place. Added to which, with the stakes constantly being raised, it is unlikely that indigenous groups will have access to the kinds of legal support that might defend their own interests against competing *criollo*, nationalist and World Heritage claims.

Even so, as the *Aymara Today* bulletin recognizes in its claim for the return not only of the Pachamama Stele but also of Tiwanaku as a whole to Aymara peoples, if it were not for the vigilance of international organizations that have claimed the site as World Patrimony, 'it would have been dismantled already' (*Aymara Today*, December 2001).

ACKNOWLEDGEMENT

Many thanks to U. Ricardo López G. for his bibliographic searches and challenging comments during the writing of this paper.

ENDNOTE

1. This paper was originally submitted in November 2002 and discusses the situation in Bolivia at that time.

Denise Y. Arnold, an English anthropologist, directs the *Instituto de Lengua y Cultura Aymara* in La Paz, Bolivia, and is Visiting Research Professor at Birkbeck College, London. Among her publications are *River of Fleece, River of Song* (2002) and *The Rostrum of Heads: Textual Struggles, Education and Land in the Andes* (in press).

Contact address: Instituto de Lengua y Cultura Aymara, La Paz, Bolivia and Birkbeck College, London. Email: ilca@acelerate.com

Juan De Dios Yapita, a Bolivian linguist and Aymara speaker, founded the *Instituto de Lengua y Cultura Aymara* in La Paz, Bolivia, and is Visiting Full Professor at Birkbeck College London. Among his publications are *Aymara Compendio* (1988) and a series of teaching grammars of Andean Spanish for Aymara speakers.

Contact address: Instituto de Lengua y Cultura Aymara, La Paz, Bolivia (Casilla 2681, La Paz, Bolivia, South America) and Birkbeck College, London. Casilla 2681, La Paz, Bolivia, South America.

REFERENCES

Abercrombie, T.A. To be Indian, to be Bolivian: ethnic and national discourses of identity. In Sherzer, J. and Urban, G. (eds) *Nation-State and Indian in Latin America*. University of Texas Press, Austin (1991).

Abercrombie, T.A. *Pathways of Memory and Power. Ethnography and History Among an Andean People.* University of Wisconsin Press, Wisconsin (1998).

Albó, X. *Bolivia plurilingüe. Guía para planificadores y educadores.* 2 tomos. UNICEF y CIPCA, La Paz (1995).

Arnold, D.Y and Yapita, J.de D. *El rincón de las cabezas: Luchas textuales, educación y tierras en los Andes.* UMSA and ILCA, La Paz (2000). English version to be published by the University of Pittsburgh Press.

Arnold, D.Y. and Yapita, J.de D. The nature of indigenous literatures in the Andes. In Valdés, M.J. and Kadir, D. (eds) *Literary Cultures of Latin American: A Comparative History of Cultural Formations, Part 3. The Presence of Amerindian Cultures*. Oxford University Press, Oxford and New York (2004).

Astvaldsson, A. *Las voces de los Wak'a*. CIPCA Cuadernos de investigación 54, La Paz (2000).

Aymara Today. Pieza religiosa aymara sufre agresión en La Paz. *Aymara Today* (Aymar Jichur Urun) No. 07, December 2001: http://www.aymaranet.org/AymaraToday007.html

Bigio, I. El avance de los partidos campesinos en los comicios bolivianos, 12 de Julio de 2002. http://www.altopilar.com/ISAACBIGIO (2002).

Bouysse-Cassagne, T. Pertenencia étnica, status económico y lenguas en Charcas a fines del Siglo XVI. *Tasa de la Visita General de Francisco de Toledo*. Edición de Noble David Cook. Universidad Mayor de San Marcos. Dirección Universitaria de Biblioteca y Publicaciones, Lima, Peru (1975) 312–328.

Bubba, C. Los rituales a los vestidos de María Titiqhawa, Juana Palla y otros, fundadores de los ayllus de Coroma. In Bouysse-Cassagne, T. (ed. Compiler) *Saberes y memorias en los Andes. In Memoriam Thierry Saignes.* CREAL-IFEA, Lima (1997) 377–400.

Cerrón-Palomino, R. Examen de la teoría aimarista de Uhle. In Kaulicke, P. (ed.) *Max Uhle y el Perú antiguo*. Pontificia Universidad Católica del Perú, Fondo Editorial, Lima (1998) 85–120.

Comisión Económica para América Latina y el Cáribe (The United Nations Economic Commission for Latin America and the Carribean) (CEPAL). *Etnicidad, 'raza' y equidad en América Latina y el Caribe*. LC/R.1967/Rev. 1, 7 de agosto de 2000. Autores: Alvaro Bello y Marta Rangel. CEPAL (2000).

Cook, A.G. *Wari y Tiwanaku: Entre el estilo y la imagen*. Pontificia Universidad Católica del Perú, Fondo Editorial, Lima (1994).

Crespo, R. Radio broadcast. Universidad Pública de El Alto, La Paz (2000).

Fernández, M. *La ley del ayllu. Práctica de jach'a justicia y jisk'a justicia (Justicia Mayor y Justicia Menor) en comunidades aymaras*. PIEB, La Paz (2000).

González de la Rosa, M. Les deux Tiahuanaco, leurs problèmes et leur solution. *Paper presented to the XVI Congreso Internacional de Americanistas (Viena)*. A. Hartleben's Verlag, Wien und Leipzig (1910) 405–428.

Harris, O. Response to O. Starn, 'Rethinking the politics of anthropology: the case of the Andes'. *Current Anthropology* 34 (1994) 13–38.

Instituto Nacional de Estadística. *Censo nacional de población y vivienda*. La Paz: INE (1993).

Kolata, A.L. *The Tiwanaku: portrait of an Andean Civilization*. Blackwell, Oxford (1993).

Loza, C.B. Du bon usage del quipus face à l'administration coloniale espagnole (1550–1600). *Population* 1-2 (1998) 139–160.

Mamani Condori, C. History and prehistory in Bolivia: what about the Indians? In Layton, R. (ed.) *Conflict in the Archaeology of Living Traditions*. Unwin Hyman, London (1989) 46–59.

Mamani Condori, C. *Los aymaras frente a la historia: dos ensayos metodológicos*. Aruwiyiri, Chukiyawu (1992).

Manifiesto de Jach'ak'achi. Published in *Aymara Today* on the Internet, 9 April 2001. (2001).

Medina, J. *Diálogo de sordos. Occidente e indianidad. Una aproximación conceptual a la educación intercultural y bilingüe en Bolivia*. CEBIAE, La Paz (2000).

Nación Originaria Uru. *Kiriwill qamanakztan nijz cheqanchistanpacha tiy wajtha qalltiniki uruz. Estatutos orgánicos y reglamentos de la Nación Originaria Uru*. Serie 'Marka' 19. CEDIPAS (Centro Diocesano de Pastoral Social) and NOU, Oruro (2000).

Pacheco Balanza, D. Visiones sobre la territorialidad y el desarrollo rural. Manuscript, Fundación Tierra, La Paz (2001).

Platt, T. *La persistencia de los ayllus en el norte de Potosí de la invasión europea a la república de Bolivia*. Fundación Diálogo, etc., La Paz (1999).

Rowe, W. Memoria, continuidad, multitemporalidad. In Leinhard, M. (ed.), *La memoria popular y sus transformaciones*. Vervuert/Iberoamericana, Madrid (2000) 43–51.

Silverstein, M. Contemporary transformations of local linguistic communities. *Annual Review of Anthropology* 27 (1998) 401–426.

Torero, A. Lenguas y pueblos altiplánicos en torno al siglo XVI. *Revista andina*, 10. Centro Bartolomé de las Casas, Cusco (1987) 329–372.

Torero, A. El marco histórico-geográfico en la interacción quechua-aru. In Dedenbach-Salazar Sáenz, S., Arellano Hoffman, C., König, E. and Prümers, H. (eds) *50 Años de Estudios Americanistas en la Universidad de Bonn*. Verlag Anton Sauerwein, Bonn (1998) 601–630.

Velasco Reckling, E. La Reforma Educativa boliviana: Una (Re) Visión Estratégica. *Noche Parlamentaria*. Konrad Adenauer Stiftung, Asesoría Parlamentaria, La Paz (1994).

Yapu, M. Balance desde las aulas. La Reforma y la enseñanza de la lecto-escritura en el campo. *T'inkasos*, revista boliviana de ciencias socials (1999) 601–630.

Museums and communities in Africa:
facing the new challenges

Lorna Abungu

ABSTRACT

Established during the colonial era, the majority of museums in Africa were modelled on their European counterparts. The period of Africanization that followed the independence of many African nations witnessed a dramatic increase in the number of Africans receiving higher education and specialized training. Institutions such as museums began to come under the leadership of indigenous Africans but, in most cases, the exhibits and their condition(s) remained the same. Today, African museums face new challenges: how can they become more relevant, both to the local communities they serve and to foreign visitors? How can they attract more visitors, especially from local communities? This article discusses the notion of 'indigenous' in an African context. It looks at the development of museums in Africa and their current metamorphosis into dynamic cultural centres that address pertinent social, cultural and even economic issues – in the face of dwindling government funding and increased modernization and globalization. It discusses several museums and how they are meeting these challenges, and how organizations such as AFRICOM (International Council of African Museums) and programmes such as SAMP (African–Swedish Museum Network) are contributing to the positive changes currently taking place.

INTRODUCTION

The vast majority of museums in Africa were established during the colonial era, either by the colonial authorities themselves or by members of the European elite. As a result, they were modelled upon European museums – or at least the European idea of a museum: a place where the upper classes could come to marvel at exotic artefacts belonging to the indigenous peoples of the particular country. Some museums, such as the National Museums of Kenya, were also established as repositories of natural history specimens; again, these specimens were housed and displayed for a particular group within the local population – invariably the white elite.

However, in the latter part of the 20th century many African nations gained independence from their colonial masters, and an increasing number of Africans received further education and specialized training. As a result, many government institutions and private companies underwent a period of 'Africanization'. Today, museum directors throughout the continent and, indeed, most of the staff themselves, are indigenous Africans. However, the basic set-up of the museums remains the same: endless glass cases with (often) dusty natural history or ethnographic specimens. Does this type of exhibit truly satisfy the needs of today's African museum visitor, whether a member of the local community or a tourist? The answer, increasingly, is 'no'.

CHALLENGES FOR THE FUTURE

So where do African museums go from here? Should these existing museums be demolished and written off as an undesirable hangover from a painful colonial era? Or do they adapt themselves to fit the new requirements of the local communities and other visitors alike? This is indeed a major challenge that faces African museums today. One of the most pressing questions in this scenario, however, is what does 'indigenous' mean?

WHO IS INDIGENOUS?

It is important here to address the term 'indigenous' as it applies in an African context. While there has been much hype recently about 'indigenous people', it is a term that is perhaps not very relevant on the African continent. In other countries, such as the USA, Canada, Australia and even parts of Europe, 'indigenous peoples' are those who have been marginalized through colonialization, and later by immigration, and who now make up a minority of the nation's population; examples would be the Australian Aborigines, Native Americans (or First Peoples) or the Sami of Sweden. In Africa, despite colonialism, indigenous Africans remain in the majority and so almost every person walking the street, whether in traditional attire or a suit and tie, is in fact 'indigenous'. A Maasai in full regalia in his hut in the Rift Valley is equally as indigenous as a Kikuyu businessman in Nairobi dressed in an imported Armani suit.

So, in an African context, it is much more common to talk about the needs of local communities, and how museums can become relevant to the communities they serve. The word 'indigenous' is often used to refer to mostly minority, disadvantaged or culturally exploited groups.

INVOLVING COMMUNITIES

Already in Africa, many museums are facing up to the challenges of the 21st century – problems of reduced government funding, low visitor numbers, stagnant exhibitions and high staff turnover, among others. Some issues, such as government funding and 'brain-drain', are beyond the immediate control of an individual museum. However, museums in Africa can and are addressing some of the other challenges. In order to encourage more visitors, new exhibitions and education programmes are being initiated, and increasingly these are community-driven and designed to address pertinent social issues. The museums are increasingly adopting the function of a neutral space of exchange and dialogue among people of different ethnicities and religions.

At the National Museums of Kenya, the Ethnography Department initiated a community-driven project that resulted in the Asian-African Heritage exhibition. The Asian community in Kenya joined together to draw up a story line, gather objects and actually construct the exhibition. The exhibition, officially opened in February 2000, was a resounding success and to this day is a huge attraction to visitors. Another project of the department was on Peace and Conflict Resolution. This time, elders from various rural communities such as the Maasai assisted in putting together both information and material that culminated in a book and an exhibition. It was realized that modern urban societies can indeed benefit from the traditional methods of peace and conflict resolution as espoused by elders in the rural areas.

Other museums in Africa are adopting similar attitudes towards education and exhibit programmes. The Village Museum in Dar es Salaam, Tanzania, serves as a venue for people from the surrounding communities to come and recreate their traditions for the general community to enjoy. There are 'Ethnic Days' where people from a particular ethnic group prepare traditional foods and entertain visitors with traditional songs, dance and storytelling. Not only do such programmes serve to involve the communities and encourage sharing, they play a role in promoting cultural diversity and ensuring the survival of local traditions in the face of rapid urbanization and globalization.

In South Africa, the District Six (Cape Town) and South End (Port Elizabeth) Museums serve an important role in representing a common memory of communities evicted from their homes during the Apartheid era. They serve to educate the local people about what happened and to restore their dignity. These museums also serve as a painful reminder of the dangers of intolerance and prejudice.

THE CHANGING FACE OF MUSEUM EDUCATION

While traditionally the role of a museum has been to display collections for the educated elite, their role as institutions for educating the wider public is increasing. As mentioned above, many museums are using exhibitions to entice more visitors and involve local communities. It should also be noted that more and more museums are breaking away from traditional types of education programmes such as film shows and guided tours. Instead, dynamic, interactive education programmes are being developed, not only to teach the children but also to encourage them to think critically and analytically.

The National Museums of Kenya's *Museum Interactive* project conducts regular 'studios', bringing schoolchildren into a specially designed and equipped room to learn about various scientific or cultural topics through active participation. The project also initiated the 'Young Researcher Club', which involves children aged between 8 and 13 years coming to the museum three times a year for a morning filled with hands-on fun and learning. Each Young Researcher's Day focuses on a specific topic (e.g. ornithology, archaeology, art, etc.) and the children gain knowledge through a combination of games and serious learning, with the assistance of 'real' researchers from the relevant department at the museum.

In Botswana, the National Museum developed the *Desert Zebra* outreach programme, which 'takes the museum' to people in rural areas and promotes research into oral traditions. This type of initiative is important because, in so many African countries, a museum located in a major city or town is not accessible to the majority of the population who live in rural areas.

It is obvious that African museums are playing an increasingly important role in supplementing the national curriculum in schools.

INTERNATIONAL INITIATIVES

The International Council of Museums (ICOM) realized that African museums have particular needs. Its AFRICOM Programme was born out of a series of meetings in Benin, Ghana and Togo in November 1991, with the aim of addressing the role and the relevance of museums for the African continent. This programme was very successful and, in 1999, the Constituent Assembly of AFRICOM convened in Lusaka, Zambia and resolved to establish AFRICOM as a pan-African organization.

Today, AFRICOM is an international NGO registered by the Government of Kenya, with its headquarters in the capital city, Nairobi. AFRICOM in its new form seeks to contribute to the positive development of African societies by encouraging the role of museums as generators of culture and as agents of cultural cohesion. It aims to do this through developing projects that facilitate exchange and the sharing of experiences.

Currently, AFRICOM, together with the West African Museums Programme (WAMP), is updating the *Directory of Museum Professionals in Africa* (first published by ICOM/WAMP in 1993). This important project will allow the continent to have an accurate record of both human and institutional capacities in museums on the African continent. With this knowledge, AFRICOM will be better placed to understand and assess the needs of various museums to develop appropriate programmes. Both WAMP and AFRICOM have recognized the importance of local communities, and both are developing programmes that will encourage community participation while at the same time highlighting the role of these local communities within the museums themselves.

Through ICOM's AFRICOM Programme, the Museum Education Programme of Africa (MEPOA) was developed and the first phases were carried out with funding from UNESCO. In 1999 a workshop was held in Zimbabwe. From the workshop came the inspiration for a pilot project that would highlight the importance of the work done by women in the community, thus bringing museums closer to their local communities.

In 2001 an exhibit entitled 'Pottery of Burkina Faso – Women's Skilled Hands' was organized at the Museum of Civilisations in Poni, in Burkina Faso's Gaoua province. The project also included meetings with local teachers, competitions for school children and the creation of a resource pack to encourage other museum professionals to set up similar projects in their countries. This is but one example of a successful programme that invited local communities to participate and highlighted the contributions of a particular group within the community, namely women.

Along similar lines, in 1984 the Swedish National Committee of ICOM set up the African–Swedish

Museum Network (SAMP). Based in Stockholm, since its inception SAMP has been spearheading a unique programme of exchange and 'twinning' between African and Swedish museums. The programme has initiated special exhibitions and training workshops, and also developed a project to connect more museums in Africa to the Internet. Community involvement in museums has always been an important facet of SAMP, and it has actively promoted the idea of 'Museums without Walls': bringing the museum out to the people, including outdoor activities, such as the Village Museum in Tanzania. Museums in Africa need to be places where people from the local communities can come and actively engage in stimulating activities that are at the same time entertaining and educational.

One of SAMP's most successful projects was a traditional music 'festival' held at the Skansen open-air arena in Stockholm, Sweden in 1998. Each African museum in the SAMP network was asked to identify groups of traditional musicians from the rural areas. The groups selected had little – or preferably no – exposure in urban areas. Another criterion was that they must never have performed outside Africa. The aim was to show how contemporary urban African music owes much to tradition 'folk' music from the villages. The concert, dubbed 'Music from the Villages' was a resounding success and gave relatively unknown rural musicians international exposure. This particular project culminated in the production of a CD that reflects the diversity and talent of the various artists.

CONCLUSION

Over the years it has become evident that African museums have special needs. Although set up according to European models, they are now re-evaluating their missions and their role within contemporary society. They must address the needs not only of a privileged elite or of international tourists, but also of the urban population and the local communities in rural areas. In order to be sustainable and relevant, they must address current social, economic and sometimes even political issues. They must be places of social interaction that teach tolerance and acceptance in the face of increased globalization and cultural diversity.

Not only are African museums learning more from local communities but they are also reaching out to encourage the participation of these local communities in the museum and its activities. Through local, regional and international initiatives, African museums can grow to be more socially relevant, more entertaining and more educational. They are destined to become symbols of national pride and unity.

Lorna Abungu worked from 1987 to 1999 with the National Museums of Kenya as an archaeologist, first in the coastal town of Mombasa and later at the Museums' headquarters in Nairobi. Since August 2000 she has directed AFRICOM (the International Council of African Museums), an umbrella body for museums and museum professionals on the continent, serving to facilitate exchange and the sharing experiences beyond geographic and linguistic borders.

Contact address: International Council of African Museums (AFRICOM), P.O. Box 38706, Ngara 00600, Nairobi, Kenya. Email: l.abungu@africom.museum; website: http://africom.museum

REFERENCE

International Council of Museums/West African Museums Programme (ICOM/WAMP) (eds) *Directory of Museum Professionals in Africa*. International Council of Museums, Paris (1993).

Talking about others: archaeologists, indigenous peoples and heritage in Argentina

María Luz Endere

ABSTRACT

In the process of creating the Argentinean nation, the indigenous peoples were dispossessed of their lands and their sacred sites. The indigenous past was therefore neglected in a nation that was thought to be formed by European immigrants. As a result, pre-Hispanic heritage was considered part of the public domain of the State and a subject of scientific enquiry. In the last few decades, legal and political changes have encouraged indigenous peoples' claims on heritage issues. The aim of this paper is to analyse a number of contested heritage issues in which indigenous communities were involved, as well as a few examples in which archaeologists, authorities and indigenous groups have succeeded in building a dialogue regarding the care of specific archaeological sites. These issues are further discussed in the context of the current socio-political and economic crisis in Argentina.

INTRODUCTION: INDIGENOUS PEOPLE AND NATIONAL HERITAGE

During the second half of the 19th century, the Argentinean ruling elite treated national history as a means of breaking away from native traditions and the colonial past. Indigenous peoples were excluded from the new sense of nationhood, which was designed by, and composed of, European immigrants (Alberdi, [1852] 1979).

At the time, the intellectual elite was strongly influenced by social Darwinism, which provided a scientific basis for research (e.g. Ameghino, 1880) and also justified the political agendas of the new nation state (Politis, 1995: 198–199). The publicly vaunted claim that the 'barbarism' of native peoples was inferior to 'civilized' European values (Sarmiento, [1845] 1967: 59) was inspired by dominant political and scientific ideology that denied any value to native cultures. Indigenous people were considered to be 'savages' or a 'sterile race', thus relegated to the role of obstacles in the path of progress and civilization (Zeballos, [1878] 1986).

Along with the conquest of lands still controlled by indigenous groups, material elements of indigenous heritage were appropriated by the State. Academic institutions' intellectual ownership over archaeological sites and collections, and the emphasis on national history in formal education and museums were all used to dispossess the indigenous peoples of their past and to create a 'National Heritage'. Pre-Hispanic ruins and artefacts were considered to be the 'relics of ancient cultures' that should be collected before they disappeared. Governmental interest in the study of native cultures was demonstrated by the construction of national museums to store and exhibit both artefacts and human remains from a number of different ethnic groups (Politis, 1992, 1995; Podgorny and Politis, 1992; Endere, 2002a). The nation state continued the colonial process of excluding indigenous peoples from their traditions, sacred landscapes and heritage, in order to assimilate them into the national identity. The model of cultural homogeneity or the 'racial melting pot' was adopted by the new Nation State of Argentina, in order to deny any ethnic differences that could challenge national consolidation or promote any socio-political fragmentation (Balazote and Radovich, 1992: 17–18; Slavsky, 1992: 72).

During this period, Argentina enacted its first heritage legislation (Law 9080/13), in order to avoid its collections being 'looted by private collectors and sold to European museums' (Rojas, 1909: 461–462). This created the basis of the current legal system for heritage protection, in which the State becomes the legal and exclusive owner of pre-Hispanic sites, and assumes the responsibility for the protection of all archaeological heritage (Berberián, 1992; Endere 2000).

From the 1930s onwards, Argentina's pre-Hispanic past became increasingly less important in the construction of the 'national history', which glorified the Spanish Catholic tradition and highlighted national heroes. Formal education and textbooks contributed to reinforcing European traditions, and the information they provided about the indigenous population and their ancient occupation of the territory was prejudiced against native people (Podgorny, 1990, 1994, 1999; Oliva, 1994: 114). As a consequence, heritage protection focused predominantly on those monuments dating to the European colonial and national patriotic periods (e.g. Law 12.665/40 concerning museums, monuments and historic sites).

Until 1983, the government aimed to unify national culture around historic heroes and the defence of Christian values (Podgorny, 1994: 413). Thus, indigenous peoples, non-European immigrants and religious minorities were absent from or misrepresented in official history and museums. Throughout the 20th century, the status of indigenous peoples evolved from 'exponents of an inferior race' to 'lower class members' of the national society, although their ethnic diversity and rights were not legally recognized until the 1980s (Law 23.515/85). The democratic process, begun in 1983, marked a turning point in official ideology with the idea of a pluralist society being emphasized in arenas ranging from political speeches to educational curricula. Amendments to the National Constitution recognized a new set of civil rights regarding both cultural heritage and indigenous communities, thus generating new responsibilities for the Nation State. Moreover, in 2000, Argentina ratified the International Labour Organization (ILO) Convention 169 concerning Indigenous and Tribal Peoples in Independent Countries, which states that 'governments shall consult the peoples concerned ... whenever consideration is being given to legislative or administrative measures which may affect them directly' and shall also 'establish means by which these peoples can freely participate ... at all levels of decision-making in elective institutions and administrative and other bodies responsible for policies and programmes which concern them' (ILO, 1989: article 6 clauses a and b; see also Hualpa, 2003). However, social integration of indigenous peoples seems to be an even more complex process, as the permanence of the 'stigma of being Indian' is still present in a country in which indigenous peoples are a minority with little political power.

THE RECOVERY OF INDIGENOUS HERITAGE

Until the 1980s, alternative voices regarding the ownership and display of archaeological heritage were considered a curiosity, a product of people's ignorance or a potential threat to science, and were both underestimated and neglected by researchers. Northwestern people's reactions against the removal of human remains, for example, were considered 'superstitious', and an obstacle to research (e.g. Ambrosetti, 1907). In some cases, these views were also considered to be ancient beliefs that should be recorded before they disappeared (e.g. Boman, 1908). As a result, indigenous peoples' link to archaeological sites has been traditionally denied, and they have not been considered as a potential audience for heritage places.

During the 1980s, the shift in official ideology to acknowledge the pluralistic nature of the Argentine nation was welcomed by some archaeologists who were in favour of discussing contested issues, such as repatriation and popular culture versus scientific knowledge (e.g. the 'Workshop about the Uses of the Past' undertaken in the La Plata Museum in June 1989), and encouraged local people's involvement in museum activities (e.g. Casanova Museum in Tilcara;

Guillermo Madrazo, personal communication, 19 April 2001).

These academic changes, however, did not produce the expected impact on indigenous groups. It was not until 1992 that the official 'celebration' of the 500th anniversary of the 'discovery' of America generated a strong reaction from indigenous organizations with public protests that drew attention to the inconsistency between the official rhetoric and the reality of what indigenous people were experiencing. On that occasion, several indigenous groups commemorated the 'last day of freedom before the Spanish Conquest', performing ceremonies at archaeological sites that they identified as part of their own cultural heritage (e.g. the *Kolla* Centre at the Pucará of Tilcara and the Indigenous Community of Quilmes at Fuerte Quemado).

At present, indigenous groups are still struggling 'to participate in the management of natural resources and other matters in their interest', a right introduced by a 1994 amendment to the National Constitution (art. 75, clause 17), which in practice has been of little consequence for indigenous heritage issues.

Repatriation of indigenous human remains

Claims for the return of human remains held in museums (and legally designated as national heritage) became the first issue regarding indigenous heritage to be contested between indigenous organizations and national authorities (see Podgorny and Politis, 1992; Podgorny and Miotti, 1994). Since the 1970s, these claims had focused on the remains of several well-known 19th century Tehuelche-Araucano chiefs, most of them held at La Plata Museum. Only two of these claims have succeeded because of the need to enact a specific law for each case in order to authorize the delivery of the remains to the communities. The first law of repatriation, passed in 1991, ordered that the remains of the Tehuelche chief Inakayal be returned to his homeland in Tecka, Chubut province (Law 23.940). The restitution was not carried out until 1994, as many bureaucratic problems had to be overcome, along with political and academic resistance (Endere, 2002a). The second law, passed in July 2000, authorized the return of the mortal remains of the Ranquel chief Panquitruz Güor – better known by his Christian name Mariano Rosas – from the La Plata Museum to the Ranquel Community in La Pampa Province (Law 25.276). In June 2001 the remains of Mariano Rosas were delivered in an official ceremony of 'reparation to the Ranquel people', which was widely covered by the press (Camps, 2001; Cornejo 2001; Debesa and Galmarini, 2001.

In December 2001 a general law concerning repatriation was passed. It aims to have a considerable impact on museums and research activities because it states that the human remains held in museums must be delivered to the indigenous peoples or communities that have claimed them (Law 25.517/01, art. 1). The law also declares that those human remains that have not been claimed may continue to be held under the custody of the museums and institutions that have kept them, although they must be treated with respect (art. 2). It finally states that any scientific activity that involves indigenous communities – including their historic and cultural heritage – should previously be agreed with these communities (art. 3).

This brief law brings a substantial change in heritage legislation, since previous laws had unanimously declared archaeological heritage to be under the exclusive ownership of the State (see Law 9080, Civil Code, art. 2339 and 2340). However, the potential benefits of the new law may be diminished because of the lack of any provision regarding a number of key issues. Law 25.517 does not state how the communities should claim the remains, the criteria that museums should apply to assess these claims nor in which cases researchers should request permission from the communities to carry out their activities. All these issues must be ruled in the decree that enforces the law; until then, the parties involved (i.e. archaeologists, museum curators and indigenous groups) are not able to discuss its terms. It is regrettable that the passing of such a key law was not preceded by an open debate of its implications among the different interest groups. This could have avoided the confusion and uncertainty felt by museums and researchers regarding the scope of their legal obligations.

In 2003, a new law (25.743) concerning archaeological and palaeontological heritage was passed. This new rule, which repealed Law 9080, has not made any provision on indigenous peoples' rights to their own cultural heritage.

Archaeologists and indigenous peoples

Occasionally, archaeologists have recognized indigenous peoples' concerns and have invited them to participate in research projects (e.g. Proyecto Arqueológico Quilmes, in Buenos Aires province; Quatrin de Rodriguez, 1999). But, even today, most Argentinean archaeologists do not consider the socio-cultural contexts of their work, and are therefore not prepared to discuss their research aims with non-professional groups (i.e. the indigenous peoples). Complaints about the arrogance of archaeologists (particularly those who do not live in the area) remain vociferous among indigenous peoples of the Northwest (see Endere, 2002b).

Fortunately, there are some examples of good practice to be considered. The Añelo museum and the Ñorquinco community's sacred site in Lanín Park, both in Neuquén province, constitute interesting, although exceptional, examples of indigenous communities' participation in site preservation and management.

The Añelo site museum concerns a 500-year-old hunter-gatherer cemetery discovered in 1988 on land traditionally occupied by the Painemil Mapuche community. The site was partially excavated by a research team with the participation of several Mapuche families. Even though the human remains found were not their ancestors, the indigenous community asked to be in charge of the protection of the remains so that 'children could learn about the history of the ancient people' (Font et al., 1997: 2). The site was covered by a shelter and opened as a museum in 1989 (Biset, 1989). At present, it is under the guardianship of a member of the Mapuche Community and is visited by thousands of school children as part of an educational programme exploring regional history from the earliest human occupation to the present day (Cúneo and Rodríguez de Torcigliani, 1993; Font et al., 1997: 2). This museum was also the starting point of several fresh initiatives to create community museums in the same province (Cúneo, 2004).

Another landmark in the process of recognition of indigenous peoples' rights to their cultural heritage in Argentina was the decision taken by the Administración de Parques Nacionales (the national park service) in 2000 to give to the Ñorquinco Mapuche community custody of their sacred site situated in the Lanín National Park, Neuquén province (Molinari, 2000). At present, draft legislation is awaiting consideration at the National Congress in order to return 341ha to this community, including a rock art site located in this area. A joint committee formed by representatives of Administración de Parques Nacionales and the Ñorquinco Mapuche community will discuss future policies for the management of the site.

Traditional festivities

In the last few decades, various indigenous groups and organizations have begun to publicly perform traditional ceremonies, encouraged by a more pluralistic and democratic environment. In Andean Patagonia, the Mapuche people organize an annual ritual ceremony called *camaruco* – which used to be forbidden by the authorities during the era of military governments – while the celebrations of *Pachamama* (Mother earth) and *Intiraimi* are regaining popularity among Northwestern indigenous peoples. This revival of traditional festivities is sometimes encouraged by local authorities, with the aim of promoting tourism (e.g. *Pachamama* festival in Amaicha; carnival in Tilcara, etc.). In other cases, the ceremonies are organized by indigenous organizations who perform them in sacred landscapes or in archaeological sites that are identified as part of their own cultural heritage. The reconstructed ceremonial centre of 'Pucará of Tilcara', for example, is one of the most requested places for ritual use in the Northwest. Its use as a sanctuary, however, is beginning to generate some tension between heritage managers and indigenous groups regarding public access to the sites, since some of these groups claim the right to perform secret ceremonies there (Elena Belli, personal communication, 29 May 2000).

Legal disputes

Indigenous people's concerns about their cultural heritage have had only limited debate through legal cases. A number of juridical, practical and financial difficulties have prevented indigenous peoples from expressing their knowledge and feelings concerning the care and protection of sacred sites in order to preserve their sacredness and cultural value. Two examples of indigenous heritage claims are presented in this section. The first concerns the mummies found in the Llullaillaco volcano, the second the use and management of the Quilmes' Ruins.

1. The case of the Llullaillaco's mummies

In 1999 the first attempt to obtain legal recognition for a sacred site was made by the indigenous association 'Los Airampos' on behalf of the *Kolla* community. It alleged that the excavation of three Inka mummies from the Llullaillaco volcano, Salta Province, by an international archaeological team (see Reinhard, 1999), was a violation of the community's rights. According to the complaint, the *Kolla* community felt that (1) 'they are the living descendants of those who inhabited the Inka province *Kollasuyo* during the Inka period'; (2) the high-peak sanctuary, where the mummies were found, is 'a sacred site located within the boundaries of the *Kollasuyu* province' and therefore 'the mummies belong to the *Kollasuyu*'s indigenous people'; (3) the mummies constitute an indigenous shrine from which messages have been sent to the indigenous people before and after the Spanish conquest; (4) the '*Kolla* people should have been asked for authorisation before the mummies were exhumed', according to art. 75, clause 17 of the National Constitution (Case 523/30.04.99, 'Alemán, América c/ Autores a establecer s/ Denuncia', Juzgado Federal, Primera Instancia Penal 2, Salta). The Federal attorney rejected the claim, stating that 'the archaeological expedition had satisfied the legal requirements because it had been authorised by the provincial government'. On 3 May 1999, the judge considered that there was no crime and ordered the closure of the case. The indigenous community did not challenge this decision (América Alemán, personal communication, 23 September 2001).

In November 1999, the University of Salta organized a 'round table' to discuss the ethical implications of this type of discovery for archaeologists. As a result of this meeting, several recommendations concerning its legal and administrative framework were made. They emphasized that legislation and political authorities should take into account local communities' and indigenous peoples' rights to participate in cultural heritage management (app.1. d). Regarding professional practices, they recommended the adoption of ethical standards for site and collection management and conservation, and endorsed the participation of local communities and indigenous peoples in heritage management (app. 2. b) (Centro Promocional de las Investigaciones en Historia y Antropología (CEPIHA), 1999). Despite the fact that these recommendations did not change local government's attitude towards the mummies, they constitute an important precedent because, for the first time, a group of specialists recognized the need to guarantee, as a moral duty, the participation of local and indigenous communities in managing archaeological sites (see also discussion about this case in Politis, 2001). At present, several indigenous leaders are campaigning against the exhibition of these mummies in a new museum in the city of Salta. Two indigenous representatives presented a declaration against the exhibition, which was approved in the Plenary Session of the XV National Congress of Argentine Archaeology in 2004.

2. The case of the Quilmes' Ruins

In the late 1970s, the reconstruction of the Quilmes' Ruins in Tucumán province formed part of the military government's nationalistic agenda, which claimed that the pre-Hispanic past was a vital component in the construction of 'True Argentine' nationhood (e.g. Montiel Forzado, 1981). As a result, these archaeological remains were heavily disturbed and exploited, yet poorly studied, interpreted and preserved. Indigenous groups and researchers cite the case of the Quilmes' Ruins as a classic example of governmental mismanagement of archaeological heritage (e.g. González, 2000: 260–261; Francisco Chaile, personal communication, 22 July 2000). This is due not only to the site's poor reconstruction and the building of a hotel complex over the remains, but also to the fact that the site management was given in concession to an entrepreneur, whose relationship with the local indigenous communities is one of great conflict (see Endere, 2002b).

The members of the Indigenous Community Quilmes (ICQ), officially recognized in 1990, have a long record of land claims to the Quilmes' Ruins and the surrounding area. In the last few years, they have instigated a legal case contesting the renewal of the 'concession' to run the ruins as a commercial venture, and the final decision was against the renewal. At present, the entrepreneur is still in control of the ruins even though his concession has officially expired. The members of the ICQ are currently campaigning to eject him from the ruins and to discussing their future involvement in the management of the ruins with the provincial authorities.

CONCLUSIONS

Encouraged by the amendments to the National Constitution and changes in the official ideology, some positive moves towards the recognition of Argentina's indigenous peoples' rights to their cultural heritage (such as the repatriation laws) have taken place in the last few years. These improvements, however, have not been the consequences of a new integrated national heritage policy, but the result of isolated efforts. Law 25.743 is a clear example of how discordant new rules may be regarding constitutional statements on indigenous peoples' rights. Furthermore, their participation in the management of archaeological sites is a subject commonly ignored by provincial heritage laws and most provincial authorities are not keen to listen to indigenous organizations' claims.

Indigenous groups face major obstacles in order to gain recognition of their appeals. Most authorities and archaeologists regard indigenous activists with suspicion, and entertain doubts about the sincerity of their concerns. The fact that indigenous groups have not registered their claims officially until recently is the main argument usually employed in denying the legitimacy of their claims. Furthermore, internal division and conflicts of leadership among indigenous groups have prevented them from developing a strong and clear position on heritage issues. As a result, the heritage of Argentina's indigenous communities is commonly presented at most archaeological sites and museums as part of another's past, distant in time, ethnic origin and cultural traditions from current citizens, without acknowledging any link with contemporary indigenous groups.

However, the recent formation of regional, national and supranational indigenous organizations, and the emergence of a young indigenous intellectual elite, may presage the consolidation of an indigenous discourse over the next few years. This may result in increasing tensions if 'indigenous heritage' is neither recognized within the heritage legal system nor among archaeologists.

In the context of Argentina's recent severe economic and social crisis, heritage has become a minor topic in the long list of social issues. However, recent interest in heritage derives from a mixture of factors, including middle-class local/nationalist reaction to drastic socio-economic changes, and the need for alternative sources of income. In this sense, the State's virtual abandonment of its obligations concerning archaeological heritage seems to correspond with an increased involvement by civil society in heritage issues. Many heritage places are being reassessed in terms of their value to local/indigenous or national traditions, or as tourist attractions. The growing pressure to open sites to the public without developing any strategy for their long-term preservation often generates conflict among researchers, local communities, politicians and private investors (see Mazzanti and Quintana, 1999; also *menhires* of Tafi Valley case, García Azcárate, 2000; Endere, 2002b).

There is an urgent need for archaeologists to join with indigenous groups (and with civil society as a whole) in order to co-ordinate their efforts to preserve archaeological sites. In this sense, the increasing public demand for substantial changes generated by the socio-political and economic crisis as well as the 'ethnic emergency' may offer an opportunity to encourage new kinds of partnerships in dealing with heritage issues.

ACKNOWLEDGEMENTS

This paper partially derives from my Ph.D. thesis. I am very grateful to my supervisors Professor Peter Ucko and Kathy Tubb. I also thank Dr Bill Sillar and Lawrence Owens for their helpful editing. Finally I owe a great debt to the Programme FOMEC-UNCPBA for having funded my studies in the UK, as well as Fundación Antorchas (Awards No. 14.116/151 and 14248/65) and Programme INCUAPA for funding my subsequent research projects.

María Luz Endere is a Lecturer in Law and Cultural Resource Management and a full-time researcher at the Department of Archaeology, Universidad Nacional del Centro de la Provincia de Buenos Aires (UNCPBA), Argentina. Her formal education includes a BA in Law, Universidad Nacional de Buenos Aires, 1988, BA in Anthropology, UNCPBA, 1995; MA in Museum and Heritage Studies, Institute of Archaeology, University College London, 1998 and a Ph.D. in Archaeology, UCL, 2002.

Contact address: INCUAPA, Departamento de Arqueología, Facultad de Ciencias Sociales, Universidad Nacional del Centro de la Provincia de Buenos Aires. Avda. Del Valle 5737 – 7400 Olavarría, Argentina. Email: mendere@soc.unicen.edu.ar

REFERENCES

Alberdi, J. *Bases y Puntos de Partida para la Organización Política de la República Argentina.* Centro Editor de América Latina, Buenos Aires ([1852] 1979).

Ambrosetti, J. Exploraciones arqueológicas en la ciudad prehistórica de La Paya. *Publicaciones de la Sección Antropología* 3 (1907).

Ameghino, F. *La Antigüedad del hombre en el Plata.* G. Masson, Paris and Buenos Aires (1880).

Balazote, A. and Radovich, J. Introduction. In Balazote, A. and Radovich, J. (eds) *La Problemática Indígena. Estudios Antropológicos sobre Pueblos Indígenas en Argentina.* Centro Editor de América Latina, Buenos Aires (1992) 7–25.

Berberián, E. *La Protección Jurídica del Patrimonio Arqueológico en la República Argentina.* Córdoba: Comechingonia (1992).

Biset, A. El Museo de Sitio de Añelo. *Actas, Jornadas sobre el uso del pasado, Symphosium Administración de Recursos y Manejo de Bienes Culturales Arqueológicos.* Universidad de La Plata, La Plata (1989).

Boman, E. *Antiquités de la région andine de la République Argentine et du désert d'Atacama.* Paris (1908).

Camps, S. Ya están en el desierto pampeano los restos del cacique Marino Rosas. *Clarín* 24 June (2001) 42.

CEPIHA (Centro Promocional de las Investigaciones en Historia y Antropología). Mesa Redonda. Hallazgos arqueológicos, entre la ciencia y la identidad. *Andes* 10 (1999) 245–248.

Cornejo, J. El cacique volvió a sus raíces. *La Nación* 23 June (2001). Website: http://www.lanacion.com.ar/01/06/23/dg_314645.as (accessed 25 June 2001).

Cúneo, E. Huellas del pasado, miradas del presente: la construcción social del patrimonio arqueológico del Neuquén. *Intersecciones en Antropología* 5 (2004), 81–94.

Cúneo, E. and Rodríguez de Torcigliani, M. Evidencias prehistóricas: antiguo poblamiento y coexistencia cultural. In Bandieri, S. and Favaro, O. (eds) *Historia del Neuquén.* Plus Ultra, Buenos Aires (1993) 11–63.

Debesa, F. and Galmarini, M. Restituyeron los restos del célebre cacique pampeano Mariano Rosas. *Clarín* 23 June (2001). Website: http//ar.clarin.com/diario/2001-06-23/s-04215.htr (accessed 25 June 2001).

Endere, M. *Arqueología y Legislación en Argentina. Cómo proteger el patrimonio arqueológico.* Tandil: Departamento de Publicaciones, Universidad Nacional del Centro de la Provincia de Buenos Aires (2000).

Endere, M. The reburial issue in Argentina: a growing conflict. In Fforde, C., Hubert, J. and Turnbull, P. (eds) *The Dead and their Possessions: Repatriation in Principle, Policy and Practice.* Routledge, London (2002a) 266–283.

Endere, M. Management of archaeological sites and the Public in Argentina. Unpublished PhD Thesis. University College London (2002b).

Font, L., Cúneo, E., Billinger, E. and Muelas, N. El Museo y la Escuela. Algunos aportes sobre la base de la experiencia desarrollada en la Provincia de Neuquén. *Paper presented at the VII Encuentro Educativo El Museo y La Escuela.* Archivo y Museo Históricos Dr. Jauretche, Buenos Aires (1997).

García Azcárate, J. Diagnóstico y situación actual de los menhires en el parque. Unpublished Report presented to the Comisión Nacional de Museos, Monumentos y Lugares Históricos (2000).

González, A. *Tiestos dispersos. Voluntad y azar en la vida de un arqueólogo.* Emecé, Buenos Aires (2000).

Hualpa, E. *Sin despojos. Derecho a la participación mapuche-tehuelche.* Cuadernos de ENDEPA, Trelew (2003).

ILO (International Labour Organization) *Indigenous and Tribal People's Convention 169* (1989).

Mazzanti, D. and Quintana, C. Mar del Plata ¿Un futuro sin pasado? *Nexos* 10 (1999) 5–8.

Molinari, R. ¿Posesión o participación? El caso del Rewe de la comunidad Mapuche Ñorquinco (Parque Nacional Lanín, Provincia de Neuquén, Argentina). *Paper presented at Segundo Congreso Virtual de Antropología y Arqueología.* Facultad de Filosofía y Letras, UBA. October (2000) http://www.naya.org.ar/congreso2000/ponencia/Roberto_Molinari.htr (accessed 10 April 2002).

Montiel Forzado, L., Prefacio. In Pelissero, N. and Difrieri, H. (eds) *Quilmes, Arqueología y Etnohistoria de la Ciudad Prehispánica.* Gobierno de la Provincia de Tucumán and Universidad Nacional de Buenos Aires, San Miguel de Tucumán (1981) 9–10.

Oliva, F. Education as a means of protection of the archaeological heritage in the districts of Buenos Aires Province. In Stone, P. and Molyneaux, B. (eds) *The Presented Past. Heritage Museums and Education.* Routledge, London (1994) 109–119.

Podgorny, I. The excluded present: archaeology and education in Argentina. In Stone, P. and MacKensie, R. (eds) *The Excluded Past: Archaeology and Education.* Unwin Hyman, London (1990) 183–189.

Podgorny, I. Choosing ancestors: the primary education syllabuses in Buenos Aires, Argentina, between 1975 and 1990. In Stone, P. and Molyneaux, B. (eds) *The Presented Past. Heritage Museums and Education.* Routledge, London (1994) 408–417.

Podgorny, I. *Arqueología de la Educación. Textos, indicios, monumentos. La imagen de los indios en el mundo escolar.* Sociedad Argentina de Antropología, Buenos Aires (1999).

Podgorny, I. and Miotti, L. El pasado como campo de batalla. *Ciencia Hoy* 5 (1994) 16–19.

Podgorny, I. and Politis, G. ¿Qué sucedió en la historia? Los esqueletos araucanos del Museo de La Plata y la Conquista del Desierto. *Arqueología Contemporánea* 3 (1992) 73–79.

Politis, G. Política Nacional, Arqueología y Universidad en Argentina. In Politis, G. (ed.) *Arqueología en América Latina Hoy.* Biblioteca Banco Popular, Bogota (1992) 70–87.

Politis, G. The socio-politics of the development of archaeology in hispanic South America. In Ucko, P. (ed.) *Theory in Archaeology. A world Perspective.* Routledge, London and New York (1995) 197–228.

Politis, G. On archaeological praxis, gender bias and indigenous peoples in South America. *Journal of Social Archaeology* 1 (2001) 90–107.

Quatrin de Rodriguez, Z. Conflicto de intereses en la preservación del patrimonio cultural de Quilmes. *Actas XII Congreso Nacional de Arqueología Argentina II.* Universidad Nacional de La Plata, La Plata (1999) 316–320.

Reinhard, J. A. 6,700 metros niños incas sacrificados quedaron congelados en el tiempo. *National Geographic* 5 (1999) 36–55.

Rojas, R. *La Restauración Nacionalista.* Imprenta de la Penitenciaria, Buenos Aires (1909).

Sarmiento, D. *Facundo.* Biblioteca Argentina Fundamental. Centro Editor de América Latina, Buenos Aires ([1845] 1967).

Slavsky, L. Los indígenas y la sociedad nacional. Apuntes sobre políticas indigenistas en la Argentina. In Balazote, A. and Radovich, J. (eds) *La Problemática Indígena. Estudios Antropológicos sobre Pueblos Indígenas en Argentina.* Centro Editor de América Latina, Buenos Aires (1992) 67–79.

Zeballos, E. *La Conquista de las Quince Mil Leguas.* Hyspanoamérica, Buenos Aires ([1878] 1986).

The making of the Heart of the World:
representation and the Kogi

Alan Ereira

ABSTRACT

The Kogi of Colombia's Sierra Nevada have maintained a culture isolated from colonial contact since 1600. Living in the 'Heart of the World' they call themselves 'Elder Brother'. They consider themselves the world's caretakers and the keepers of a traditional knowledge long since lost by the invasive and destructive colonizing 'Younger Brother'. An invitation from a BBC filmmaker to provide a medium for the Kogi to contact the outside world was accepted. The result was a film that the Kogi planned and devised to warn Younger Brother to stop his destructive behaviour.

INTRODUCTION

In 1988 I was shown an article on 'Ciudad Perdida', or the 'Lost City of the Taironas', in a relatively inaccessible region of Colombia: the Sierra Nevada de Santa Marta. The BBC asked me to investigate the possibility of making a programme about the people of this region and, as I was planning a shoot in Bogota, it seemed a reasonable request. That was how I came to learn about the Kogi.

Being the highest coastal mountain massif in the world, the Sierra Nevada acted as a beacon for passing ships. However, its steep jungle presented a significant geographic barrier to invasive settlement and was a primary reason for the lack of Spanish colonial activity in the area. During the 16th century, the largest Spanish colonial city in the area, Santa Marta, was witnessing a widespread exodus of indigenous people and a large amount of acculturation throughout the region. Conversely, the relative geographical isolation of the mountain communities meant they were able to maintain a great deal of cultural integrity. Though a war broke out between the colonists and the highland Indians in the late 16th century, it ended in a stalemate in 1600 and, since then, contact between mainstream Europeanized Colombian society and the Kogi has been minimal.

Such isolation is particularly noticeable on the steepest north face of the Sierra: this is where the 'Lost City' was 'discovered'. These northern slopes comprise the principal territory of the Kogi, who remain the least acculturated of the indigenous people of the Sierra. Their acceptance of 'civilized' technology came to an abrupt end in 1600, and since then they have remained profoundly conservative. Though not rejecting the innovations that had been adopted up to 1600, there was, and remains, great resistance to the acceptance of any later inventions. Thus, the use of iron farming implements (such as machetes and hoes), the farming of Spanish-introduced animals and crops, the use of the sugar-press and the wearing of pantaloons by the men were all integrated into traditional culture before the strictures against foreign adoption were implemented. Even though these foreign elements appear within Kogi culture, there remains a clear awareness of what was introduced and what belongs to the older tradition.

Writing, however, was never accepted within Kogi society and nor were shoes. Even greater resistance existed among the Mamas (the political and spiritual leaders of the Kogi) regarding the use of electricity, radios, tape recorders, commercially spun cotton and other pieces of modern technology (which they refer to as 'moths'). While these items were used – with some anxiety – on the frontier, a real effort had been made to keep them out of the Kogi heartland.

By the time I made contact with the Kogi, seeking help in understanding the 'Lost City', I was already aware of many aspects of their lifestyle and the traditional manner in which they lived: as farmers, that their 'towns' were meeting centres and usually unoccupied, that they wore only simple traditional costumes, without shoes, and that the Mamas were regarded with nothing short of awe. I was also aware of their successfully maintained isolation from governments, missionaries and filmmakers. Having read the work of Geraldo Reichel-Dolmatoff (e.g. 1985), the only living anthropologist with significant knowledge of the Kogi, I made contact with him and he was profoundly discouraging about my prospects.

I also knew that the Mamas were not only the guardians of the culture, which was entirely oral, but also considered themselves as caretakers of the world, describing the indigenous people of the Sierra as 'The Elder Brother'. Outsiders were known as 'The Younger Brother', a nomenclature imbued with meaning; we 'Younger Brother' clearly needed to be looked after and were inherently dangerous and incompetent.

The term 'Younger Brother' refers to all people who do not belong to what the Kogi recognize as a common cultural framework. One form of shorthand for this definition is that 'Elder Brothers' are 'people who use the *poporro*', the gourd of lime powder that is taken with coca leaves and which the men carry. The other indigenous people of the Sierra are also Elder Brother, and the Mamas believe that the whole region (Central and South America) was populated by Elder Brother before the conquest. I took pictures of the Lacondon Maya to the Mamas, and their first reaction was that they were *kaggaba*, real people, and therefore Elder Brother. Closer examination of the pictures led to the statement that they must be completely surrounded by Younger Brother, and I was asked to find out if they knew how to make offerings. Over the last decade it seems that the Kogis' sense of who might be Elder Brother has been changing as they have become more conscious of other indigenous groups, and they now feel that they have a duty to help other groups return to and reinforce their ancient traditions (or, as they put it, their Law of Origin).

It was with this knowledge that I made my first tentative approach to the Kogi, hoping that if they had such a profound sense of responsibility the Mamas would want to pass on some advice for taking care of the world before they withered away. This seemed to be my best chance of getting some insight into the functioning of the 'Lost City', which seemed to be entirely a product of their (pre-Conquest) culture. Not wanting to risk a direct meeting at this stage, I passed messages through intermediaries to three Kogi towns. Six months later I received the reply. 'We are waiting to work with you. Come.'

FIRST MEETINGS

Six months after that I was in the government's Office of Indian Affairs in Santa Marta, ready to go into the Sierra. But first I was given a severe lecture by Adalberto Villafaña, a stern indigenous leader from the Ika, a closely related group in the Sierra. Adalberto was a most impressive figure, over six foot tall and dressed in a long belted white cotton robe, white cotton trousers and a flat-topped conical white hat over shining hair rippling onto his shoulders. He angrily complained that by communicating with three separate towns I had been trying to divide the society, hoping that if two said 'no', the third might still choose to work with me. This, he explained was how Younger Brother operated to split and weaken indigenous communities and ultimately destroy them.

The Mamas had set up their own organization, Gonawindua Tairona (GT), which must act as the sole point of communication with the Kogi. GT was controlled by the Mamas, and he was its senior officer (*cabildo gubernador*). Before going any further, I must agree only to deal with the Kogi through GT. Having given that undertaking, I was allowed to go to the meeting-place, a large circular meeting-house in a Kogi town, explaining to a large gathering of Mamas from all over the Sierra what a film is, why I thought they might want to use the opportunity, what dangers and problems I could foresee being created, and saying (to the local equivalent of applause) that they would decide on making the film for reasons that I would not understand, and that if they said 'No' they would never see me again.

All discussion had been through an indigenous translator, who, I learned, had been trained in history and the theory of translation (finding appropriate metaphors) by the Mamas, and then had been sent off to learn Spanish, so that they would be able to communicate on their own terms with the Younger Brother. I was dismissed, and told that I would be summoned again the next day, after a divination.

The next day's meeting was a great surprise. 'Have you a machine that remembers what we say?' 'Yes.' 'Turn it on.' There followed a lengthy speech, given in relay by five Mamas. It began with the origin of the world: 'In the beginning there was nothing, nothing at all, neither sun nor moon, only Aluna, the Mother. And Aluna was not a person, she was memory and possibility'. The process of creation was described, the world being established around its heart, the Sierra Nevada, the birth of humanity – first Elder Brother, then Younger, in the perfect environment of the Sierra. They then described the expulsion of Younger Brother to a place where he could do no harm, across the sea, having been given the gift of knowledge of technology. Finally, his eventual return as Columbus, the story of the Conquest, and its continued encroachment into the Sierra, the Heart of the World was recounted (cf. Ereira, 1990).

Now, I was told, the process was coming to an end. Younger Brother was pushing into the Sierra, and this final stronghold was about to fall to the Conquistadors. The Heart of the World was threatened. And as this happened, the Younger Brother's rape of the Mother was intensifying – the world was being ripped apart for profit and, as a result, watercourses were drying up, the snows were melting and the world was heating up. 'We know what you have done with the clouds. You have sold the clouds.'

I sat like a stunned fish, as the terms, nature and form of the film they intended to make were issued to me as a commission. It was to be a warning to the Younger Brother to change his ways. To authenticate themselves, the Mamas would demonstrate that they are the true heirs of their ancient civilization. I would return with whoever and whatever I needed, and they would ensure that the job would be done.

This was all very sudden, and I was concerned about the size of the cultural divide between us. I knew nothing about them, and the Kogi had no conceptual framework for the kind of work we were going to do. I said that I needed a year to prepare, and to learn. And I suggested that they, too, should take a year to prepare for this, talking about it and thinking about it. I was told that they only needed six months, as they had started work already, but that it was true that I would need a year. And I was told that I would also need a contract, which the (illiterate) Mamas dictated and signed with thumb-prints.

This was an extraordinary reversal of the Kogis' attitude to the outside world. Up to now they had attempted to remain as closed as possible, as can be seen from the failure of both the Colombian government and earlier anthropologists to ascertain the size of the population. In 1987, Professor Reichel-Dolmatoff had published an estimate of 6000: three times his first estimate, but only half of the actual population. The difficult terrain means that there were some Kogi towns that had never seen a non-indigenous visitor – and in any case, when people arrive uninvited, they normally find the towns deserted.

I offered them a domestic DV camera and a Polaroid camera, so that they could better grasp what I was offering to do. They looked at them in a fairly cursory way, taking some pictures with both and then returning them politely – and asking pointedly about the safety of the Polaroid prints, and the possibility of telling lies with the DV camera.

To help with the planning, an anthropologist, Dr Graham Townsley, went to spend some time in the Sierra. He was to do nothing to promote the idea of making the film, as only the full commitment of the Mamas would allow the film to proceed. The Kogi refused him entry to their territory for some time, and then gave him limited co-operation. When I visited the Sierra after six months, Graham and the local representative of the Office of Indian Affairs told me that the Kogi were still debating the issue and needed more time to make up their minds. I was escorted into their territory assuming that we would cancel the project. But on my first night, I was visited by three senior Mamas who simply declared 'The Mamas do not speak with two tongues', and left. Filming was to proceed on schedule.

FILMING

When filming began, the Mamas were in complete control. Production meetings were held every three days, at which they agreed what was to be shot, where, when and with whom. When the crew was late for a location they would arrive and demand that work begin. Although they do not make images (perhaps to avoid resurrecting the Conquistadors' assault on 'Devil worship' amongst the Tairona) they clearly understood their significance. It was their idea to show the entry to their territory at a bridge over a ravine, where they built a symbolic gate, to convey the gulf between our worlds and their control over access between them.

I gradually realized that they were also controlling everything we saw. The towns we were allowed into were populated with specially selected families. The individuals we filmed were there because they had been ordered to be there – often as a form of discipline.

I had been puzzled by the remarkable cohesion of Kogi society, which produces virtually no renegades or deserters despite the constant feuds and schisms between towns and families. Part of the answer lies in the astonishingly sophisticated man-management techniques of the Mamas, who praise rebels and load them with responsibilities that teach them to value themselves and their culture. This also consists of leading group discussions, whose end point is a unanimous endorsement of their own point of view. This is orchestrated through an elegant process in which the Mamas' agree with the group consensus – whatever it might be – and then proceed to guide the group into raising problematic issues with the consensus until they find their way to the Mamas' perspective and solution. These gently ruthless techniques are accompanied by enforced discipline applied, to the extent that someone who has misbehaved first has to accept that they need to be punished.

The film was essentially a message from the Mamas to 'Younger Brother', and to ensure that it was easily and clearly understood I decided to use voice-over (with the original sound audible in the background) rather than sub-titles. This had the additional advantage that it allowed the Kogis' rhetorical style to be used; given the Kogis' are an oral culture, the deliberate and significant nature of their oration could hardly be adequately replaced by the written word. This is an issue in ethnographic filmmaking, where there is a consensus that sub-titles are to be preferred as they allow the original voices of the speakers to be clearly heard. However, the Kogi were not making a strictly ethnographic film, and the only times I used sub-titles were over conversations that were not placed in the film as messages for the viewer.

As filming drew to an end, I observed to the Chief Mama that the pieces of film we had shot were threads that had been spun, and that I now had to take them away and weave them into a garment. He looked at me somewhat cynically and said 'We'll see'.

PERCEPTIONS OF THE FILM

He got his chance to see when I brought the completed film back to Santa Marta, in a version that did not include the voice-overs (so the Kogi could hear themselves) and gave them Spanish sub-titles and a Spanish commentary. I showed the film twice, once to the Kogi alone and once to an assembly of local people and dignitaries, where the Kogi could see how it was received by 'Younger Brother'. Some forty families trekked down the mountain for this event.

I was told by them 'You speak Kogi!', and that they had spoken well, though the film structure was somewhat criticized on the basis of their own rules of rhetoric, elements of which include: number of repetitions, use of cut-aways, and time and emphasis devoted to different issues.

A detailed critique concerned the way in which I had used a group of tomb-robbers as a narrative device, attempting to build suspense as they were seen hunting for treasures. The Kogi criticized this, and I was told that the film had returned to them too often. When we went through the sequences in detail, it emerged that the Mamas had counted the number of cut-aways there were to the tomb-robbers. Arguing that these increased the emphasis on that part of the story and gave it too much weight, the Mamas were well aware of the impact of these techniques, employing them within their own oral traditions. On reflection, I think they were right.

The Kogi Mamas had a clear sense of their purpose and of how they wanted to represent themselves. This was based on their sense of who *we* are. That sense does not appear to contain a vision of us as altering over time: they have observed us as naturalists observe animals. So when modern government officials behave differently from Conquistadors, they do not say 'Younger Brother has changed' but 'Younger Brother does that as well'. They were therefore addressing an audience composed, in their eyes, of modern bandits, 16th century adventurers, bigoted missionaries and ineffectual place-men. In order to get their message across, the film had to be received with respect for the Kogi, and to do so, emphasis had to be placed on their guardianship of traditional knowledge.

The Mamas held many meetings with their own people to emphasize this. 'They want to know if we still eat salt. We do still eat salt.' The reference is to animals returning, generation after generation, to the same salt-lick. The Mamas return, generation after generation, to the teachings of the Mother.

Their understanding of the audience was exactly right, of course. The fact that the Kogi do not wear t-shirts or baseball caps or sneakers, that they do not have radios or spectacles, gives them a visual authority that many indigenous people do not possess. Their maintenance of a true frontier, which consciously repelled modern technology, was visually evocative of their mental discipline; the film drew much of its strength from that.

Any notion that these are 'simple' people, who needed to be guided by the 'sophisticated', or worldly, knowledge of the filmmaker, would be very wide of the mark. The leaders of Kogi society are highly intelligent, extremely well-informed and quick-witted, as well as profound analytic thinkers. Our simplicity was a constant puzzle to them: how did we have such an advanced technology when we have such weak intellects and such a brutal society? We were sometimes referred to, ironically, as 'civilized'.

AUDIENCE

The Mamas had wanted a film that would appeal to as wide an audience as possible, to be heard by Younger Brother all over the world (whatever that meant). From this standpoint, their mission was achieved. It was shown on BBC1 to considerable acclaim, with high viewing figures, and as a result quite literally of popular demand it was run again on BBC2 within six weeks. A shortened version was shown by the PBS series 'Nature' in the USA as its tenth anniversary celebratory transmission, and it was shown widely around the world – though not on Colombian television.

The film has had some effect in Colombia. It was seen by the President's family, and so played a role in the Presidential decision to visit the Sierra and announce that Colombia would assist the indigenous people there to recover their lost lands. It contributed positively to an on-going process of giving value to the Kogi within Colombia. This process had already begun, and the film served as an added stimulus.

I established a charity for the Kogi, the Tairona Heritage Trust. This originally concentrated on helping with land purchase, and has subsequently assisted with the physical side of creating an administrative infrastructure that allows the indigenous people of the Sierra to deal directly with government and non-governmental organizations that have an interest in the territory.

The Trust operated, until recently, by holding money for land purchases made by GT. Once GT had identified a farm that it wished to buy, and had negotiated a price, the Trust would supply the finance, plus additional sums for GT's administration and health programmes – but no money was to be allocated for these without an associated land purchase. In recent years other NGOs and the Colombian State have assisted in land purchase, so the Trust's significance has diminished. Two substantial projects have been part-financed by the Trust in this new situation: the construction of a new Indigenous House in Santa Marta, and the supply of computer-mapping hardware, software and training to allow GT to exercise control over information about the Sierra in its dealing with the Colombian government and large corporations. This work is done not by Kogi but by members of closely related and more acculturated tribes. Officially, the Lost City is now under the care of the local indigenous population. However, the reality of the situation is constantly changing.

Since making the film, the situation in the Sierra has changed fundamentally. On my last visit (January 2005) I found that Paramilitaries now control the whole of the lower region. Guerrillas are an all-pervading presence in the higher parts of the massif, and the army is establishing itself there with the intention of destroying them. Military bases have been established in indigenous territory. In the Mamas' terms, the conquest that began with Columbus has now been completed.

GT now represents all the indigenous people of the Sierra – Kogi, Ika and Wiwa. But there is clearly a significant problem for the organization's functionaries, based in Santa Marta, to maintain contact with the Mamas. One obvious problem, apart from the sheer difficulty and danger of arranging consultative meetings, is that the working language of GT is Spanish, which the Kogi Mamas have difficulty understanding.

One new development is that GT has begun making its own short films. As a consequence of their involvement with National Geographic, who published an article on the Sierra in October 2004, they have acquired three good-quality mini-DV cameras and a semi-professional video editing kit, together with some training. Their 'Indigenous Media Project', which includes members of all three groups, is making what are, in effect, public relations videos in the hope that this is a way to make their voice heard in a difficult situation. It seems that their experience of speaking through film has been encouraging.

Alan Ereira studied Law and History at Queens' College, Cambridge. In 1962 he began a career as a radio and television producer, specializing in history. His credits include *Battle of the Somme*, which won the Japan Prize in 1978; *Armada*, which was winner of the Royal Television Society's Best Documentary Series of 1988 and numerous history documentaries. He is the author of *The People's England*, *The Invegordon Mutiny*, *The Heart of the World* and co-author with Terry Jones of *Crusades* and *Terry Jones' Medieval Lives*. He has set up his own film production company, Sunstone Films.

Contact address: Sunstone Films Ltd, 19 Bolsover Street, London W1W 5NA, UK. Email: aereira@aol.com

REFERENCES

Davis, W. Sierra Nevada Indians. National Geographic, October (2004) 50–69.

Ereira, A. *The Heart of the World*. Jonathan Cape, London (1990).

Reichel-Dolmatoff, G. *Los Kogi: Una tribu de la Sierra Nevada de Santa Marta, Colombia*. 2 Vols, 2nd edition. Centro Editorial, Universidad Nacional de Colombia, Bogota (1985).

Social images through visual images: the use of drawings and photographs in the Western representation of the aborigines of Tierra del Fuego (southern South America)

Dánae Fiore

ABSTRACT

This paper analyses the creation of social images (culturally biased representations) about Fuegian aborigines through the production of visual images (drawings and photographs) by European voyagers, missionaries and ethnographers. The images are evaluated as records that offer rich and complex information about both the recorder and the recorded subjects through a consideration of the context in which they were published and the prevailing socio-historical situation. The creation and manipulation of visual records by Western agents has dual elements, in which the representation of the social 'other' (the Fuegians) bears a clear relation to the representation of the social 'self' (the Europeans). However, the Fuegians themselves were not necessarily passive subjects, but could act as active agents, negotiating who was photographed and in what situations. Over time, the prevailing representation of Fuegians changes from an initial idealization of their status as aboriginals, to a population of potential religious converts, and finally to their portrayal as 'unpolluted' aborigines in ethnographic photography. The paper concludes by considering how Fuegian societies and the impact of Western people have been re-considered through a re-contextualization of these same images within a recent museum display in Argentina.

INTRODUCTION: VISUAL REPRESENTATIONS OF FUEGIAN ABORIGINES

Tierra del Fuego has been inhabited for at least 11,000 years, but the most dramatic changes to Fuegian culture took place after the first European expedition to the region in the 16th century. After this date, the Fuegian population was decimated by slaughter and acculturation, and by ecological and health disasters (Borrero, 1995; Orquera and Piana, 1999; Orquera, 2002). Paradoxically, it was during this destructive colonial process that Europeans formed a rich record of the vanishing Fuegian life style. This record includes both written texts and visual images (drawings, photographs and films). While the former have been used both in historical and archaeological studies, the latter have mainly been considered to be illustrations, and little analysis has focused on them as actual sources of information.

This paper will provide a diachronic panorama of the ways in which drawings and photographs have been produced and manipulated by Westerners (mostly Europeans) to create representations of the Fuegian aborigines. These images serve a dual purpose, containing information about the biases, intentions and perceptions of their creators, in addition to data about Fuegian cultural life. I will focus on the former aspect, particularly on the contexts in which these representations were produced and, when information is available, on their intended viewers.

The social significance of the images of the Selk'nam, Haush, Yámana and Alacaluf aborigines obviously changed according to the socio-historical context in which the drawings and photographs were produced and/or manipulated. What I intend to show here is *how* and *why* some of these strategies of representation took place.

STRANGE NOVELTY: THE IDEALIZED ABORIGINAL STATUS

The first visual representations of the aboriginal inhabitants of Tierra del Fuego were created in the late 16th and early 17th centuries. These engravings and drawings illustrate texts and maps of the exploratory journeys made by voyagers such as De Weert, Van Noort, Van Spielbergen, L'Hermite and Narborough (see, for example, reproductions in Brüggemann, 1989; Gusinde, 1982, 1991; McEwan *et al.*, 1997). They were published in books that described these journeys, providing information about the geography of the newly explored territories, as well as some descriptions of the 'new' and 'exotic' peoples that were encountered. Such books were presumably intended mainly for other navigators, individuals engaged in organizing, funding and profiting from such trips, and 'erudite', upper-class persons interested in learning about the newly 'discovered' places and peoples.

Many of these initial representations depict encounters between the Europeans and the aborigines. These include both scenes of a violent nature in which the two groups are shown fighting and static scenes in which the aborigines are shown 'posing' motionless, facing the draughtsman/viewer. The static scenes compare with poses depicted in European paintings of the time, and also anticipate later photographic poses.

Fuegians are sometimes shown fighting with bows and arrows, but are also represented retreating (running away) or defeated (lying on the ground, probably dead). Europeans are always represented in 'aggressive/triumphant' attitudes, attacking the aborigines. This happens even in scenes that depict in the foreground a 'peaceful' interaction between Europeans and Fuegians, but in the background the Europeans are shown engaged in some form of combat with the aborigines (see Fig. 1). Such mutliple-scene pictures may have represented a chronology of events within a single image (i.e. arrival of Europeans, violent conquest and resulting domination of the Fuegians). All these features of the images suggest that they may have been used by the European voyagers-draftsmen as a means of self-glorification (showing their power over the Fuegians). These types of image were likely to please the intended European readers, and the

Figure 1. A. One of the first Dutch illustrations of the Alacaluf (originally published in S. de Weert, 1646: 24–25, reproduced in Brüggemann, 1989: 15). B. Representation of the first encounter of the Dutch with the Alacaluf (originally published in Barent Janz Porgieter, 1599; reproduced in Gusinde, 1991: plate 1).

opposition of European and 'exotic (defeated) others' may have been a contributing factor in the construction of a European identity.

These 'Renaissance-style' drawings/engravings mostly show an idealized image of the Fuegian aborigines, represented with seemingly European physical features (build, posture, haircut, male facial hair, etc.) that do not correspond with the features of any known Fuegian population. Also, with only one known exception,[1] they are not represented as physically deformed (e.g. as giants, like their Patagonian neighbours, see Prieto, 1997). Instead, the Fuegians were visually identified as 'other' by their (semi)nakedness and by their material culture items (bow-arrow, harpoon, basket, canoe, cloak, etc. – though some of these resemble European objects).

This 'good savage' image was maintained throughout the 17th and 18th centuries, though it did not coincide with many of the written European descriptions of the Fuegians, which described them as rough, rude, dirty and even as cannibals (e.g. Walbeek, 1643, in Gusinde, 1937: 50–53). The reasons for this discrepancy are difficult to ascertain, but they are likely to have been related to the conceptual and aesthetic interests, ideals and canons of the draftsmen. Additionally, these drawings/engravings may not have been made *in situ*, but may post-date the actual instance of contact. It is even possible that some of these depictions are the result of the artist having seen a sketch, or having heard a verbal description of Fuegian natives. This latter situation is evidenced by cases in which several versions of a specific image are re-drawn and re-published in different issues of a book, or in different books, possibly by different artists (see, for example, Fig. 1 A and B).

It is clear then that 'documentary detail' and accuracy were not central to the creation of these visual representations, and that at this time the emphasis was placed on depicting the Fuegians as semi-naked hunter-gatherers in order to indicate their 'savage' state.

REPULSIVE DIFFERENCE, JUSTIFIED DOMINATION

Considerable changes occurred in the 19th century. Different types of interaction and new visual recording techniques generated new representations. An example of this new trend is the set of drawings by Conrad Martens, who took part in the *Beagle* expedition (1831–1836) commanded by Robert FitzRoy, in which Charles Darwin was the naturalist on board. This marks a difference with the previously discussed visual representations, in that Marten's drawings can, to an extent, be considered as 'first-hand' visual records composed *in situ*.

The drawings illustrate the books in which FitzRoy and Darwin write their accounts about the expedition. The selection of illustrations varies according to the date and place of issue of each book, and such variability might have been related to the perceived audiences for each volume (though other issues such as availability of images and the publisher's rights over them were likely to play a role). Initially, the accounts of the *Beagle* expedition were published as a voyage of scientific interest (geographical, geological, botanical, zoological, 'ethnographic'). Hence, their audience must have ranged from members of the British navy, interested in the geographical features and newly discovered maritime routes, to members of the academic world. The nautical significance of this voyage is evidenced by the publication of a version of these books by the Biblioteca Oficial de la Marina (Argentina) in 1932–1933. The audience for these books also increased widely after the publication of Darwin's theory of evolution – the rudiments of which were gleaned from observations made whilst aboard the *Beagle*.

Darwin's text includes many contemptuous expressions about the Yámana. For example, he wrote (1845: 224–225) that these were, 'the most abject and miserable creatures I anywhere beheld ... Viewing such men, one can hardly make oneself believe that they are fellow-creatures'.[2] To an extent, Marten's drawings support the same ideas. They represent the Yámana with bristly facial features: wide noses, big coarse lips, tangled hair and a lost/baffled look in the eyes (see Beer, 1997: 148, 150).

Within the climate of 19th-century ideals and incipient concepts of social evolution, such explicit written concepts and accompanying visual images provided an implicit justification for the acculturation of the Fuegians. Such an attempt had been put in practice by FitzRoy and Parker

King during the first voyage of the *Admiralty* and *Beagle* (1826–1830), when four Fuegians (Oran'delico (Jemmy Button) – a Yámana; Iokusulu (Fuegia Basket), El'leparu (York Minster) and Boat Memory – all Alacaluf) were taken to England. These aborigines had been taken as hostages, on separate occasions, through conflicts such as the theft of a whale-boat and the attempt to recover it (which involved the death of one Fuegian). One of them (Jemmy) had been traded for a mother-of-pearl button (hence his English name; FitzRoy in Gusinde, 1986: 79). Parker King decided to keep them on board and try to teach them English (ibid.: 369). Besides the practical reasons of being able to communicate with the aborigines, this was also important for the British expeditionaries because:

> I became convinced that so long as we were ignorant of the Fuegian language, and the natives were equally ignorant of ours, we should never know much about them, of the interior of their country, nor would there be the slightest chance of their being raised one step above the low place which they then held in our estimation. (FitzRoy, in Gusinde, 1986: 79).

In England, they stayed in Walthamstow with Rev. William Wilson, where they were taught English, religion, carpentry, horticulture, etc. (Sosa, 2001: 194). They were also presented to King William IV and Queen Adelaide in Saint James' Palace, where the Fuegians received several gifts (ibid.: 195). Yet, there is no information to suggest that they were displayed privately or publicly as curiosities, unlike latter Fuegians who were displayed as public attractions at 'freak shows' (see below).

After their stay in England, the three surviving Fuegians (Boat Memory died in October 1830) were taken back to Tierra del Fuego, where they were expected to transmit their newly acquired English cultural habits and language to their fellow natives (though Darwin had some doubts about the potential success of the enterprise; Darwin, 1845: 240–241).

This 'experiment' was commemorated through a unique visual record: a drawing that includes portraits of Fuegia, Jemmy and York (McEwan *et al.*, 1997: 147). Six portraits are aligned in two parallel vertical rows, which, at first glance, appear

Figure 2. Illustration by C. Martens comparing different portraits of Fuegian aborigines (originally published in Darwin, 1845; reproduced in McEwan *et al.*, 1997: 149).

to represent the transformation of the Fuegians from savage to civilized human beings (see Figure 2). However, when examined in more detail, a number of significant variations can be found in the construction and presentation of the visual information. The drawings are organized in pairs according to the represented subject. In the first pair of portraits, the left-hand picture shows Fuegia wearing a Western dress, a necklace and tied/short hair (the caption reads 'Fuegia Basket in 1833'). The picture on the right is a portrait of a woman of similar facial features, though 'coarser': she has bigger lips, a broader nose, a doltish look in her eyes, long untidy hair and she is depicted slouching and wearing a skin cloak – she is clearly an 'uncivilized' aborigine. But the caption states that this is 'Jemmy's wife in 1834'; therefore, in spite of the overall visual resemblance, this is not Fuegia (moreover, according to Darwin (1845: 239) Fuegia was 'married' to York). Yet the explicit comparison between the 'civilized' Fuegia and the 'uncivilized' wife of Jemmy is still evident.

The second pair of portraits depicts Jemmy in his 'savage' and 'civilized' states. Again, the visual features used to picture him as a 'typical' Fuegian are long hair, a broad nose, full lips, a big forehead and a sombre look in his eyes. His 'civilized' portrait shows him with short hair, European clothes, a straighter physical position (i.e. not slouching), wide-open eyes with a more attentive look, a flatter forehead and thinner lips. However, besides these conspicuous visual features, which are clearly propaganda to show the benefits of the 'civilization process', the arrangement of both portraits is also revealing. The picture on the left, depicting the 'savage Jemmy' is captioned 'Jemmy in 1834', while the picture on the right, depicting the 'civilized Jemmy' is captioned 'Jemmy Button in 1833'. Therefore, the transformation that could be inferred by reading the illustrations from left to right does not correspond to the chronological sequence of Jemmy's different appearances. Instead, these portraits show Jemmy's 'involution' from 'civilized' back to 'savage', a change which deeply disappointed Darwin (1845: 240–241) when he met Jemmy again a year after the Fuegian had returned home. As Beer (1997: 151) rightfully pointed out, while Darwin could have admired Jemmy's ability for adaptation – a key point of the theory of evolution he would develop years later – he read this process as degradation.

Finally, the third pair of portraits represents York. In the left portrait he is facing to the front, while in the right he is shown in profile, in the style of a natural history specimen. York is only shown in his 'acculturated version', with Western clothing and haircut, and with 'Westernized' facial features. A chronological comparison is suggested by the captions: 'York Minster in 1832' (left portrait), 'York in 1833' (right portrait) but it is not clear why there is no visual information about his 'uncivilized' appearance.

While the two first pairs of portraits involve a certain manipulation of visual information to illustrate the comparison of the before-and-after acculturation states of the Fuegians (i.e. using the portrait of another person, or changing the chronological order of the portraits), there is no intention to hide this by manipulating the captions. These texts clearly indicate the identity of the persons depicted and date of the representations. There was also no intention of 'deceiving' the viewer/audience by creating 'fake' portraits of the Fuegians in their 'uncivilized' states to fit the aims of the illustration. This suggests that, in this case, visual representations may have been regarded as 'scientific' visual information that should not be tampered with in order not to alter the 'accurate' records of events and not to mislead the readers, which may indicate a change in outlook as to the purpose and accuracy required from these illustrations.

Visual records of other voyages went beyond the representation of 'stunted' Fuegians and acculturation attempts, and involved their exhibition as curiosities, and recording their annihilation. In the Great Exhibition held in Paris in 1889 a group of Alacaluf were kept in cages and exhibited as cannibals in the *Jardin Zoologique d'Acclimatation*. To achieve the desired effect on the public, the group were starved and then, shortly before visitors arrived, were given raw meat to eat, which obviously they devoured (Borrero, 1989: 25). Souvenir-postcards of the exhibition, presumably aimed at a wide audience of the general public, show photos of the Alacaluf alone and with a European man (M. Maitre) holding a conspicuous cane, similar to those used to tame wild beasts (Chapman *et al.*, 1995; Prieto and Cárdenas, 1997). Interestingly, neither the images nor the captions on these postcards make reference to the supposed cannibalism of these Fuegians.

Photographs were taken not only to document the Fuegian 'others', but also to record their extermination. In 1886, Julio Popper was financed by the Argentinean government to search for gold in Tierra del Fuego. During his stay, Popper had violent encounters with the Selk'nam, and some were killed. According to Gusinde, when the gold business was no longer profitable, Popper was hired by the owners of some 'estancias' (large farm-estates) to 'hunt' Fuegians (Gusinde, 1982: 54). When the Argentinean government confronted Popper about his violence against the Fuegians, he spoke and wrote in favour of them (Popper, 1887, 1891) with a verbosity that Gusinde (ibid.) rightly qualifies as hypocritical.

Popper's raids were recorded in a series of photographs in which he and his men are shown aiming and firing their guns. At least three photos show them next to the dead body of a Selk'nam

Figure 3. One of the photographs that documents Popper's actions in Tierra del Fuego (original photograph from 1886–1887, published in Brüggemann, 1989: 85).

man lying on the ground, still holding his bow (see Figure 3). The copies of Popper's photographs held in the Royal Geographical Society show printed captions (embedded within the photo), which range from self-indulgent texts ('Arrows were coming from everywhere'), to those one would now consider outrageously cynical ('Dead in the field of honour' in reference to the dead Selk'nam man).

The reasons why these photographs were taken are not entirely clear: they may have ranged from propaganda aimed to obtain more funding for Popper's raids, justifications of them in case his actions were criticized, to mementos for personal consumption. However, it is clear that photographs, and captions 'adjusting' their messages, were used to justify and glorify the annihilation of 'the other', a process that was nevertheless conveniently denied by Popper when confronted by critical authorities.

DESIRABLE TRANSFORMATIONS: MISSIONARY VISUAL RECORDS

Besides voyagers and explorers, European Missionaries developed strong contacts with the Fuegians. From 1850 onwards, British Anglican missionaries began to travel to Tierra del Fuego and established missions along the shores of the Beagle Channel and of various southern islands. A considerable number of their texts include abundant information about Yámana customs (e.g. Parker Snow, 1857; Despard, 1861; Bridges, 1897, 1933), but their visual records (mostly drawings of landscapes, ships, missions and a few representations of aborigines) are scanty.[3]

Salesian missions were established in northern Tierra del Fuego from 1889 onwards. The missionaries, mostly of Italian origin, recorded in their published books (e.g. Beauvoir, 1915; De Agostini, 1924; Borgatello, 1929), with a varied degree of detail, Selk'nam customs and activities of the missions. These included written texts and visual records, mostly photographs. In a few cases, the published photographs were explicitly intended to raise money and support for the mission and to thank for previous contributions (e.g. a photo of two Selk'nam girls framed in a heart ornamented with flower girdles, captioned 'From the **Heart** of Tierra del Fuego – Rio Grande. Two *Shelknam* girls of 10 and 6 years old, which the Salesian Mission gathered in Rio Grande. The charity of our contributors maintains [them]. They salute you and thank you from their **Hearts**'. Beauvoir, 1915: 226, emphasis in original).

The most important collection of photographs made by the Salesians were taken by De Agostini, and published in a number of his books (De Agostini, 1924; 1941; 1945; 1955; Fig. 4). These are mostly structured as records of his trips in Tierra del Fuego, with a great emphasis on the geography and natural landscapes. They also provide information about some Fuegian customs, and recorded the two main processes of acculturation developed by the Salesian missions:

Figure 4. Pa'ciek, a Selk'nam man, women and child in a hut. Photo by De Agostini (originally published in De Agostini, 1924 and currently sold as a postcard).

the Catholic mass and the employment of aborigines in mission workshops. In doing so, they show a number of underlying biases. The record of the Fuegians acculturation involves in some cases the 'forging' of their identities and of some of their customs by staging and/or editing the photographs. The following are examples of these artifices:

1. The photographs of Selk'nam men wrestling show them wearing skin cloaks, when other texts and photos confirm that they wrestled naked (Gusinde, 1989; Prieto and Cárdenas, 1997: figs 51–52).
2. The editing of a photo of an Alacaluf man (De Agostini, 1924: 267), whose face was cut and pasted into the photo of a Selk'nam man (ibid. 265), in order to show him dressed in a skin cloak, instead of Western clothing (Prieto and Cárdenas, 1997: 30).
3. A photograph of two Yámana women (Yayosh and Lakutaia) has been published in different books identifying them as, variously, Yámana, Alacaluf and Selk'nam (e.g. Borgatello, 1929; De Agostini, 1945; Stambuk, 1986; Mordo, 2001) showing how this photograph was used more as an illustration than an ethnographic document. In addition, the women are dressed in big skin cloaks, like those worn by the Selk'nam, possibly because they were originally wearing Western clothing (hence did not look like 'typical Fuegians').

While previous records used nudity to characterize the Fuegians as the 'other', De Agostini avoided nudity in order to shorten the distance between Western people and the Fuegians, providing a fake record of the latter's 'Western decency'. But at the same time, De Agostini wanted them to appear in some of his photos wearing 'typical clothing', even if it was not typical of their own society, thus providing a fake record of 'ethnographic purity'.

DESIRABLE EXOTICISM: ETHNOGRAPHIC PHOTOGRAPHY

Ethnographic photography started in Tierra del Fuego as early as 1882 with the French *Mission Scientifique du Cap Horn* (MSCH), which established an observation station on Navarino Island for a year and explored thousands of kilometres along the shores of the Beagle Channel. Besides the rich and systematically presented ethnographic texts (e.g. Martial, 1888; Hyades and Deniker, 1891) this metereologic-geographical mission generated numerous photographs (most published in Chapman et al., 1995) and some drawings, which can be considered the first ethnographic[4] visual record of Yámana culture (Fig. 5). Many of these photographs are clearly posed: the subjects are staring at the camera/photographer/viewer or are photographed in front and profile, as in a typical physical anthropology specimen illustration (e.g. Edwards, 1988). Such

Figure 5. Athlinata, a Yámana man, hafting a multibarbed harpoon. Photo by the Mission Scientifique du Cap Horn (original 1882–1883, published in Chapman et al., 1995: 108).

poses are mainly related to the interests of the photographers in recording certain activities, attitudes or features of the Fuegians, rather than to photographic-technical limitations, since the use of the dry-gelatin bromide procedure allowed them to take almost instantaneous photographs (Prieto and Cárdenas, 1997: 15). Yet this photo collection also provides detailed information about Yámana culture that was previously unknown. Some of the photographs and drawings show artefacts isolated from their context, which suggests a new interest by the observers in material culture that focused on the objects of the 'other' as subjects for observation, collection and exhibition.

Forty years later, Gusinde produced the most varied collection of photographs of Fuegian societies.[5] Though he was a clergyman, Gusinde (1931, 1937, 1989, 1991) made four fieldtrips to Tierra del Fuego between 1919 and 1924, not as a missionary but as an ethnographer. In his texts, Gusinde maintained a constant paradox: he insists that the Fuegians are on the verge of imminent extinction because of their contact with Europeans, but also views these societies as unchanged and frozen in pre-contact times. Such inconsistency is quite visible in Gusinde's photographs. Although he acknowledged that the Fuegians had mostly changed their clothing because of European influence (Gusinde, 1919: 22–23), he chose to picture the Selk'nam wearing traditional clothing as much as possible, or to edit the photos to avoid such 'cultural pollution' (e.g. one photograph was cropped in order to remove a man wearing a Western hat – uncut original published by Bridges, 1951: plate XL). But other photographs show the opposite situation. For example, the Yámana, who were already deeply influenced by the Anglican missionaries, appear in all of Gusinde's photographs wearing Western clothes (Fig. 6). Even in situations where traditionally they were expected to be naked (such as the male initiation ceremonies), they still appear wearing a loin-cloth. Such detail suggests both the degree of acculturation of the Yámana to Western clothing customs, as well as the choices they made based on such newly acquired patterns: they agreed to pose for Gusinde but not to be photographed entirely naked (as the Selk'nam did, see below).

Figure 6. A group of Yámana men and women (adults and youngsters), together with Gusinde (left) and Koppers (right), ornamented and holding dancing wands for the *chiéjaus* initiation ceremony (published in Koppers, [1924] 1997: fig. XIIa). Note the Western clothes worn by the Yámana individuals.

Unlike the Yámana, the Selk'nam did not always agree to being photographed. They feared the camera, because, 'they were convinced that if captured with that little box, their souls or their vital spirits would perish inside of it' (Gusinde, 1982: 82). For this reason, they called Gusinde *Mink'en*, which meant 'shadow hunter or image hunter' (ibid.). They also refused to pose wearing their traditional clothes, because they considered this a 'savage' practice of 'ancient times' (Koppers, [1924] 1997: 38). Therefore, Gusinde tried to accustom them to this technique, by showing them photographs and making them look through the camera. He also paid them with money, goods and copies of the photographs.[6] Through these means, he could photograph the Selk'nam, mostly wearing traditional clothing and also naked, during their male initiation ceremonies.

This questions the biases within a 'representative' record that had to be constantly negotiated, and is likely to have depicted situations that were not always spontaneous. Nevertheless, systematic studies of photo collections taken by different photographers help indicate to what extent they actually document socio-cultural Fuegian patterns (both their everyday life and their attitudes towards photography) and whether these were broken by the staging of the photo (Fiore, 2002). For example, Gusinde's photographs show different degrees of acculturation by the Yámana and the Selk'nam in relation to their 'traditional' clothing (their access to it, knowledge to make it and willingness to wear it). In addition, this demonstrates that, faced with the same photographer, the Selk'nam and the Yámana had different reactions to photography, which strongly suggests that not only the photographer but also the photographed subjects were active agents in the process of ethnographic photography.

REGRETTED LOSS (OF DIFFERENCE): RE-PRESENTING REPRESENTATIONS

Images of the Fuegians have been re-used on numerous occasions to re-evaluate and re-present their society, and the impact of European contact in books, newspapers, museums, postcards, tourist souvenirs, art productions such as paintings and sculptures and, lately, on the Internet. An example of this is the exhibition *En el Confín del Mundo* (At the Uttermost Part of the World), held since 1996 in the Museo Etnográfico 'J.B. Ambrosetti' (Facultad de Filosofía y Letras, Universidad de Buenos Aires). The museum's audience is quite varied, ranging from groups of school children, to families, and tourists from foreign countries. Guided tours are offered to the visitors, particularly during the weekends.

The ideological and conceptual perspective of the exhibition is clearly summarized in two phrases painted on the walls of the exhibition-rooms: 'What a curious paradox that of the Western [world], who cannot know without possessing, and cannot possess without destroying', and 'These peoples, who fascinated the Westerners, are not here anymore. They have been massacred in few decades, and not by the "conquistadores" of the XVI century, but by our grandparents, less than 100 years ago'.

Thus, the main aim of the exhibition is to introduce the audience to the two-fold process entailed by the Western 'discovery' of the Fuegian societies, which involved building (biased) knowledge about them while at the same time their territories were occupied and most of the aborigines were killed or acculturated. Its display occupies two rooms. The first one (the entrance) is a sinuous corridor whose walls are covered by collages of images. The right wall illustrates the European expansion from the 15th century onwards; the left wall shows photos, drawings and a map of Tierra del Fuego showing its landscape, fauna and inhabitants, including the European drawings of idealized Fuegians. These images are presented without specifying their dates, artists or subjects depicted (they range from the 16th to the 19th centuries; some of them have been published by Gusinde, 1982 and Brüggemann, 1989). Texts about the socio-historical facts and processes represented are placed underneath the collages. This entrance shows the main aim of the exhibition: to identify the two social agents of the colonization of Tierra del Fuego (Europeans and Fuegians) and to point out that no account of the latter should ignore the presence and biases of the former.

Matching the introductory function of this room, images are used mainly illustratively, to give a sense of the geographical and socio-historical contexts in which the expansion took place. Their display in collages and the lack of individual captions contributes to this: by making each image blend with the next, their limits fade, creating a visual continuum that invites the viewer to walk through the corridor rather than to observe each picture in detail. Therefore, the images here have mainly an illustrative and aesthetic use, while their potential as records that contain visual information (which would involve showing the entire image, captioning them individually, etc.) is not highlighted.

The second room, of rectangular shape, combines sets of images (individually framed) and glass-cases with artefacts, which alternate along the two longer walls (Fig. 7). The logic of display is continued from the entrance: right, European-Creole colonizers; left, Fuegian aborigines. The centre of the room is occupied and divided longitudinally by a Yámana canoe. Against the far end wall are placed four life-size silhouettes cut out of photographs (taken by Gusinde in 1923) picturing Selk'nam men wearing very intricate ceremonial body painting designs. The selection and display of these images seems to have been based on the potential aesthetic and eye-catching effect generated by the body paintings' designs on the viewers, as well as on the striking sense of difference (with the viewer) generated by the painting on the men's naked bodies. These effects, in turn, are clearly enhanced by the large size of the pictures. Yet the lack of textual information directly related to these silhouettes leaves their display in a more ambivalent situation than the rest of the exhibited photographs (see below).

The presentation of the photographs displayed on the two walls entails a re-signification process, which involves the use of written captions. For example:

- the caption of a photo of Yámana aborigines taken by the French *Mission Scientifique du Cap Horn* indicates that one of them has his head shaved because moulds of his head were taken, hinting towards the use of aboriginal populations for the racial typologies of physical anthropology and social evolution;
- one of Popper's photographs depicting the shooting of Selk'nam men is captioned, far from its original self-complacent manipulation, as evidence of his 'indigenous hunting' campaigns;
- photos of the Salesian missions' workshops are captioned mentioning the indigenous labour

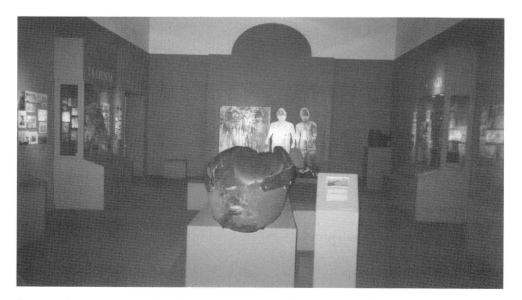

Figure 7. Second room of the 'Confín del Mundo' exhibition, Museo Etnográfico J.B. Ambrosetti, Universidad de Buenos Aires. Note the Yámana canoe in the centre of the room, the several photographs on the right and left walls, and the life-size silhouettes of Selk'nam men, cut out from photographs, in the far end wall.

force they employed, and their economic importance as a source of funding for the missions;
- photos of a Fuegian skull with a bullet wound and others from archaeological collections are presented, hinting towards the murder and collection of aboriginal skeletons by Western invaders and scientists;
- other photos represent the Fuegians not as victims of Western actions but as producers of varied cultural habits, and as active social agents in the most recent period of their history. For example, as informants of more modern anthropologists (of the 1960s), and as 'representatives of the current society', such as Angela Virginia Choinquintel (the 'last pure Selk´nam', who died in 1999) and Ruben Maldonado, President of the Ona Association.

Therefore, captions are used to provide contextual information about recorders, intentions and recorded contents, and give the photo the status of reliable contemporary documents instead of prejudiced or fanciful illustration. At the same time, the captions guide the viewer's gaze towards certain details of the images that help the viewer appreciate them from a critical standpoint. Genocide, acculturation and science are thus critically introduced in the exhibition by the written (re)interpretations of images, which are mainly shown as visual documents of events and processes. Such a combination of image and text creates a new representation based on previous representations of the Fuegians.

VISUAL REPRESENTATIONS, WRITTEN CONCLUSIONS

This brief diachronic panorama of the different Western visual representations of Fuegian aborigines demonstrates how the representations changed depending on the biases and interests of the European-Creole societies, both in relation to the aborigines as 'the other', and to their own self-images.

The visual records of the Fuegians are illustrative of changes in the kinds of topics that were desirable/suitable for representation: nakedness, domination, death, acculturation, 'tradition', diversity.

Variation in the ethics of representation are also recognizable: early engravings copied motifs from previous illustrations with little care towards accurate representation, while from the late 19th century onwards the aim of ethnographic photographs became more explicitly directed towards scientific depiction. Even so, the posed scenes, fake details and photographic editing were not disclosed, because of the apparent desires of the ethnographer/publisher/museum curator to create an acceptable and palatable representation of aboriginal groups for (Western) society.

It is very unlikely that the Fuegian aborigines were aware of, or had any power over, the uses that Westerners were making of their visual representations from the 16th to mid-19th centuries, particularly because of the kind of techniques of representation (drawing, engraving), which did not necessarily entail the active involvement of the subjects. With the beginning of ethnographic photography (a technology that requires a certain predisposition of the photographed subject) in late 19th and early 20th centuries, the Fuegians became, in some cases, active agents in the photographic process by choosing how and/or when to be photographed. Thus, they contributed to shaping their own image, and sometimes became consumers of these images when they were paid with photographs by the ethnographers.

To the best of my knowledge, there is no available information about the opinions of the current Yámana and Selk'nam descendants about their (past and present) representations made by Westerners. In the case of the exhibition in the Museo Etnografico, the current descendants of Fuegian communities were not consulted about the content and format of the exhibition. Yet the images of living aborigines (and of Western anthropologists, whose photos were also exhibited without consultation) were selected and displayed upon two basic criteria: that they were images of 'public people' (such as the president of the 'Ona association') and/or that they were images that had been previously published in other media (newspapers, etc.) with agreement of the photographed person (Kurk, A., personal communication, 2002). This indicates an interest in using the images of persons as documents of historical processes that involve active social agents and not as illustrations of passive exotic subjects.

The museum also made some attempts to invite members of the present communities of Fuegian descendants to the exhibition, but these were not successful. Other aboriginal communities, such as the Mapuche from Patagonia and the Toba from the Northern region of Argentina, have visited the exhibitions. According to the museum curators, their opinions are ambivalent, including a sense of unease towards the loss of cultural heritage resulting from the process of colonization (which included the formation of museum collections with important pieces of such cultural heritage). At the same time, however, 'they feel that this museum represents them in a dignified way' (Kurk, A., personal communication, 2002). Concordant with the prevailing values of current social and academic trends, the South American colonization process is thus represented from a critical standpoint. Still, the construction of these representations does not involve, so far, the active inclusion of members of aboriginal communities. In Argentina, this is of the utmost necessity, in order to introduce most of the 'general public' to the existence of descendants of numerous aboriginal societies (including but vastly exceeding the Fuegians) still surviving in Argentina,[7] but also to ensure that these images can be used in future aboriginal claims.

In conclusion, exploring the past and present biases of visual representations can contribute to building a greater self-awareness of the intentions and ethics that underlie our creation and manipulation of visual records/representations. This sort of examination can also contribute to acquiring information about these aboriginal groups, long after traditional cultural practices have ceased.

Clearly, visual images can afford more than one meaning, and it is this multifaceted potential that was manipulated in the construction of representations of the Fuegians. Through the re-use of earlier representations, by re-signifying some visual details (or focusing on different ones) social identities were manipulated and constructed using visual representations. The use of words and images were then often interlinked in the creation and display of depictions of Fuegians and, just as in this paper, result in the construction of new representations of the Fuegians.

ACKNOWLEDGEMENTS

I would like to thank Bill Sillar for inviting me to contribute to this publication, for his interest in this research topic and for his detailed and stimulating comments on earlier versions of this paper. To Stephen Shennan, Jeremy Tanner and Bill Sillar for their many comments on my PhD thesis, from which this paper developed as a 'side-topic'. To the Royal Geographical Society, Archivo Salesiano, Biblioteca del Museo Etnográfico 'J.B. Ambrosetti' (Universidad de Buenos Aires), Luis Orquera, Ernesto Piana, Estela Mansur and Luis Borrero for giving me access to their Fuegian visual records collections; and to Alicia Kurk, Silvia Calvo and Marcelo Dimentstein for their helpful assistance in my numerous visits to the 'Confín del Mundo' exhibition. The results presented here were partly developed during my PhD research, which was generously funded by University College London, the Council of Vice-Chancellors and Principals of the United Kingdom, and Fundación Antorchas (Argentina).

END NOTES

1. An illustrated map, 'Tabula geographica regni Chile', shows, among many non-deformed aborigines, a tailed-man (see detail in Gusinde, 1982: 40).
2. This opinion was not extended to all Fuegians, since he considered that the Haush from Good Success Bay were physically better built and 'a very different race from the stunted, miserable wretches farther westward' (Darwin, 1845: 216).
3. Much later, photographs taken by L. Bridges (1951) – son of Rev. Bridges – provide a reliable (i.e. apparently not staged or retouched) visual record of the Fuegians, mostly of the Selk'nam.
4. Any visual record can provide ethnographic information, even if not made for such a purpose. This collection was at least partly made with such specific systematic intention.
5. Other photographic collections relating to Fuegian ethnography include the work of Barclay (1926), Furlong (1917), De Agostini (1924, 1941), Koppers ([1924] 1997), Lothrop (1928), and L. Bridges (1951). From the 1950s onwards, Emperaire (1955), Chapman (1982), Klevansky (in McEwan et al., 1997) and others took photographs of the last surviving Fuegians and their descendants, who were deeply acculturated to the Western mode of life.
6. Similar negotiations are quoted in Bridges (1951, referring to F. Cook), and by Dabbene (1911, possibly referring to Barclay).
7. Currently, a community of Yámana descendants is located in Puerto Williams (Navarino island, Chile). The 'comunidad Ona Rafaela Ishton', which gathers Selk'nam descendants and is represented by the Ona Associacion, obtained in 1999 by provincial law number 405 the right to 36,000 ha located near Tolhuin, in the centre of Isla Grande de Tierra del Fuego (Argentina). Such land claim and restitution was fostered by article 75 of the national constitution of Argentina, reformed in 1994, which for

the first time recognizes 'the ethnic and cultural preexistence of the indigenous peoples of Argentina' and 'the community possession and property of the lands which they traditionally occupy, as well as the regulation of the restitution of other [lands] apt and sufficient for human development'.

Dánae Fiore studied archaeology at the Universidad de Buenos Aires (1993) before completing an MA (1997) and a PhD thesis (2002) on the body painting of Selk'nam and Yámana societies from Tierra del Fuego at the Institute of Archaeology, University College London. Her research interests include archaeological theory and methods, and the analysis of art from technical, visual-cognitive and economic perspectives. Dánae is currently a researcher at CONICET (National Council of Scientific and Technological Research, Argentina), studying the portable art and the ethnographic photography of Tierra del Fuego, and the rock art of Patagonia.

Contact address: CONICET, Asociación de Investigaciones Antropológicas, Rivadavia 1379 11 'F'. C.P. (1033), Buenos Aires, Argentina. Email: danae_fiore@yahoo.es

REFERENCES

Barclay, W. *The Land of Magellan*. Methuen and Co., London (1926).
Beauvoir, H.M. *Los Selknam: indigenas de la Tierra del Fuego. Sus tradiciones, costumbres y lengua*. Tipografía Salesiana de Artes y Oficios, Buenos Aires (1915).
Beer, G. Travelling the other way. Travel narratives and truth claims. In McEwan, C., Borrero, L. and Prieto, A. (eds) *Patagonia. Natural History, Prehistory and Ethnography in the Uttermost End of the World*. British Museum Press, London (1997) 140–152.
Borgatello, M. *Patagonia meridionale e Terra del Fuoco*. Societa Editrice Internazionale, Torino (1929).
Borrero, J.M. *La patagonia trágica*. Americana, Buenos Aires ([1957] 1989).
Borrero, L.A. El registro arqueológico del contacto: enfermedad y discontinuidad poblacional. *Palimpsesto* 5 (1995) 202–207.
Bridges, L. *Uttermost Part of the Earth*. Hodder and Stoughton, London (1951).
Bridges, T. An account of Tierra del Fuego (Fireland), its natives and their languages. Unpublished document held by the Royal Geographical Society. Copy held by R.N.P de Goodall (1897).
Bridges, T. *Yámana–English Dictionary*. Goodall, Zagier and Urruty, Ushuaia ([1933]1987).
Brüggemann, A. *Der Travernde Blick. Martin Gusindes Fotos der letzlen Feuerland-Indianer*. Museus für Volkerkunde, Frankfurt (1989).
Chapman, A. *Drama and Power in a Hunting Society: the Selk'nam of Tierra del Fuego*. Cambridge University Press, Cambridge (1982).
Chapman, A., Barthe, C. and Revol, P. *Cap Horn 1882–1883: reencontre avec les indiens Yahgan (collection de la photothèque du Musée de l'Homme)*. Editions de la Martinière, Museum National d'histoire Naturelle y Photothèque du Musée de l'Homme, Paris (1995).
Dabbene, R. Los indígenas de la Tierra del Fuego (contribución a la Etnografía y Antropología de los fueguinos). *Boletín del Instituto Geográfico Argentino*. XXV (1911) 163–226, 247–300.
Darwin, C. *Journal of Researches in Natural History and Geology of the Countries Visited During the Voyage of HMS Beagle Round the World Under the Command of Capt. Fitz-Roy (R.N.)*. Henry Colburn, London (Second edition) (1845).
De Agostini, A. *I miei viaggi nella Terra del Fuoco*. Societa Salesiana, Milan (1924).
De Agostini, A. *Andes Patagonicos. Viajes de exploracion a la cordillera patagonica austral*. Peuser, Buenos Aires (1941).
De Agostini, A. *Paisajes Magallánicos*. Punta Arenas. (1945).
De Agostini, A. *Treinta años en Tierra del Fuego*. Peuser, Buenos Aires (1955).
Despard, G.P. Letters and fragments of his journal. In *The Voice of Pitty for South America*. IV–VIII (1857–1861).
Edwards, E. Representation and reality: science and the visual image. In Morphy, H. and Edwards, E. (eds) *Australia in Oxford*. Pitt Rivers Museum, Oxford. (1988) 27–45.
Emperaire, J. *Les nomades de la mer*. Gallimard (Collection L'Especie humaine), Paris (1955).
Fiore, D. Body painting in Tierra del Fuego. The power of images in the uttermost part of the world. Unpublished PhD Thesis. Institute of Archaeology, University College London (2002).
Furlong, Ch.W. Some effects of environment on the Fuegian tribes *The Geographical Review* 3 (1917) 1–15.
Gusinde, M. Expedición a la Tierra del Fuego (informe del Jefe de Sección). *Publicaciones del Museo de Etnología y Antropología de Chile* II (1919) 9–43. [AQ1]
Gusinde, M. *Die Feuerland Indianer*. Band I: Die Selk'nam. Anthropos, Mödling bei Wien (1931).
Gusinde, M. *Die Feuerland Indianer*. Band II: Die Yamana. Anthropos, Mödling bei Wien (1937).
Gusinde, M. *Die feuerland Indianer*. Band III: Die Alakaluf. Anthropos. Modling bei Wien (1974).
Gusinde, M. *Los indios de Tierra del Fuego. (Los Selk'nam)*. 1 (1 & 2). CAEA, Buenos Aires (1982).
Gusinde, M. *Los indios de Tierra del Fuego. (Los Yamana)*. 2 (1, 2 & 3) CAEA, Buenos Aires (1986).
Gusinde, M. *Los Indios de Tierra del Fuego: resultados de mis cuatro expediciones en los años 1918 hasta 1924, organizadas por el Ministerio de Instrucción Publica de Chile. Antropología Biológica*. CAEA, Buenos Aires (1989).

Gusinde, M. *Los indios de Tierra del Fuego (Los Halakwulup)* 3 (1 & 2) CAEA, Buenos Aires (1991).

Hyades, P. and Deniker, J. *Mission scientifique du Cap Horn (1882–1883).* 7. Anthropology and Ethnography. Official Edition, Paris (1891).

Koppers, W. *Entre los Fueguinos*. (Translation of *Unter Feuerland-Indianer eine forschungsreise zu den Sudlichsten bewohnern der erde mit M. Gusinde [1924]*). Universidad de Magallanes and Programa Chile Austral de la Unión Europea, Punta Arenas (1997).

Lothrop, S.K. *The Indians of Tierra del Fuego*. Museum of the American Indian, Contributions 10. Heye Foundation, New York (1928).

Martial, L.F. Histoire du voyage *Mission Scientifique du Cap Horn (1882–1883)*. Official Edition, Paris (1888).

McEwan, C., Borrero, L. and Prieto, A. (eds) *Patagonia. Natural History, Prehistory and Ethnography in the Uttermost End of the World*. London: British Museum Press (1997).

Mordo, C. *La herencia olvidada*. Fondo Nacional de las Artes, Buenos Aires (2001).

Orquera, L.A. The late XIX century in the survival of the Magellan-Fuegian littoral natives. In Briones, C. and Lanata, J.L. (eds) *Living on the Edge: Native Peoples of Pampa, Patagonia and Tierra del Fuego*. (Bergin and Garvey Series in Anthropology) Greenwood Publishing Group, Westport CT (2002).

Orquera, L.A. and Piana, E.L. *La vida material y social de los Yámana*. EUDEBA, Buenos Aires (1999).

Popper, J. Exploración de la Tierra del Fuego. *Boletín del Instituto Geográfico Argentino* VIII (1887) 74–115.

Popper, J. Apuntes geográficos, etnológicos, estadísticos é industriales sobre la Tierra del Fuego. *Boletín del Instituto Geográfico Argentino* XII (1891) 7–8, 130–170.

Prieto, A. Patagonian painted cloaks. In McEwan, C., Borrero, L. and Prieto, A. (eds) *Patagonia. Natural History, Prehistory and Ethnography at the Uttermost End of the Earth*. Princeton University Press, Princeton NJ (1997) 153–172.

Prieto, A. and Cárdenas, R. *Introducción a la fotografía étnica en Patagonia*. Comunicaciones, Punta Arenas (1997).

Snow, W.P. *A Two Year's Cruise off Tierra del Fuego, the Falkland Islands, Patagonia and in the River Plate (A Narrative of Life in the Southern Seas)*. London (1857).

Sosa, N. *Mujeres indigenas de la pamga y la patagonia*. Emece, Buenos Aires (2001).

Stambuk, P. *Rosa Yagán. El último eslabón*. Andrés Bello, Santiago (1986).

What is a museum for?
The Magüta Museum for the Ticuna people, Amazonas, Brazil

Constantino Ramos Lopes

ABSTRACT

After working for several years in the Ethnography Section of Brazil's National Museum, Maria Jussara Gomes Gruber helped found the Magüta Museum in the town of Benjamin Constant, in Amazonas (close to Brazil's border with Peru and Colombia). Jussara Gruber believed that an ethnographic museum, with objects selected, displayed and explained in ways that made sense to the Ticuna Indians of the area, would help them to sustain social and cultural values in the face of continuing colonization by non-Indian society. The Ticuna are one of Brazil's most populous indigenous groups, with some 95 villages mainly scattered along the banks of the Upper Solimões River and its tributaries. Ticuna efforts to establish land boundaries and reclaim their own territory have met substantial opposition from non-Indian loggers, landowners and storekeepers. In this article (compiled from a letter and subsequent telephone interview translated by Maria Renata Franco Peters and edited by Bill Sillar) Constantino Ramos Lopes explains his role as director of the museum and its significance for the Ticuan people.

I am a member of the Mutum clan of the Ticuna people; my Ticuna name is Füpeatücü. I was born on the 21st of January 1966 on an island called San Jorge, municipality of San Paulo de Oliveca, Amazonas, Brazil. I had been a teacher for four years at a village school in San Leopoldo when, in 1988, I was invited to go to the city of Benjamin Constant to become the director of the Museu Magrita. At that time I did not even know what a museum was, because in the area where we live, in the middle of Amazonia, there are no museums. There are only museums in the big cities – for me, 'museum' was just a word.

Maria Jussara Gomes Grueber is an anthropologist and an artist who has worked with us for 25 years; she first began to discuss the idea of a museum with the Ticunas in 1980. One of the reasons she wanted to work with us to create a museum was to help us defend our culture and our lands. The Ticunas are one of the largest native populations in Brazil today, but our territory stretches over three countries: 26,000 of us live in Brazil, 7500 in Colombia and 5000 in Peru. Fortunately we have free access between these three countries and we are a well-integrated group. The Ticunas were one of the first groups to be contacted by the early conquistadors and we have been in touch with non-indigenous people for almost 400 years. After all this time, and with pressure from white people – a pressure for us not to be Indians anymore, our people have assimilated many white people's habits. There was a danger that this would be our end, our history, everything was going to disappear. The chiefs of all the Ticuna villages got together to discuss the idea of the museum and they agreed to support Maria Jussara in this project, and she agreed to search for funding.

Maria Jussara had already worked at Museu Nacional in Rio de Janeiro for 10 years, so when she came to Amazonia she already knew about us, and she sort of knew our history because of her previous research on the Ticuna. She had photos of the Ticuna collection in the National Museum. So, she would explain to me about the objects in the photos, because sometimes I did not know these objects either. But, with the help of these photos, we managed to find even some of the oldest artefacts. In the beginning of 1989 I went to many villages to meet with the village people and talk about the Museu Magüita – the museum where I would work – although I was not yet sure what I would really have to do in the museum. But, during 1989 I began to understand better the meaning of the word Museum and that it would be a good thing for our people.

The main objective of the museum was to keep and preserve the objects of the Ticunas, so that the young people and the children could know our history, through our traditional objects, like the *igaçaba* (funeral urn), *panela de barro* (cooking pot), *prato* (plate), *colher de pau* (wooden spoon), *arco* (bow), *bolsa* (bag), *rede* (hammock, net). For example, nobody uses the *zarabatana* (blowgun) or curare poison anymore, if it had not been for the museum this may have been forgotten. The objective of this museum was to preserve these objects so that the young people who visit the museum could, for example, see the blowgun and the curare that are no longer prepared by the Ticuna. Sometimes the artefacts we collected belonged to someone in particular and they would give them to us. Sometimes we had to buy them. Other objects had to be manufactured after the National Museum photos. In such cases I showed the men the pieces in the photographs and explained that we would pay for the men to make copies for us, and that we would put their names along with the objects so that they could be seen by tourists, students and other visitors, so that all these people would know who made the objects. They frequently asked what I wanted their Ticuna names for. They did not normally say their names in their own language due to embarrassment after years of pressure from non-indigenous people. Sometimes the artisans had to travel for three days to bring the objects they had manufactured to the museum. A log book was made and a number given to each piece and a form filled in with all the necessary information, such as the size of the piece, where it was from, what it was used for and the name of the person who made it.

I spent three years collecting material, and by the end of 1991 we put together 380 pieces, of which 170 were selected to be in the permanent exhibition. The museum was located in a house that already existed, it had been built by a non-indigenous person, but we bought it and refurbished it [ICCO, the Dutch Interchurch organization for development cooperation, sponsored the refurbishment of the museum – editor]. We organized the objects according to how they were used, those we used for cooking, for hunting, and festivals and so on. The masks and some other bigger objects were hung on the walls. Some of the small objects were placed in glass cases. The exhibition was very beautiful and the dream finally came true. We arranged to open the museum on the 6th of December 1991, and Ticunas from the nearer villages came to take part in the inauguration – a novelty for them.

Unfortunately the inauguration did not happen, because the non-Indian people from Benjamin Constant were against the museum, they wanted to throw petrol on it and burn it down. We only just managed to stop this because we managed to call the army to protect the museum. The army responded and sent two helicopters with twenty soldiers.

Here I need to explain why the non-Indians did this to us. Representatives from Funai (Brazil's National Bureau for Indigenous Affairs) and INCRA (the federal government land agency) had been in our villages since 1975 to decide about the land demarcation. They first came when I was still a little boy, and they said that the non-Indians and Indians could not live together anymore, that the non-Indians had to go somewhere else, to Benjamin Constant or wherever. After this subject of the demarcation of our land had been raised, the non-Indians changed the way they related to us Indians. Because until then we had lived together and worked together, we were friends. But, when Funai came and said the non-Indians had to leave our lands the situation changed completely. After a few years, in 1986, the first six areas of the Ticunas were defined, and then the Sao Leopoldo area was defined as well – that was where we lived, and my family still live there now. After the demarcation of the lands the non-Indians became even more our enemies, the non-Indians who lived there changed their attitude, the same ones who a few years before were our friends, our *compadres*! In 1988 a massacre happened in Sao Leopoldo, because of the dispute over the demarcation of the lands. The massacre happened on the 28th of March 1988 when 100 Indians from four different Ticuan communities had been holding a meeting at Capecete Creek, a group of men with guns were sent by the white settlers and opened fire upon us. On that day 14 Ticunas died, six of them were children, 23 other people were injured. I was one of the survivors of this massacre. After that, the police arrested the murderers, but later they released them again. It seems here in Brazil justice is too slow. [In March 2001 a federal court in Manuas sentenced the men responsible for this massacre to prison, these were the first ever convictions in Amazonas under the 'genocide law', which carries a sentence of between 12 and 30 years for the crime of genocide of Indians – editor.]

When the inauguration was to happen, in 1991, the situation was tense, the land disputes and the massacre were still recent, and the authorities in Benjamin Constant were all loggers and white settlers – antagonistic to us Indians. The thing is that the museum, besides keeping our artefacts, was a means of communication with other places, because we had a telephone line and a fax machine there, it was a source of protection for us as well. Because of the museum we had direct connection with Brasilia and Funai. Everybody knew about this and the non-Indians said that information was leaking from the museum, that from there information was sent to Rio de Janeiro, Brasilia and even to other places. And it was true. They figured that the museum was a sort of power for us; it could be used to legitimize our cause. So, when we distributed the invitations to the inauguration, it was transformed into a protest. Jussara Gomes Gruber had her life threatened several times and, because of these threats, she had to leave the city the day before the inauguration of the museum; she was escorted away by the army for her own protection. We called from the museum requesting help, and fortunately soldiers did come from Tabatinga. Tabatinga is a city a short distance from here, it is close to the national frontier and it has a military base, but we did not call Tabatinga directly, we called Brasilia and then they ordered the soldiers to come from Tabatinga using their two helicopters.

It seemed that this was the end of our work for the museum, work we had been doing with affection and much sacrifice – it ended with much sadness for all us who had been working so hard for three years. But, only 15 days later we returned and we were able to open the museum, although without any inauguration ceremony.

Then the local people started visiting the museum, and from 1992 we were always working on advertising the museum, we made posters and spread them around and we gave interviews on local TV, to tell them we had Ticuna art and that families would be welcome. We also worked on the museum agenda with the city and state schools to gain their trust, the library in Museu Magüita had about 300 books available for indigenous and non-indigenous people. This work in our library was quite successful, it made the non-indigenous students appreciate our work; the children of those who only a few months earlier had wanted to burn down the museum. We worked with all grades, from elementary to high school and even college. Ours was the only library in the city. I also guided the visitors to the museum and tried to explain to the students who were studying to be teachers in the future that the Indians, even though they could not read or write, were artists, and that the knowledge that could be seen in the museum belonged to the Indians. And these 'teachers to be' did not know that those artefacts and knowledge were as important as their careers, so I taught them how to respect all that knowledge. Our work was done in order to end the bias that these students' parents had against the Indians.

In 1995 the museum was awarded the title of 'Symbol Museum of Brazil', by the International Council of Museums (ICOM) Brazilian Committee, because it was run by Indians and because of the way it was run. This was why, later in 1995, I was invited to the International Council of Museums Congress in Norway, and I went there to represent Brazil. There, we explained the work we were doing in Brazil. Our work had gone much beyond what we had expected. The Dutch saw our work and said they were interested in showing it in Holland. On the second day of the conference they called me and proposed an exhibition of Ticuna

Art at the Royal Tropical Institute in Amsterdam. That was how we were invited to go to Holland to discuss this, and then the Dutch came to Benjamin Constant and bought a very similar range of objects to those that were shown in our museum exhibition. We spent one week in the villages buying these objects and I helped by explaining to the Dutch what the objects were used for and why they were important for the Ticunas. All of these were objects that were still in everyday use such as: baskets, necklaces, bows, *peneiras* (strainer). This new collection was also very complete (we did not take anything from our own museum collection). The Dutch came over two more times to oversee the collection and packing of the objects, which were then sent to be exhibited in Holland.

With regard to the land dispute, about 90% of our lands have now been officially recognized and delimited. In 1992, we got in touch with a secretary from the Austrian government, and they gave us US$500,000 and along with Funai and the Brazilian government we completed a large part of our negotiations for land in 1993. We still have not finished it all because the Brazilian government say they cannot afford it; we still have seven areas to be defined. The research has been done but it cannot be executed because of the lack of funds.

When we went to Norway and then to Holland, we were doing beautiful work and managing to put our message across well. We were given an award and part of this award was money to keep the museum going, so that we could pay for our electricity and water bills, and the people who worked for us. We were even making some money from a little shop selling crafts to the tourists. But then a group of white people who had previously worked with Jussara became jealous. They did everything they could to throw us out of the museum. It all happened when we were away organizing a three month exhibition in Manaus, a project with the participation of Universidade do Amazonas, Universidade de Coimbra and Universidade do Porto, Portugal ... I was the co-ordinator of this exhibition so I was in Manaus when the white people, who were once friends of Jussara, closed the museum. When I heard about it, it had been closed for a week already. In the end it was locked for a whole year. Today the museum is rather run-down because the people there do not understand the work of making a museum for the Ticuna.

This was my work as director. I no longer work there; I left the Magüta Museum in 1997, although I am still asked to lecture on the museum and on land disputes. The museum was of great significance for us, especially for me. As a director I gained a lot of knowledge on how museums work and function, because I have been visiting museums in Norway, France, Germany, Italy, Austria, Switzerland, Belgium and Britain. With this knowledge I currently work as the secretary of a centre providing education and qualifications for new Ticuna teachers, part of the General Organization of the Bilingual Ticuna Teachers (OGPTB). [The Ford and the Getúlio Vargas Foundations jointly recognized the work of OGPTB by giving the organization an award under their Public Management and Citizenship 2000 Program – editor.]

Constantino Ramos Lopes, is a Ticuna Indian. He was working as a teacher before becoming director of the Magüta Museum from 1988 to 1997. He currently works for the Organization of Bilingual Ticuan Teachers based in Benjamin Constant.

Contact address: Av. Castelo Branco 245, 69630-000 Benjamin Constant. Amazonas, Brazil.

Artefacts, archaeologists and American Indians

Joe Watkins

ABSTRACT

Archaeologists traditionally have observed the style and technology of artefacts and used this to classify archaeological assemblages, describing the repeated association of artefact groups as a 'Culture'. We continue to place overwhelming reliance on our ability to derive meaningful information about past culture from artefacts, yet the importance these objects had for the members of the cultural group (past and present) is not adequately considered. The typological approach sidelines the creative role of the artisans, we find out a little about their economy, gain momentary glimpses of their religion, but learn almost nothing about their humanity. Archaeologists tend to focus on the physical, technological or esoteric attributes of an artefact, while indigenous populations tend to focus on the object's ritual or social importance. This is most apparent in the treatment of funerary artefacts. Until recently, many American Indian tribal groups have seen no distinction between 'grave robbing' and 'archaeological excavation'; it made no difference to them whether the dead were disturbed by looters or by qualified archaeologists. By involving indigenous populations in the design, practice and dissemination of archaeological research, we can add humanity to our study of the human past, and take a step toward a truly worldwide archaeology.

ARTEFACTS, ARCHAEOLOGICAL 'CULTURES' AND LIVING CULTURE

The primary focus of most archaeological studies is the cultural refuse of past archaeological cultures, but the focus we as archaeologists choose leads us to practice what Martin Wobst (2001) decries as the '... glorification of materiality in archaeology'. Our vision of a culture is flawed when we develop models based on artefacts without openly recognizing and acknowledging that we cannot examine the entire spectrum of the culture that produced these artefacts. Mainstream archaeology, as it is practiced today, is full of limiting factors that are usually unrecognized, or at least unstated. The reliance on durable artefacts as 'type fossils' has led to the definition of 'cultures' that probably have no reality other than in the minds of the archaeologist that first described them, yet archaeologists continue to talk about them as if their constructs are reality. Although morphological typologies allowed archaeologists to compare technological attributes of a site and to group sites with similar technological tendencies, the discussion of archaeological sites as 'cultures' is misleading. Future archaeologists of the USA might establish '.30-06 caliber' cultures or '.38 caliber' cultures or '9mm' cultures to describe hunting camps found in wilderness today, perhaps by correlating the caliber of the spent rifle shell with the beverage containers associated with them ('It seems that the 9mm culture had a stronger reliance on bourbon than whiskey, although the higher incidence of wine containers in parts of the south is noteworthy. In contrast, the occurrence of ritually killed beer cans within the .22 caliber culture implies that this group did not find it necessary to use higher-powered ammunition to ceremonially dispatch their quarry').

Thus archaeology itself defines the meaning and significance of artefacts and removes our ability to describe Culture with a capital 'C' rather than merely the products or technology of culture. It places ultimate importance on the analyst or scientist and disregards many of the intellectual choices made by the individual of the culture under study. To describe a Folsom point, or any other specialized tool, in technological terms certainly increases the scientific understanding of certain aspects of that item, but such an action prevents the culture that produced the artefact from being adequately described.

When we focus on artefacts, we are looking at Culture twice distilled – the most durable artefacts of a culture distilled from the entire range of artefacts that the culture produced, and then the further distillation by the craftsperson of the entire range of cultural ideals. Archaeologists additionally present a distorted view of prehistory when the majority of artefacts used to define the culture and chronology are the technologies of male-oriented tasks.

We do not 'know' any past culture – we know only tiny pieces of their economy, momentary glimpses of their religion and almost nothing of their humanity. Our knowledge is skewed not only by the differential preservation of their artefacts but also by the focus of our researches. We continue to place overwhelming reliance on our ability to derive meaningful information about past culture from artefacts whose importance to the cultural group is not adequately questioned. We equate technological processes, time invested in artefact production and aesthetic qualities of an artefact's final appearance with 'worth' and 'value' as filtered through our own ethnocentric myopia, and fail to acknowledge that these cultural biases are of our own construction. But there is nothing inherently 'significant' about an artefact, for, without context, an artefact has no scientific value and no scientific reality.

While artefacts are tangible relics of the past, the way they are viewed by indigenous populations and archaeologists is tempered by cultural differences. Archaeologists tend to focus on the physical, technological or esoteric attributes of an artefact, while indigenous populations tend to focus on the ritual or social importance of the artefacts.

The apparent dichotomy between the wishes of non-American Indian scientists and American Indian people is perhaps more of an unintended by-product of the reality of the current social situation. When Janet Spector asked, 'What are the ramifications of the fact that until fairly recently academic knowledge has been produced almost exclusively by white, middle-class men of European descent, socialized in cultures that discriminate on the basis of race, sex, and class?' (Spector, 2000: 134), she began an internal questioning that led her to become, 'acutely aware of the exclusion of Indian people from the creation of archaeological knowledge about their histories and cultures' (ibid.: 134). Archaeologists and indigenous people are working toward the same goal of protecting archaeological sites, although their motives for protecting those sites might be different.

> Indians wish to preserve archaeological sites... because these sites are an integral and irreplaceable part of their cultural identity and their history as a people ... to which they retain their links through legends and myths about the land and its people. Archaeologists and concerned non-Indians... wish to preserve and protect archaeological sites primarily to protect a nonrenewable data base that holds part of the record of human adaptive evolution. (Anyon, 1991: 216)

Scientists, on the other hand, view the past as information that should be available to everyone. They want to record, discuss and analyse the past so that they can bring it into the present, depersonalize it and then conveniently move on to another quest (the 'been there, done that, got the t-shirt' attitude). Until archaeologists realize and acknowledge the ways our cultural perceptions colour our research, we will be destined to continue our struggle to communicate the scientific significance of artefacts to indigenous populations.

FUNERARY ARTEFACTS

In the USA, a major problem in protecting grave sites and funerary artefacts is that American Indian grave localities are often considered to be abandoned since there are usually no visible grave markers. If a cemetery is abandoned, it is often no longer afforded protection, even though the abandonment might not have been voluntary.

From 1968 through 1970, a private collector named Leonard Charrier excavated what came to be known as the Tunica Treasure from numerous graves of Tunica Indians from the 18th century town of Trudeau, a well-known Tunica Indian village whose location had been lost over time. The collector 'excavated' the graves of the dead to obtain the artefacts that had been buried with them and offered the collection for sale. Ultimately, Charrier sued the owners of the land on which the archaeological site existed for the collection he had made under Louisiana's Treasure Trove law (Brain, 1979, 1988).

Under *Charrier v. Bell*, (496 So. 2d 601, La. Ct. App.), the Louisiana Supreme Court found that a burial ground discovered on private land was not considered abandoned and allowed descendants to prevent the disinterment of the deceased relatives. The Court made a distinction between loss and abandonment and ruled that funerary items found at the burial site were not 'abandoned' because the tribes that left them there did not do so with the intent that anyone could come and lay claim to the objects. The result of ruling otherwise would be that people could dig up graves the moment after they were filled.

In the USA, the sanctity of the grave is held as an important issue and, while burial protection statutes vary greatly (cf. Price, 1991; Yalung and Wala, 1992), most provide criminal punishment for the intentional disturbance of graves and associated funerary objects. Although a distinction between 'grave robbing' and 'archaeological excavation' has often been made, to many American Indian tribal groups it makes no difference whether the disturbance is caused by grave looters or by qualified archaeologists: 'To them, the only difference between an illegal ransacking of a burial ground and a scientific one is the time element, sun screen, little whisk brooms, and the neatness of the area when finished' (Mihesuah, 1996: 233).

SPIRO MOUNDS: A STUDY IN ARTEFACTUAL IMPORTANCE

The Spiro Mounds complex in the Arkansas River valley of eastern Oklahoma is perhaps one of the best-known mound complexes in the southeastern USA (Fagan, 1995: 444). 'Spiro is well known to southeastern archaeologists for two reasons: the extraordinarily rich litter burials of the elite and the shameless looting of the burial mounds during the Depression' (Bense, 1994: 223).

In 1935, two men hired unemployed coal miners to dig craters and tunnels into the mounds in search of artefacts and even resorted to dynamiting the mounds in an attempt to gain quicker access to the graves within them. As the rich archaeological materials became known, private collectors and museum agents converged on the site, with artefacts often being sold on the spot. Phillips and Brown (1978) offer a partial list of some of the grave goods found with the burials: monolithic stone axes, engraved shell cups and gorgets, shell and copper beads, freshwater pearls, carved stone pipes, fabric robes and even embossed copper plates. These artefacts are indeed special in their size and workmanship, but they are also funerary objects and grave goods.

Most of the artefacts pillaged from the Spiro Site were lost to private and museum collections throughout the world, but some still exist within the collections of the new Sam Noble Oklahoma Museum of Natural History on the campus of the University of Oklahoma. This new museum was constructed to replace the aging structures that made up the University's Stovall Museum of Natural History and to provide a new showcase for the artefacts that made up its collections. The museum questioned which current-day American Indian tribe (if any) should be considered culturally affiliated with the remains interred at Spiro Mound and the rightful 'owners' of the Spiro artefacts.

In discussing the identity of the inhabitants of the Spiro area, Wyckoff (1980: 533) recognized that, 'the post-A.D. 1400 remains from the Arkansas Basin are markedly different' from sites attributed to the historic Caddo Indians, and suggests, 'one or more of the Wichita tribes appear to be the most likely descendants of the Arkansas Basin Caddoans' (Wyckoff, 1980: 534). Rohrbaugh agrees that the people who had flourished at the Spiro cultural complex were most likely, 'the historic Kichai, a linguistically distinct group associated *at various times with both the southern Caddo and the Wichita*' (Rohrbaugh, 1982: 238–239, emphasis added).

On 10 December 1996, the President of the University of Oklahoma and the Director and

Curator of Anthropology of the Sam Noble Oklahoma Museum of Natural History met with the Chairman of the Caddo Tribe, the President of the Wichita Tribe and other elected officials of each tribe regarding the disposition of artefacts from Spiro Mound that were in the museum's possession.

The pronouncement that the museum wished to exhibit the Spiro artefacts in the new museum was met with mixed response. The Chairman of the Caddo Indian Tribe of Oklahoma noted that the artefacts were grave goods and indicated that the Caddo Tribe would eventually request the return of the artefacts for exhibit in the Heritage Centre of the Caddo Tribe, to demonstrate the high level of accomplishment of the Caddo tribe in the past and as a source of pride to contemporary tribal members. The President of the Wichita and Affiliated Tribes agreed with the Chairman of the Caddo Tribe that the artefacts were grave goods but felt that they should be reburied. In his opinion, the artefacts were not meant to be displayed but were meant to be away from the sight of individuals who had no right to view them.

And so the museum was placed in a dilemma. If the descendants of the Spiro Mounds are indeed the Kichai, should the Caddo or the Wichita have the authority to determine the ultimate use of the objects? University officials left the meeting with an idea of the complexity of options available to American Indian tribes regarding the disposition of grave goods, but they also left with the Spiro artefacts firmly within their control.

SUMMARY

In 1991, Knudson wrote: 'We all have a right to our past, and our past is the worldwide record of the human experience' (Knudson, 1991: 3). But while archaeologists expound the idea of a collective past, according to Zimmerman, in reality archaeologists want to maintain an upper hand. 'The problem is control. I sense that ... most archaeologists would be reluctant to relinquish control' (Zimmerman, 1995: 66).

So where do we go from here? We can continue to view artefacts as technological objects divorced from their cultures, or we can try to integrate their cultural context into the way we view them. We need to breathe life into cold, impersonal, objective science and to add humanity to our study of the human past. By involving indigenous populations in our research, we can take a step toward a truly worldwide archaeology.

Joe Watkins is an American Indian and an archaeologist. His primary research interest is the study of anthropology's relationships with descendant communities and aboriginal populations. He has a Ph.D. in archaeology from Southern Methodist University and was an archaeologist for the Anadarko Agency of the U.S. Bureau of Indian Affairs in Oklahoma prior to taking up a position at the University of New Mexico.

Contact address: Department of Anthropology, University of New Mexico, Albuquerque NM 87131, USA. Email: jwatkins@telepath.com

REFERENCES

Anyon, R. Protecting the past, protecting the present: cultural resources and American Indians. In Smith, G.S. and Ehrenhard, J.E. (eds) *Protecting the Past*. CRC Press, Boca Raton FL (1991) 215–222.

Bense, J.A. *Archaeology of the Southeastern United States: Paleoindian to World War I*. Academic Press, San Diego CA (1994).

Brain, J.P. Tunica treasure. *Archaeological and Ethnological papers of the Peabody Museum of Archaeology, Harvard University*. Harvard University Press, Cambridge MA **71** (1979).

Brain, J.P. Tunica archaeology. In *Archaeological and Ethnological papers of the Peabody Museum of Archaeology, Harvard University*. Harvard University Press, Cambridge MA **78** (1988).

Fagan, B.M. *Ancient North America: The Archaeology of a Continent*. Second Edition. Thames and Hudson, London (1995).

Knudson, R. The Archaeological Public Trust in context. In Smith, G.S. and Ehrenhard, J.E. (eds) *Protecting the Past*. CRC Press, Boca Raton FL (1991) 3–8.

Mihesuah, D.A. American Indians, anthropologists, pothunters, and repatriation: Ethical, religious, and political differences. *American Indian Quarterly* **20** (1996) 229–250.

Phillips, P. and Brown, J.A. *Pre-Columbian Shell Engravings from the Craig Mound at Spiro, Oklahoma*. Peabody Museum Press, Cambridge MA (1978).

Price, H.M., III. *Disputing the Dead*. University of Missouri Press, Columbia MI (1991).

Rohrbaugh, C.L. Spiro and Fort Coffee Phases: Changing Cultural Complexes of the Caddoan Area. Unpublished Ph.D. dissertation, University of Wisconsin-Madison, University Microfilms, Ann Arbor (1982).

Spector, J.D. Collaboration at Inyan Ceyaka Atonwan (Village at the Rapids). In Dongoske, K.E., Aldenderfer, M. and Doehner, K. (eds) *Working Together: Native Americans and Archaeologists*. Society for American Archaeology, Washington DC (2000) 133–138.

Wobst, H.M. Matter over mind: perishables and the glorification of materiality in archaeology. In Drooker, P.B. (ed.) *Fleeting Identities: Perishable Material Culture in Archaeological Research*. Center for Archaeological Investigations, Southern Illinois University, Carbondale IL (2001) 43–57.

Wyckoff, D. Caddoan Adaptive Strategies in the Arkansas Basin, Eastern Oklahoma. Unpublished Ph.D. dissertation, University of Washington, Pullman. University Microfilms, Ann Arbor (1980).

Yalung, C.B. and Wala, L.I. Statutory survey: a survey of state repatriation and burial protection statutes. *Arizona State Law Journal* 24 (1992) 419–433.

Zimmerman, L. Regaining our nerve: ethics, values, and the transformation of archaeology. In Lynott, M.J. and Wylie, A. (eds) *Ethics in American Archaeology: Challenges for the 1990s*. Society for American Archaeology, Washington DC (1995) 64–67.

Honour thy ancestor's possessions

Edward Halealoha Ayau

ABSTRACT

This article addresses the ethics of reclaiming *moepū* (funerary items) for reburial. It centres around a case involving *moepū* that were removed from a burial cave, conserved by the Bernice Pauahi Bishop Museum, and reburied. Most significant amongst the funerary items removed from the burial cave were four carved wood images of ancestral deities called *kiʻi aumākua* and other personal possessions of high-ranking chiefs. To explain the traditional practice of placing items with the dead, an overview of the traditional role of *moepū* is provided. Two opposing perspectives in response to the reburial are then presented. The article concludes that, as with *iwi kūpuna* (ancestral bones), the conservation of *moepū* is improper and museums should support efforts to return them to their deceased owners. Only by restoring *moepū* to their original context – and thereby their original function – can the responsibility of caring for the ancestors be properly maintained and higher levels of traditional cultural understanding be achieved.

THOU SHALT NOT STEAL

In 1905, David Forbes, William Wagner and Friedrich Haenisch explored a burial cave located on the island of Hawaiʻi. Commonly referred to as 'Forbes Cave' the true identity of this cave was kept *huna* (secret) and not otherwise recorded in Hawaiian history. Several mummified *iwi kūpuna* (ancestral bones) and *moepū* of high-ranking chiefs were consequently looted. Forbes, a lawyer and part-time judge, sketched a plan of the cave interior indicating its chambers and the locations of its significant contents (Brigham, 1906: 3). The plan established the funerary function of the items including four *kiʻi aumākua* (carved wood images of ancestral deities). The four *kiʻi aumākua* were situated immediately fronting a cache of *iwi poʻo* (skulls) in a sealed chamber.

A few days later, Forbes wrote to William T. Brigham, Director of the Bernice Pauahi Bishop Museum in Honolulu, to inform him about the 'collected' items and to ask if the museum was interested in purchasing the prized collection. Forbes included with his letter a photograph of the stolen funerary items (Forbes, 1905: 1). In his reply, Brigham confirmed his awareness that the funerary items were illicitly acquired, cautioned Forbes about the severity of existing burial laws and offered the museum as the ideal location to hide the theft:

> [y]our find is of great interest and importance, but is impossible to put a price upon the articles without a careful inspection ... In the meantime, keep the matter quiet for there are severe laws here concerning burial caves, and I shall not make the matter public, of course, until you say so. If you should wish to keep the collection or part of it, the coming from this place [Bishop Museum] would throw any suspicious persons off the scent. (W. Brigham to D. Forbes, 11 November 1905, Bernice Pauahi Museum Archives)

Later Brigham wrote to Forbes with an appraisal of the collection of stolen human remains and funerary items (W. Brigham to D. Forbes, 21 November 1905, Bernice Pauahi Museum Archives). Eventually, Bringham acquired the majority of the Forbes Cave collection for the Bernice Pauahi Bishop Museum, including three of the *kiʻi aumākua*. There was some doubt expressed as to whether the carved wood images were, in fact, funerary. It was postulated that the images were temporarily placed in the cave for the purpose of safe-keeping following the fall of the traditional Hawaiian religious system. Brigham promptly dismissed these assertions as baseless when he stated in a 1906 museum report,

> [i]t has been suggested that [the four wood images] form the paraphernalia of a temple and were hidden, as so many of the idols were, at the time of the general destruction of the idols in 1819 in the hope that the storm would blow over and better times ensue, but there is absolutely nothing in the collection to support such a view. The two gods or aumakua were household deities, the other articles might be the private property of some chief or priest, and two things, the fan and bit of porcelain are such keepsakes as were commonly deposited with the dead to whom the articles had belonged. (Brigham, 1906: 3)

Interestingly, Brigham acknowledges the understanding that the funerary items were owned originally by the deceased with whom they were placed.

The actions of the Bernice Pauahi Bishop Museum and Hui Mālama I Nā Kūpuna O Hawaiʻi Nei were the topic of a heated debate 95 years later, following the reburial of the Forbes Cave collection.[1] The debate pitted traditional cultural values of respecting the deceased and their possessions through reburial against contemporary demands for continued museum conservation to educate and inspire the living regarding significant works of art.

HOʻOMOEPŪ ʻIA (PLACED WITH THE DEAD)

In Hawaiʻi, from ancient times, items were placed with the deceased as a sign of respect and affection. These would include a person's favourite keepsakes as well as items intended to provide nourishment, comfort and protection in the next world. These items were fondly referred to as *moepū*, which means 'to sleep with', and were considered *kapu* (sacred), possessing *mana* (spiritual essence, power) and vital to the *pono* (balance, well-being) of our ancestors and ourselves.

Once placed together, the *moepū* belonged to the deceased. This relationship was considered permanent in that the items served the needs of the ancestors in the afterworld until the long journey toward complete deterioration resulted in a melding of elements with the land and a completion of the cycle of life. An *ʻolelo noʻeau* (wise saying) provides insight into how native Hawaiians traditionally viewed the sanctity of *moepū* by prohibiting their removal.

> *Mai lawe wale i nā mea i hoʻomoepū ʻia.*
> Don't wantonly take things placed with the dead.

Implicit in this *ʻolelo noʻeau* was the respect given to the original decision to place the items with the dead. There was a recognition that the relationship between the *iwi kūpuna* and *moepū* is to be maintained as part of the requisite care and protection provided to the *kūpuna* (ancestors). The removal of *moepū* by one who was not part of the original placement was considered an egregious transgression against the individual and a violation of the sanctity of the grave.

Pualani Kanakaʻole Kanahele, a Native Hawaiian *kumu* (cultural resource leader) provided further insight into *moepū* when she discussed cultural traditions relating to items placed with the dead, including deceased high-ranking chiefs,

> [t]he interdependency of life cycles was well thought out and practiced among our *kūpuna* [ancestors]. The care of an individual from prenatal to post life was an established process. Especially if the person was of high rank or highly regarded because he/she had proven themselves and was accepted by the greater population for his/her intelligence and skill. The post-physical existence of an individual would require his/her personal acquisitions. Funerary objects are personal articles for the individuals who have passed from this temporal life into the next realm. Some of these acquisitions were for the purpose of protection, others were personal favorites, others to honor the rank and responsibility of the individual, others were gifts from family members to the deceased, others were gifts to the ancestors who were waiting on the other side... (Kanahele and Ayau, 1999: 8).

Burial imbues the land[2] with the *mana* (spiritual essence) of the people and their possessions, which is necessary for the physical and spiritual nourishment of the living. *Moepū* belong to the *iwi kūpuna* and both belong to *pā'ele'ele*, the darkest of darkness and to the Earth Mother *Haumea*. The *kuleana* (responsibility) of the living is to respect their final resting-places and maintain the integrity of their funerary possessions.

HONOUR THY ANCESTORS' CHOICES

Pursuant to a Federal law, the Native American Graves Protection and Repatriation Act (NAGPRA), the Bernice Pauahi Bishop Museum consulted with Hui Mālama I Nā Kūpuna O Hawai'i Nei[3] and other interested Native Hawaiian organizations over a period of seven years regarding the classification of the cultural items removed from Forbes Cave. Consultation culminated with the decision to classify the items as funerary objects, thereby qualifying them for repatriation. The Bernice Pauahi Bishop Museum allowed us to transport the *iwi kūpuna* and *moepū* back to the island of Hawai'i. In order to restore *pono*, we ceremonially reburied them and secured the site.

In completing reburial, Hui Mālama I Nā Kūpuna O Hawai'i Nei honoured the original decisions made by the ancestors to place the *iwi kūpuna* and *moepū* together. Our actions were founded on the traditional understanding that *moepū* are the inalienable possessions of the dead and are meant to be buried. Where these have been removed from their intended resting place, Native Hawaiians have a duty to restore *moepū* to their originally intended function.

Pualani Kanaka'ole Kanahele provides further insight into the treatment of *moepū* and the interdependence between the past, the living and the future:

> [f]unerary objects are very personal to the individual, who through his/her lifetime has done all the requirements to earn these objects. They knew the depth and breadth of the value, merit, function and use of these things. It is not for us, who live at this time, to decide the fate of these objects. The decision was made long ago when the personal articles were placed in the cave. As Hawaiians today, our function is simple, it is to see that the initial decision is realized and respected. Let's respect the wise practices of our ancestors as we hope that our progeny will see the wisdom in our decisions and practices. (Kanahele and Ayau, 1999: 9)

Many understood and supported the actions taken by Hui Mālama I Nā Kūpuna O Hawai'i Nei. Their response to the reburial of the Forbes Cave collection was that the reunification of the *iwi kūpuna* and *moepū* should be honoured as a necessary element of the responsibility to provide care and protection. However, not all agreed that traditional treatment was proper.

CONSERVATION PROVIDES FOR THE LIVING

Some people felt that the interests and needs of contemporary Native Hawaiians, researchers and the general public would be better served through the continued conservation of these items by the Bernice Pauahi Bishop Museum, regardless of their intended funerary nature. The educational value derived from studies, contemplation and inspiration represented *bona fide* benefits such that the important needs of the living should be allowed to outweigh traditional funerary practices.

The people who advocate this contemporary view maintain that there is always a responsibility to ensure that the *iwi kūpuna* and *moepū* are well cared for, but that significant examples of items such as the *ki'i aumākua* should be exempted from traditional treatment. Although the separation of outstanding *moepū* from the *iwi kūpuna* for the benefit of the living represented a departure from tradition, these people consider this change a necessary step in the evolution of Native Hawaiian culture. The carved wood images should be considered masterpieces of indigenous craftsmanship and not the personal possessions of the dead. As such, presentation and preservation through museum conservation is regarded as the most responsible treatment of *ki'i aumākua* today (Kalāhiki, 2000). Many people have even justified museum conservation on the basis that the four *ki'i aumākua* were not funerary at all, having been placed in the cave for safe-keeping. This view ignored the placement of the carvings with the *iwi kūpuna*.

Opposition to the reburial of the Forbes Cave collection sought to shift the focus from the needs of the dead to those of the living, even though implementation of this contemporary view would have required a second looting of the *moepū*. The merits of these two opposing positions were carefully considered.

THE COST OF CULTURAL SURVIVAL

The contemporary view reflects the Western practice of objectifying *moepū* as artefacts with inherent educational value, rather than as items intended to serve specific needs of the deceased. The question becomes whether it is healthy for Native Hawaiians to embrace this departure from traditional thought. Specifically, 'should the educational and inspirational needs of the living, including academics and the general public, be allowed to supersede the personal funerary wishes of deceased Native Hawaiians?'. The answer is: 'absolutely not'.

It seems that what were once fundamental values and beliefs to the ancestors regarding funerary practices are now foreign to many in the contemporary generation. It is in this climate, where a lack of understanding of cultural tradition, supported by colonized attitudes toward knowledge and learning, has given rise to a shift in focus from providing care to the ancestors to demanding a benefit from them. Despite the appearance of striving to increase cultural knowledge, implementation of the actions required by those who support the contemporary view would seriously undermine the ancestral foundation. In addition, advocating such a position is contrary to the traditional values and fundamental principles prohibiting the wanton taking of items placed with the dead.

Living Native Hawaiians have inherited the *kuleana* (responsibility) to care for the well-being of our *kūpuna* and their possessions. We have also inherited countless cultural items from our ancestors that serve to educate, inspire and provide insights into our identity as a people. There was a time when it was instinctually understood that such cultural items did not include *iwi* and *moepū* as those belong solely to the *kūpuna*. Moreover, it was understood that our duty is to assure that the *iwi kūpuna* and *moepū* are properly buried and protected so that the centuries-long process of deterioration and eventual absorption back into the land may take place undisturbed.

Educational and inspirational needs are best served by learning foundational traditions and respecting and maintaining them. In doing so, we preserve the integrity of the decision to place the items with the deceased, and come to understand that such an act is a necessary element of the requisite duty of care and protection owed to the ancestors. Rather than teach our children how a *ki'i aumākua* was carved and the materials used to complete the image, we instead impress upon them the importance of respecting the choice made to place the carving with the *iwi* and the values that support such a tradition. Furthermore, we should resist the temptation to impose our contemporary views upon the *kūpuna* and instead seek to achieve higher levels of cultural understanding through adherence to critical elements of our traditional practice.

MOEPŪ CONSERVATION IS IMPROPER

The Bernice Pauahi Bishop Museum was correct in identifying the items as funerary objects as defined by NAGPRA, based upon the available evidence. Moreover, the museum was also *pono* in allowing the *iwi kūpuna* and *moepū* to be reburied, recognizing that the continued conservation of both were inappropriate as a matter of Federal law, and as a matter of respect for Native Hawaiian cultural traditions. Through reburial, the Bernice Pauahi Bishop Museum was able to rectify and bring closure to the actions of its former Director who was complicit in the theft of these funerary items by David Forbes and others.

Based on the traditional view, it is concluded that museum conservation of *moepū*, as with *iwi kūpuna*, is wholly inappropriate. Museums conserving Native Hawaiian funerary items should honour requests for reburial. Science needs to temper its thirst for knowledge, recognize that the acquisition of data is a value and not a right and should not be conducted at the expense of traditional cultural responsibilities. Moreover, Native Hawaiians need to discipline their minds to understand that the removal and conservation of *moepū* does not honour our ancestors, or ourselves, and does not result in *pono* or *lōkahi* (unity) between the past and present. An important lesson learned from this case is that we must not seek to preserve our culture at the expense of undermining foundational cultural traditions and offending our ancestors.

As Pualani Kanaka'ole Kanahele profoundly stated, the function of Native Hawaiians today regarding *moepū* is simple. It is to see that the initial decision by the ancestors is realized and respected. Moreover, it is that we do this in the hope that our descendants will see the wisdom in our decisions and practices. Maintaining the integrity of the relationship between the *iwi kūpuna* and *moepū* through reburial is an important means through which we maintain *pono* between the past, the present and the future. *Mai lawe wale i nā mea i ho'omoepū 'ia.*

ENDNOTES

1. Some of the funerary items from the Forbes Cave collection, including the fourth *ki'i aumākua*, are currently being conserved by Hawai'i Volcanoes National Park after being donated by B. Edmondson, daughter of David Forbes in 1956 (Wosky, 1956: 1–2; Cleghorn, 1996: 4–10).
2. The word for homeland in the Hawaiian language is *kulāiwi* which literally translates as 'bone plain'. The homeland therefore was considered to be the land with the buried bones of the ancestors.
3. A Native Hawaiian organization established in 1988 to provide requisite care and protection to *iwi kūpuna* and *moepū* through repatriation and ceremonial reburial utilizing traditional cultural protocols. Edward and Pualani Kanahele founded the organization.

Edward Halealoha Ayau is a graduate of Kamehameha Schools, the University of Redlands and the Colorado School of Law. He has worked for the Native American Rights Fund, Native Hawaiian Legal Corporation, US Senator Daniel Inouye, the US Senate Indian Affairs Committee and is the former director of the State Burial Sites Programme. He is a member of Hui Mālama I Nā Kūpuna O Hawai'i Nei, where he leads efforts to repatriate Native Hawaiian remains and funerary objects.

Contact address: P.O. Box 365, Ho'olehua, Hawai'i 96729. Email: halealoha@wave.hicv.net

REFERENCES

Brigham, W.T. *Memoirs of the Bernice Pauahi Bishop Museum, II (2)*. Bishop Museum Press, Honolulu (1906).

Cleghorn, J. Hawai'i National Parks NAGPRA Cultural Affiliation Project. Unpublished National Park Service Files (1996).

Forbes, D. Letter to William Brigham, 7 November. Bernice Pauahi Bishop Museum Archives (1905) Unpublished.

Kalahiki, M. Getting items back. First step to healing. *The Honolulu Advertiser* 16 April (2000).

Kanahele, P.K. and Ayau, E.H. *Proper Disposition: Relating to the Repatriation of all Funerary Objects Removed from Three Burial Caves in Honnokoa Gulch Kawaihae, Island of Hawai'i*. For consideration by the trustees of the Office of Hawaiian Affairs & Commissioners of the Department of Hawaiian Home Lands 24 November (1999) 1–14.

Wosky, J.B. Letter to Mrs Harry Edmondson, dated 14 March 1956. Hawai'i National Park Service Files (1956) Unpublished.

Indigenous claims and heritage conservation:
an opportunity for critical dialogue

Glenn Wharton

ABSTRACT

Indigenous claims of ownership and access to material culture challenge the field of heritage conservation. This article illustrates how indigenous concerns conflict with basic constructs of Western conservation, and how conservators respond to these claims. Despite efforts of inclusion, relatively few conservation projects integrate indigenous knowledge with scientific research. Redistribution of conservation authority is rarely put into practice. The article concludes by pointing to conservation as a meeting ground where collaborative decisions can be made about material culture on display. Conflict negotiation in conservation presents a potential forum for cultural representation and contested meaning of objects on display.

INTRODUCTION

In their routine work, conservators physically alter artefacts and cultural sites in the name of preservation. Their choice of what to conserve and how to conserve it affects our perceptions of exhibited material culture. Through their interventions, they inevitably perpetuate their own assumptions about the world. Conservators from dominant cultures are often unaware of this power to shape the way objects and cultures are understood, and of cultural lenses that filter their own perceptions and decisions.

Western conservation focuses attention on objects rather than the cultures that create and continue to use them. This orientation derives from a principle belief in scientific conservation (Clavir, 1998; Pye, 2001; Gilberg and Vivian, 2001). It also comes from the conception of museums and archaeological excavations as storehouses of data, where *finds* are removed from their social context and given new meaning as display objects and sources of information.

Indigenous responses to conservation include opposition to cleaning, reconstruction and routine care of artefacts and cultural sites. These reactions derive from cultural practices that conflict with static representations and display of material culture, but they are not necessarily presented in a single voice, and vary from one culture to another.

> There is not a single item in Zuni culture which is used for religious or ceremonial purposes which is meant to be preserved in perpetuity. All are gifts to the Gods which are meant to disintegrate back into the earth to do their work. (Ed Ladd, quoted in Clavir, 1997: 177)

A different perspective is provided by a Maori conservator:

> It is ... patronizing to assume that indigenous people necessarily believe that all their works should complete a natural cycle and be allowed to degrade and eventually return to the soil. Like other people, Maori wish to keep records of their achievements and history. (Heikell *et al.*, 1995: 15)

Some conservators integrate these conflicting criteria into their practice. Odegaard (1996: 122) reports from her work with Native American collections at the University of Arizona, 'while the dolls of the Zuni and Hopi may receive conservation treatment, the Kachina dolls of the other pueblos should not'.

Although surface cleaning is inappropriate for some artefacts, leaving 'ethnographic dirt' as evidence of use is patronizing to others – particularly when the same institution exhibits pristine materials from dominant cultures. The act of physical preservation conflicts with some cultural practices, including ritual destruction of Northwest American dance masks, and gradual deterioration of sacred Apache objects (Moses, 1992: 3). Other challenges to institutionalized conservation include traditional indigenous systems of care, such as ceremonial maintenance of Plains Indian sacred bundles and care of Iroquois false face masks and wampum belts (ibid.: 3).

CHALLENGING MODERN CONSERVATION

In this short paper, I address two fundamental constructs in conservation that come into conflict with indigenous claims. The first is the underlying *ethos* of 'physical preservation', in which material longevity is an assumed goal. This driving force leads to an emphasis on material analysis over cultural analysis in order to resolve problems of deterioration. The aim of most conservation analysis is to develop methods of intervention and environmental stabilization to maximize physical preservation.

The second construct is the presumed authentic, original value embodied in material culture. Conservation literature and guidelines for practice frequently refer to the preservation of 'artist's intent', the 'intrinsic nature' or the 'essence' of the object (Clavir, 1998). As Keene points out, 'At the foundation of the conservation ethic lies the precept "thou shalt not change the nature of the object"' (Keene, 1994:19).

This essentializing of the object, and search for authenticity in either its origin or a fixed moment in its history, is challenged by recent material culture scholarship on the dynamic and contested nature of things. Based on this literature, it is helpful to think of objects as 'slow events' rather than static manifestations.[1] Authenticity is found not only in some original or genuine state, but in every stage of an object's life, including its representations and facsimiles, and the relationships it has with its surrounding community.

CONSERVATION RESPONSE

The challenge posed by these differing perspectives on conservation is not as large as it may seem. Considering complex sets of conflicting values is not new to Western conservation. Arguments for honouring physical change and recognizing historical palimpsest of the built environment continue since the late 19th century (Ruskin, [1883] 1989; Riegl, [1903] 1996; Jokilehto, 1999). The practice of actively using museum artefacts is also argued in the context of functional objects such as trains, clocks and musical instruments (Mapes, 1991; Barclay, 2004).

The principles and practice of conservation are far from immutable. In fact, over the past decade the field has begun responding to claims from indigenous representatives and relativist notions of material culture. The growing body of conservation literature reflects these responses. It is beyond the scope of this article to fully analyse changes in conservation theory and practice. Instead, I provide several examples within three different arenas: revisions to charters and guidelines for practice, collaboration in the conservation process and the transfer of conservation decision-making to indigenous groups.

REVISIONS TO CHARTERS AND GUIDELINES

Conservation charters and guidelines produced throughout the 1990s incorporated an increased recognition of social values embedded in material culture (Sease, 1998; Clavir, 2001; Federspiel, 2001). The Australian *Burra Charter* broadened the scope of conservation for cultural sites to include 'all the processes of looking after a place so as to retain its cultural significance' (Marquis-Kyle and Walker, 1992; Truscott and Young, 2000). The implication of this change is that the significance of material culture may be found in its uses, associations and meanings, as well as its physical fabric. The charter encourages the co-existence of cultural values, especially where they are in conflict (Truscott and Young, 2000: Article 13).

Global heritage agencies – ICOMOS, ICCROM, ICOM and the World Heritage Organization – similarly expanded their criteria for site conservation during the 1990s to include the concerns of living traditions and active use of cultural sites (Bell, 1997; Federspiel, 1999; Cleere, 2001). The 'test for authenticity' in the World Heritage Convention guidelines was challenged for its inattention to cultural values when a Shinto shrine in Japan was rejected because it is traditionally dismantled and renovated every twenty years (Larsen, 1995). The resulting *Nara Document on Authenticity* (1994) widens the scope of authenticity to include cultural traditions, and helps shift the focus from 'universal value' towards 'local interpretation' (Larsen, 1995).

Charters and guidelines for conserving movable objects were redrafted in recent years. Reference to conserving 'intangible values' and the 'conceptual integrity' of objects are now in national codes of ethics for museum and archaeological conservators (Sease, 1998). Yet these changes scarcely reach the level of the practicing conservator. There are few examples in the literature of sharing conservation authority by placing indigenous knowledge on a par with scientific research. As advocated by a Delaware/Mohawk conservator, 'Euro-North American museum workers should look upon Native elders and recognized spiritual leaders as a professional resource in their efforts to obtain a more complete understanding of the Native materials they come in contact with' (Moses, 1992: 3).

COLLABORATION IN THE CONSERVATION PROCESS

Some conservators call for an interdisciplinary and cross-cultural approach to conservation decision-making (Odegaard, 1995). Odegaard outlines a 'matrix' model for conservation analysis, which integrates tangible and intangible information into conservation planning (Odegaard, 1996). In addition to material criteria for her model, she adds such elements as cultural context, current indigenous issues and perspectives, and use of objects by indigenous people in ceremony and celebration.

One of the few institutional models for meaningful collaboration in conservation exists at the Smithsonian's National Museum of the American Indian (NMAI).[2] Conservators at the NMAI work with spiritual leaders and artists to develop jointly conservation procedures (Drumheller and Kaminitz, 1994; Johnson *et al.*, 2003). One such project at the NMAI was the conservation of a 19th century Tuscarora beaded textile, in which a Tuscarora curator considered it an affront to exhibit their material culture with signs of deterioration and loss.[3] Using some beads from the textile and other beads of similar age, beadworkers on the Tuscarora Reservation rewove missing and damaged areas (Heald, 1997). The use of historic beads and indigenous skills in restoring museum artefacts contradicts fundamental conservation ethics of minimal intervention and re-use of 'original' materials. This collaborative project produced dialogue on conflicts between museum and Tuscarora values such as reversibility of conservation procedures, re-use of historic materials and extensive restoration. The project cultivated wider public interest through local media coverage and participation of Tuscarora school children.

The recent conservation of the bomb-damaged Temple of the Tooth in Sri Lanka similarly engaged professional conservators, government representatives, high priests and the lay guardian in dialogue over questions of minimal intervention and aggressive restoration (Wijesuriya, 2000). Underlying the complex negotiations were conflicts between the interests of religious pilgrims who preferred rendering the site as if no damage had occurred and those who argued for leaving the repairs visible. Some argued that visible cracks and repairs serve as testimony to the politically motivated damage to the temple.[4] The process of discussion and decision-making provided a platform for negotiating different opinions. Some damaged elements were completely replaced, such as carved stone elephants, whereas certain wall paintings were conserved following Western methods, which visually distinguished restorations from original painted images.

TRANSFER OF DECISION-MAKING TO INDIGENOUS GROUPS

The transfer of conservation authority to indigenous representatives rarely takes place on a voluntary basis. In some cases, legal action under legislation such as the US *Native American Graves Protection and Repatriation Act* (NAGPRA, 1990) successfully transfers ownership and care of burial materials to designated indigenous groups. In some instances repatriated objects are reburied and in others they are cared for using traditional or Western methods.

The Cultural Conservation Advisory Council in New Zealand sponsored a programme to train a group of Maori conservators in Western conservation methods (Clavir, 2002). Through her interviews with these conservators, Clavir documents how conflicts such as 'use versus preservation' and access to collections are processed within the context of Maori control (Clavir, 2002). *Kaumatua* (elders knowledgeable in Maori protocols and culture) are consulted, and physical risks to objects are tempered with Maori socio-cultural considerations. 'Because the conservators believe in the importance of both the tangible and intangible aspects of the object, they have altered the conventional conservation approach to treating the objects to ensure their preservation, in both the western sense of stopping deterioration and in the indigenous sense of continuation of cultural life' (Clavir, 1997: 409).

Interesting reversals and further conflicts arise when indigenous conservators work on colonial material culture, and when mixed-race individuals confront internal conflicts based on cultural difference. David Yubeta, whose mother is Native American and whose father is Mexican, describes difficulties in training Native Americans and Mexican Americans in caring for historic adobe structures within the US National Park Service.[5] He finds it hard to attract course participants, reporting a lack of interest, deep ambivalence for entering a 'blue collar' profession with low pay, and frustration in preserving colonial structures that symbolize the attempted destruction of Native American culture. He also describes his own internal conflict, as his mother's culture sees material decay as part of a natural cycle and his father's culture honours the Spanish/Christian history that adobe structures represent.

CONSERVATION AS AN OPPORTUNITY FOR DIALOGUE

Written guidelines alone fail to provide clear direction for practice in cases of profound and complex conflicts of interest. As Tarlow (2000) argues in the case of archaeology, codes of ethics are inevitably historical and contextual, and ethical dilemmas should be debated and discussed rather than resolved through application of rules. This is emphatically true in the realm of conservation, where actors have the power to alter the way material culture is represented, and how the past is known.

Just as models of public archaeology shift focus from 'product' to 'process' and from 'object' to 'community', drawing attention to conflicts in conservation provides stimulus for larger public dialogue. Public archaeology employs the archaeological process to engage discourse on how the past is used (Schadla-Hall, 1999; Ascherson, 2000). It seeks to provide a critical framework for archaeology that includes the political and socio-economic structures in which it operates, and promotes debate on nationalism, ethnicity, legislation and tourism. A similar *participatory conservation* has the potential for critical dialogue on how material culture is preserved, presented and used (Wharton, 2002). As yet, there is little evidence of conservation being purposefully used to stimulate debate on cultural rights and regeneration of indigenous cultures. As conservation increasingly shares and transfers its authority in response to indigenous claims, it may look to models of public archaeology to engender local empowerment and cultural revitalization.

ACKNOWLEDGEMENTS

I thank Nick Merriman, Nicholas Stanley-Price and Clifford Price for their advice on my research performed at the Institute of Archaeology, University College London. I also thank the following conservators for their thoughtful comments used in developing ideas for this article: Miriam Clavir, Ronald Harvey, Jessica Johnson, Marian Kaminitz, Kelly McHugh, Nancy Odegaard, Elizabeth Pye, Dean Sully, Kathy Tubb, Jagath Weerasinghe and Gamini Wijesuriya.

ENDNOTES

1. The description of an object as a 'slow event' was made in communication with Katharine Young (University of California, Berkeley) 5 November 2001, who reports that it was formulated but never published by Stanley Eveling (University of Edinburgh, now deceased).
2. Marian Kaminitz (National Museum of the American Indian), personal communication, 1 June 2001.
3. Susan Heald (National Museum of the American Indian), personal communication, 31 October 2001.

4. From communications with Gamini Wijesuriya, Siran Deraniyagala and Jagath Weerasinghe (Department of Archaeology of the Government of Sri Lanka), 20–23 May 1999.
5. David Yubeta (Tumacacori National Historical Park, Tumacacori, Arizona), personal communication, 21 October 2001.

Glenn Wharton is a Research Scholar at the Institute of Fine Art's Conservation Center and the Museum Studies programme at New York University. He is a practicing conservator with current research interests in conserving contested monuments, documenting contemporary artists' views on longevity and public participation in the conservation process.

Contact address: Museum Studies/Conservation Center of the Institute of Fine Arts, New York University, 240 Greene Street, Suite 400, New York NY 10003-6675, USA. Email: glenn.wharton@nyu.edu

REFERENCES

Ascherson, N. Editorial. *Public Archaeology* 1 (2000) 1–4.
Barclay, R. *The Preservation and Use of Historic Musical Instruments: Display Case or Concert Hall*. Earthscan (James & James) Publications, London (2004).
Bell, D. *Guide to International Conservation Charters, Technical Advice Note 8*. Historic Scotland, Edinburgh (1997).
Clavir, M. Preserving What is Valued: An Analysis of Museum Conservation and First Nations Perspectives. Unpublished Ph.D. Thesis. Department of Museum Studies, University of Leicester (1997).
Clavir, M. The social and historic construction of professional values in conservation. *Studies in Conservation* 43 (1998) 1–8.
Clavir, M. The future of ethnographic conservation: a Canadian perspective. In Oddy, A. and Smith, S. (eds) *Past Practice – Future Prospects*. The British Museum Occasional Paper Number 145. British Museum Press, London (2001) 57–60.
Clavir, M. *Preserving What is Valued: Museums, Conservation and First Nations*. University of British Columbia Press, Vancouver (2002).
Cleere, H. The uneasy bedfellows: universality and cultural heritage. In Layton, R., Stone, P.G. and Thomas, J. (eds) *Destruction and Conservation of Cultural Property*. One World Archaeology Series. Routledge, London (2001) 22–29.
Drumheller, A. and Kaminitz, M. Traditional care and conservation, the merging of two disciplines at the National Museum of the American Indian. In Roy, A. and Smith, P. (eds) *Preventive Conservation, Practice* *Theory and Research. Preprints of the Contributions to the Ottawa Congress September 1994*. International Institute for Conservation, London (1994) 58–60.
Federspiel, B. Our creative diversity and contemporary issues in conservation. In Bridgeland, J. (ed.) *Preprints for the ICOM Committee for Conservation 12th Triennial Meeting, Lyon 29 August–3 September 1999*. James & James, London (1999) 166–171.
Federspiel, B. The definition of the conservation profession and its field of operation: issues in the 21st century. In Oddy, A. and Smith, S. (eds) *Past Practice – Future Prospects*. The British Museum Occasional Paper Number 145. British Museum, London (2001) 5–12.
Gilberg, M. and Vivian, D. The rise of conservation science in archaeology (1830–1930). In Oddy, A. and Smith, S. (eds) *Past Practice – Future Prospects*. The British Museum Occasional Paper Number 145. The British Museum, London (2001) 87–94.
Heald, S. Compensation/restoration of a Tuscarora beaded cloth with Tuscarora beadworkers. *AIC Textile Specialty Group Postprints*. American Institute for Conservation, Washington DC (1997) 35–38.
Heikell, V., Whiting, D., Clavir, M., Odegaard, N., Kaminitz, M. and Moses, J. The conservator's approach to sacred art. *Newsletter of the Western Association for Art Conservation* (WAAC) 17 (1995) 15–18.
Johnson, J.S., Heald, S., McHugh, K., Brown, E. and Kaminitz, M. Practical aspects of consultation with communities. *AIC Objects Specialty Group Postprints*. Vol. 10. American Institute for Conservation, Washington DC (2003) 43–48.
Jokilehto, J. *A History of Architectural Conservation*. Butterworth Heinemann, Oxford (1999).
Keene, S. Objects as systems: a new challenge for conservation. In Oddy, A. (ed.) *Restoration: Is It Acceptable?* Occasional Paper No. 99. The British Museum, London (1994) 19–26.
Larsen K.E. (ed.) *NARA Conference on Authenticity in Relation to the World Heritage Convention, Nara, Japan 1–6 November 1994*. UNESCO World Heritage Centre, Agency for Cultural Affairs; ICCROM; ICOMOS, Tokyo (1995).
Mapes, M.G. (ed.) *Risks and Rewards: Perspectives on Operating Mechanical Artefacts. Publication of a Workshop on Feb 22, 1991*. Hagley Museum and Library, Wilmington DE (1991).
Marquis-Kyle, P. and Walker, M. *The Illustrated Burra Charter*. Australia ICOMOS, Sydney, http://www.icomos.org/australia (1992).
Moses, J. Indigenous perspectives on conservation. *Newsletter. International Institute for Conservation – Canadian Group* 17 (1992) 1–4.
Native American Graves Protection and Repatriation Act (NAGPRA). US Department of Interior Bureau of Reclamation. http://www.usbr.gov/nagpra/ (accessed 1 August 2002).
Odegaard, N.N. Artists' intent: material culture studies and conservation *Journal of the American Institute for Conservation* 34 (1995) 187–193.

Odegaard, N.N. Archaeological and ethnographic painted wood artefacts from the North American Southwest: the case study of a matrix approach for the conservation of cultural materials. Unpublished Ph.D. Thesis. University of Canberra, Department of Applied Science (1996).

Pye, E. *Caring for the Past Issues in Conservation for Archaeology and Museums.* James & James, London (2001).

Riegl, A. The modern cult of monuments: its essence and its development. In Stanley Price, N., Talley, M.K. and Vaccaro, A.M. (eds) *Historical and Philosophical Issues in the Conservation of Cultural Heritage.* The Getty Conservation Institute, Los Angeles CA [1903] (1996) 69–83.

Ruskin, J. *The Seven Lamps of Architecture.* Dover, Toronto [1883] (1989).

Schadla-Hall, T. Editorial: public archaeology. *European Journal of Archaeology* 2 (1999) 147–158.

Sease, C. Codes of ethics for conservation. *International Journal of Cultural Property* 7 (1998) 98–114.

Tarlow, S. Decoding ethics. *Public Archaeology* 1 (2000) 245–259.

Truscott, M. and Young, D. Revising the Burra Charter. Australia ICOMOS updates its guidelines for conservation practice. *Conservation and Management of Archaeological Sites* 4 (2000) 101–116.

Wharton, G. Conserving the Kamehameha I Monument in Hawai'i: a case study in public conservation. In *Preprints for the ICOM Committee for Conservation 13th Triennial Meeting Rio de Janeiro.* James & James Scientific Publishers, London (2002) 203–208.

Wijesuriya, G. Conserving the Temple of the Tooth Relic. *Public Archaeology* 1 (2000) 99–108.

Applied archaeology:
revitalizing indigenous agricultural technology within an Andean community

Ann Kendall

ABSTRACT

In many parts of the world European colonization, and more recent social and economic change, has radically altered and, in some cases, decimated both the social structure and the subsistence base of indigenous communities. Archaeologists have often demonstrated the sophistication and practicality of prehistoric technologies, but only rarely have they developed long-term projects to evaluate the continuing relevance of these technologies to present-day communities. In this article the first experience of applied archaeology by The Cusichaca Trust is described, showing how a rural development project was developed within specific environmental and social contexts. The Trust's main research focus was the study of the agricultural infrastructure of the Incas and their predecessors in the Cusichaca and Huallancay side-valleys of the Urubamba Valley, Cuzco, Peru. This was paralleled by a rural development project to restore to full productivity some of the abandoned terraces and canals to the benefit of the local community. Attention is drawn to the relationship between conserving and using ancient agricultural infrastructures and the degree to which community organization is central to the maintenance and use of such technologies.

INTRODUCTION

It is not common to use archaeology to find solutions to contemporary problems, but the experience of the Cusichaca Trust's work demonstrates that a combination of field archaeology and multi-disciplinary research can lead to creative new approaches for rural development, giving archaeology a truly social function.

The concept of applied archaeology was recognized in the 1980s as one of the more socially orientated developments of New Archaeology, with the study of past agricultural systems being one of the most fertile grounds for active involvement (Renfrew and Bahn, 1991). Reassessing the applicability of indigenous technologies within the context of present-day economic situations may highlight their continuing relevance as well as bringing an understanding of them into a new dimension. Through research and experimental work this can lead to renewed practical applications for these ancient technologies. However, in most cases, the difficulties and long-term social and political commitments required in the application process mean that the results are rarely implemented.

The success of the civilizations of the Central Andes was founded on innovative developments introduced to alleviate environmental risks, thus securing the sustainability of their agriculture base. Among the notable achievements of the pre-Hispanic civilizations of Peru is the creation of agricultural systems able to mitigate the inherent risks of dry land environments in varied ecological niches, from the coastal deserts to the semi-arid high altitude (altiplano). In the altiplano, a range of different solutions were arrived at, including man-made reservoirs or wet cultivation areas called *cochas* (Flores Ochoa and Paz Flores, 1986) and raised fields called *camellones* or *waru waru* at the edge of Lake Titicaca (Erickson, 1987). The Cusichaca Trust's research and rehabilitation work focused on the terraced agriculture with accompanying irrigation systems that were well developed on the sides of highland valleys.

The Incas and their immediate predecessors in the Cuzco area were skilled farmers who invested a great amount of labour in long-term agricultural developments. In their private estates and homeland the Inca rulers c. AD 1400–1532 perfected many indigenous Andean techniques for maintaining 'sustainable environments', through ambitious construction projects that belied the apparent limitations of their 'bronze-age' technology. Their main practical concern was with the production of maize, a storable crop for food security, and with tackling soil erosion and reducing the risks of climatic change, which they did by building sophisticated irrigated terrace systems (Fig. 1), moving good quality soils to create depth and drainage on high-quality valley side terraces. Irrigation on terraces secured the annual priority crop, of maize as the prime crop, also cultivated in outlying terraced areas associated with *quinoa* or *kiwicha* (both nutritious grains). In planning their irrigation the Inca are thought to have used a water-level in a container, and to have measured low gradients with poles. They used local materials – carefully selected stone (by quality and texture), clay (for sealing in water) and sand and gravel (for good drainage) – all widely available in the Andes (Kendall, 1997). They 'built to last' by choosing the right terrain, controlling the speed of water flow in the channels and adapting stonework to cope with slow and fast gradients. Their structures also endured because of a well-organized, cohesive system of maintenance responsibilities within the social and religious context of the community.

In Cuzco, along the Sacred Valley and at some other locations such as the Colca Canyon in Arequipa and Andamarca in Ayacucho, the irrigated terraces continue to be an important live agricultural heritage that sustains both indigenous and 'immigrant' populations. The potential for restoration of pre-Hispanic irrigation systems to rehabilitate agricultural terracing can be demonstrated in the Ollantaytambo District where the Cusichaca Trust worked with two communities on separate projects; the first, to be discussed here,

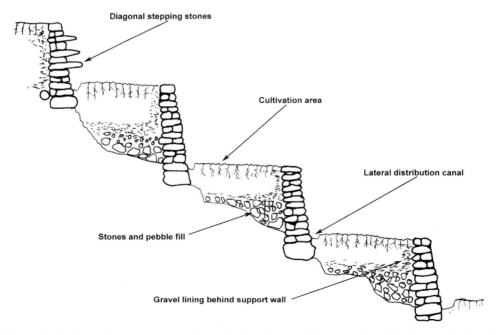

Figure 1. A schematic transverse-section of prime Inca platform terracing. Drawing by A. Kendall.

was at Cusichaca with the farming community of San Jose de Chamana.

THE LOCAL COMMUNITY: LOCAL ORGANIZATION AND PERCEPTIONS OF BENEFICIARIES

The main purpose and justification for the Cusichaca Trust's agricultural rehabilitation project was to alleviate the poverty being experienced by a present-day Andean community in an area known to have had adequate infrastructure capable of producing a large agricultural surplus in pre-Hispanic times (Fig. 2) (Kendall, 1991a). Much of the lower Cusichaca Valley (Fig. 3), which had been so intensively farmed in the Inca period, was abandoned shortly after the Spanish conquest. It was subsequently sporadically farmed by religious organizations of the Catholic church, which acquired the lands and incorporated them into their large estates, in this case the *hacienda* of Sillque, located up-valley in the Urubamba Valley. In the mid-18th century the saturation and collapse of the maize market and its transference from Cuzco to Cochabamba in Bolivia (and the rise of the Mexican and North American markets) brought in a history of poor investment. From the early 19th century the area was taken over by individual landowners who brought in Quechua-speaking settlers from further up and down the main valley to re-occupy the lower part of the Cusichaca Valley. When the project members arrived in 1977 the 8–16 families living in San José de Chamana were part of a private hacienda and owned little or no land of their own. The latest arrivals to Chamana had come from Maras with the new *haciendado* (landowner) of Chamana in 1956. These two men

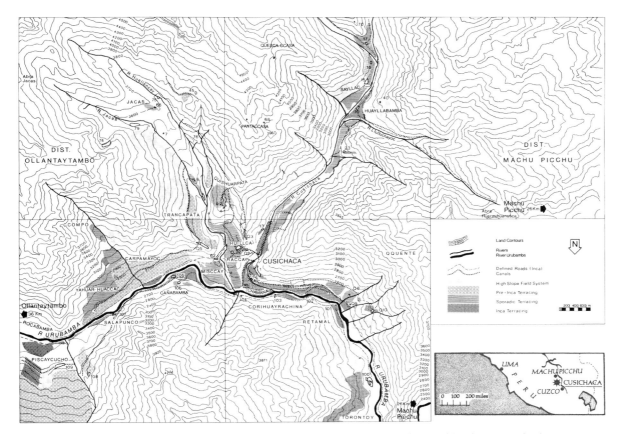

Figure 2. Map showing the present-day communities and late pre-Hispanic sites and land systems in the Cusichaca and Huallancay drainages. Source: Kendall (1984: 259, fig. 3).

Figure 3. Inca settlement and terracing at Patallacta, Cusichaca (background), with a Chamana household in the foreground, 1978. Photo: A. Kendall.

had intermarried with local women and, in the 1980s, became the dominant representatives of the growing Chamana community.

In 1980 the entire Cusichaca valley was occupied by only 145 families, with Huayllabamba in the mid-valley being the oldest and largest community of the area, where some 50 families continued to live on top of a small Inca site that their ancestors had reoccupied in colonial times. The history of poor investment and severe post-conquest depopulation brought about a major decline in the traditional agricultural systems as landowners increasingly leased out parts of their properties and were no longer concerned with maintaining irrigation to terraces or retaining a strong labour force. The majority of the indigenous population had neither the time nor the inclination to maintain the agricultural infrastructure on land they no longer owned and, as a result, the community organization necessary to sustain repairs had broken down. It was partly for such reasons that the Peruvian government implemented the Agrarian Reform, starting in 1964 under President Belaunde and greatly extended under the military government headed by General Velasco Alvarado (1968–1975). These reforms promised to return large tracts of land from hacienda estates to the ownership of indigenous communities and co-operatives. They were partly motivated by social concerns, to alleviate the exploitation of the campesinos, but it was also hoped this would lead to increased agricultural production, which was much needed by the growing urban population. It was to have the opposite effect and subsistence agriculture became even more predominant in the highlands. Although these reforms began in the 1960s, they took many years to implement in places such as Chamana at some remove from the regional political authorities. For instance, Huayllabamba became legally recognized as an indigenous community, independent of the largest local hacienda at Quente, only in 1980 (Villafuerte, 1981).

At the start of the project Chamana householders continued to work as retainers on the lands of the *haciendado*, while other households at Quishuarpata and Chakimayo were somewhat more independent. After the *haciendado* moved out, the small-scale agricultural households with very little or no irrigated land, were busy during the rainy season but had two months with little agricultural work during the long dry season.

The Cusichaca Trust recognized that the process of explaining and implementing a redevelopment project was complex and could unwittingly aggravate multiple tensions rooted in territorial concerns and distrust between local interest groups. Andean peoples have suffered a long history of reorganization and manipulation by colonial authorities, national governments, landowners and the Church. These feelings of uncertainty and mistrust had been exacerbated by raised expectations, but slow implementation, of the recent Agrarian Reform. In the case of Chamana there had been recent deception and broken promises during the negotiation of land deals with the last hacienda owner. The presence of the Cusichaca Project itself was probably a major concern for many community members. This consisted of a large multinational team of up to 80 people camping on community fields for two to three months each year, which in the early years included members of the British and or Peruvian Army. To the new owners of the Huillca Raccay and Quishuarpata tableland terraces, the Cusichaca Project was offering residents the chance to improve their quality of life through increasing the productivity of their lands and access to increased income through the selling of the expected surplus at accessible markets down valley (Villafuerte and Saico, 1980). However, at times there were differences in understanding between the type of practical and theoretical points prioritized by the project and social concerns and the more immediate practical priorities of local community members.

While the group of farmers never lost sight of the opportunity being offered to them, their caution was understandable. In a culture where constructing terraces, canals and field boundaries can be used as justification for land ownership, the farming community of Chamana was understandably wary about the intentions of a development project wanting to improve their land. Concerns included who was going to do the work? Would the project contract workers? If some workers should have to be brought in would they try to claim land rights? Basically the project had to earn their trust and clarify that the work would be carried out together with the community group, taking on board their concerns since they were the owners and would remain the owners. No-one could take away their lands if they formalized their status as a legally recognized 'Grupo Campesino'. Although their procedures to become a legally recognized community were initiated in 1979, Chamana did not fully achieve this status until 1987.

THE RESTORATION PROJECT

In the pre-Hispanic period there were some 6000ha of land under cultivation in the wider area of the Cusichaca Valley to the confluence of the Urubamba valley with the Anta valley (today the District of Ollantaytambo, which has the remains of the infrastructure of some 2500ha of Inca and pre-Inca irrigated terraces and 3200ha of high slope field systems), and were capable of feeding some 106,000 people (Fig. 2). The population in the Inca period was much the same as in 1989, about 8500 – discerned from archaeological reconnaissance of the area and aerial photographs. This suggests that about 95% of the produce could have been exported (Kendall, 1991a). However, in the 1970s very little was being exported because of the poor state of the infrastructure, transportation problems and low incentives because of the low price achieved by agricultural produce in the market place. Since the Agrarian Reform, sporadic attempts had been made to restore some old irrigation systems or build new ones. Such works usually used modern materials, for example cement, which often proved unsuitable because of inherent earth movements, a lack of flexibility and the costs and maintenance requirements placed on the community.

Terrace systems are a valuable resource against soil erosion on steep slopes. These systems had been developed, over thousands of years, as a strategy against the risks of variable precipitation, frosts and hail storms that damage agricultural production and food security (Kendall, 1997).

Four main types of terracing were documented in the Cusichaca area:

- The 79ha of high quality Inca agricultural terraces (AD 1440–1532) with integrated irrigation systems were constructed like level platforms, with inclined double-faced stone walls and some stone fill for drainage (see Fig. 1). A special feature is the retention of water/humidity, which encourages the transformation of the soil through microbiological activity and the increase of nutrients, encouraging heightened temperature (a great way to diminish climatic risks) and recycling of nutrients, which can enable continuous cultivation (Kendall, 1997; Kendall and Rodríguez, 2001).
- Inca-period rehabilitation of the late pre-Inca irrigated terracing at Huillca Raccay has some similar features to the Inca terraces but a single stone-faced support wall and less attention to drainage needs.
- Pre-Inca (c. AD 1000–1440) irrigated agricultural terracing is most visible today where 195ha survive on steep slopes up to 3700m a.s.l. Many of these terraces were constructed following the slope contours and built up at the lower end where the support wall is of the single stone-faced type.
- Although difficult to date, there is also a large amount of low-investment unirrigated terracing located on high gradients above settlements formed by stabilizing natural soil erosion through the compacting of the top soil at the lower end and placing occasional fieldstones and vegetation to encourage the formation of natural banks.

Changes in the size of the indigenous population and their social organization have had a radical effect on the construction and demise of these agricultural systems (Kendall and Rodríguez, 2001). In Inca times the *mit'a* public workforce undertook much of this construction work and local overseers were in charge of canal maintenance and use. Following the Spanish Conquest of 1532, disease contributed to the decimation of the population, administrative breakdown resulted in a lack of investment in land improvement and maintenance, and changes in land use led to the deterioration of the canals and terraces. The introduction of large-hoofed animals from Europe, such as cattle, horses and goats, replaced the delicate-footed camelids. These newly introduced animals grazed near water sources such as canals, resulting in significant damage to both the terraces and canals. In the 1980s studies by the Oficina Nacional de Evaluación de Recursos Naturales (ONERN) estimated that between 50% and 75% of terraces had been abandoned. In some areas the work of looking after community resources, such as irrigation systems, was incorporated within the political and ritual organization of native communities, where all households are obliged to work on canal maintenance at least once a year (Isbell, 1985). For instance, in Andamarca, Carmen Salcedo, Department of Ayacucho, strong commitment and enduring forms of social organization have enabled communities to continue effective maintenance programmes to keep their pre-Hispanic agricultural infrastructure in working order. However, in many other areas, the discouragement of native social and ritual practices and the imposition of external landlords meant there were no longer any social structures in place for the up-keep of the canals.

It is not surprising or untypical, therefore, that the households dispersed around Chamana had no political organization or religious institutions. The 'economic standing' of Andean peasant households is based on the extent and quality of their land holdings, their livestock, the size of their family, their ability to call on external labour and their social obligations. In order to improve the economy of the households in Chamana and the rest of the valley, the Cusichaca Project hoped to bring the community together in a cooperative labour project that would both improve the annual yield from the land and help to develop the social organization and the skills needed to maintain the canal system in the future.

In the Cusichaca area, most of the terrace systems, including some pre-Inca ones, were found to be in a remarkably good state of preservation, but some of the major irrigation canals had irretrievably broken down, causing their abandonment. The most important irrigation system to have broken down was that of the Quishuarpata canal that had irrigated the pre-Inca and Inca terraced lands of Quishuarpata and Huillca Raccay, totaling 45ha. All these lands could come under permanent agriculture again if the canal were to be restored.

At the time this was the only substantial area of land available to local people since other lands were farmed by the two privately owned haciendas. However, local people lacked the community organization and cohesion required to restore and manage the canal facilities. It was therefore decided that while on-going research would focus on the wider area, feasibility studies for the agricultural restoration project would focus on the Quishuarpata canal.

It was in this context, initially as part of its archaeological research, that the Trust investigated the Quishuarpata irrigation system and its development over a period of 1000 years (Kendall, 1991b). The investigation led to an experimental programme for its restoration. The aim of reactivating productive terrace agriculture was a strategy to alleviate poverty and improve the availability of good agricultural land in the area. The Peruvian archaeologist Julio C. Tello said in the 1960s: 'Estudiar el pasado para comprender el presente y planificar el futuro' ('Study the past in order to understand the present and plan for the future'). We found this to be a two-way benefit – that in gaining an understanding of the present to help plan for the future, this statement could be reversed: the information gained in the present, in the agricultural restoration projects, also became a feedback to help in the interpretation of the archaeological data.

BACKGROUND TO THE RESTORATION PROJECT

Study of the terrace systems

From 1977 the archaeological reconnaissance work was combined with agro-ecological studies, vegetation and soil studies, as well as small remedial support projects to assist local families in the maintenance of a few broken-down canals. Some aspects of the archaeological research were specifically designed to investigate the ancient agricultural technology, including studies of the main canal route, the complex engineering to control water velocity and its distribution (Farrington, 1984) and terrace construction in relation to present-day soil fertility (Keeley, 1980, 1982, 1984). Sociological and anthropological studies provided socio-economic evaluations of local commerce and the potential of wider markets (Michel, 1981; Villafuerte, 1981). These studies were necessary to evaluate whether or not the reconstruction of the ancient systems would provide sustainable agricultural land, whether the local residents would use these fields and whether there was a viable market for the increased production.

In the restoration of the Quishuarpata canal, traditional technology was studied and used as far as possible, using the main known and verifiable locally available materials of stone, sand and clay. These materials are freely available, thus ensuring that the community will be able to maintain the technology whatever their economic status. Canals built using traditional Inca techniques have also proven to be very effective in accommodating the extreme changes in temperature and humidity that occur in the Andean highlands (Kendall, 1997). However, it was not possible to be certain what other special materials or ingredients had been included in pre-Hispanic mortar mixes. It was later learnt that the juice of the cactus *gigantón*, could be mixed into mortar for maintaining dampness (Ignacio Aragon, mastermason, personal communication, 1983) and llama grease has been found plugging gaps between stones of an Inca canal in the Calle Loreto, Cuzco (Hernan Aráoz, personal communication, 1995).

By 1980 the technical feasibility studies for the rehabilitation project were in place. This included the hydraulic engineering studies undertaken by Binnie and Partners (Green, 1978; Becerra, 1982), and topographic studies by the British Army logistical support team. Studies of the main Huillca Raccay terrace system involved excavations, which showed that although the soils were deep and had a good structure, in order to reach appropriate fertility with irrigation they would need manure to increase the nitrogen content and provide organic material. Further test pits to study the water distribution systems and the stability of the terraces revealed that some banks contained several support walls and rubble. This interpretation was confirmed by discussing current practice when working with the community in the preparation of the land for agricultural use: local farmers removed stones from the land and threw them in front of the terrace walls. In past maintenance, these stones would, at intervals, have been reincorporated in an eroding wall or been reabsorbed by the bank. Additionally working with local people on three canals that had been kept in operation demonstrated continuities in indigenous knowledge and technological ingenuity in handling local materials (stone, sod and wood) for undertaking temporary maintenance works.

Community response

In 1980, after the basic research and feasibility studies had been completed, the project awaited the decision, or initiative, of the community group to start work. For some time there had been no sign from them and the impression was that there must be some continuing mistrust in relation to the motives of the heavily foreign interests of the project. Project personnel became increasingly despondent towards the end of the 1980 season when there was still no sign of a positive move by the community. But then Pancho Candia, the owner of terraces at the top of the agricultural system at Quishuarpata, who had consistently shown interest in the project, complained that much talk and study had taken place in offering to restore the agricultural system but there was no sign of the work starting. He, personally, was waiting for the project to begin, time was passing. This was what was needed to justify making a real move to implement the project. In a position at the top of the system his lands were in the right place to start the canal restoration – where the project must begin. No guarantees were in place for the rest of the community following suit, but if this first stage was carried out successfully with local participation, there could be no better argument for attracting the rest of the community in further stages of the project. It had already been realized that the work would take place during the dry seasons in stages over several years (during the wet season the demands of agricultural work meant that the farmers would not have time to give to the restoration project).

1981–1993. EXECUTION OF THE PROJECT

In 1981 the canal was restored from the third of the four original secondary intakes. The digging out and consolidation of 3km of canal, including the restoration of four fallen sections and of the drop structure, brought water directly to Quishuarpata. In 1982 the 2km to Huillca Raccay was completed. In 1983, following confirmation that the canal was functioning, work continued to extend the reconstruction back to the canal's original intake off the Huallancay river, at 3700 m.

In 1981 when a contract was signed with Sr. Candia, in which he became responsible for the cleaning of the canal and taking on his team of workers, the project lent him S/150,000, equivalent to US$300.00, to be reimbursed from his first harvest. This he honoured. The clearing and cleaning work was carried out by his workers who were given food during the *faenas* (community workdays) (Fig. 4). At the start of the work Candia advised that it was necessary to carry out the appropriate rituals and he undertook to provide the necessary prepared offerings for the local

Figure 4. Community farmers participating in the clearing of the canal at Quishuarpata, 1981. Photo: D. Parker.

deities to ask for their blessing through a shaman or curer. After these offerings were made the work proceeded as planned.

As expected, in September the agriculturalists were obliged to return to preparations for their main sowing season. However, given that the project had a permit and joint agreement with the National Institute of Culture (INC) and had the organization, materials and operational funding for transport and to pay for workers, the INC agreed that their mastermason and his local team of restorers could work for a week on each of the fallen sections to Quishuarpata. Ignacio Aragón, a very experienced mastermason on restoration projects, with an excellent knowledge of Inca and traditional building methods and materials, had offered to work with the local community on restoring and conserving the canal, building on local knowledge and ingenuity. This allowed the project to work with and train local people in the necessary skills, rather than buying in outside labourers. He helped them to identify appropriate raw materials of clay, sand, sod and stone, all of which were locally available. Generally the principles of traditional technology were observed closely but his knowledge of modern mixes also led to some incorporation of a cement mortar in two sections subject to soil erosion, identified by the irrigation consultants from Binnie and Partners. A graduate student of hydraulic engineering from Wageningen University and a local student agronomist were taken on to help co-ordinate and to complement the work at Quishuarpata. All this resulted in the achievement of this first phase of restoration work by November 1981.

In 1982, from January to April, further cleaning of the canal was carried out. At Quishuarpata, Candia's son-in-law moved to establish his family there to take full advantage of the newly irrigated terraces and support. The successful re-establishment of irrigation to this point attracted the full interest and participation of the rest of the community. The dry season saw the continuation of restoration works down the second drop structure to Huillca Raccay. For its inauguration in September, the canal carried water for irrigation to prepare the terraces for plowing and sowing of a potato crop (Fig. 5). Inaugurations in Peru are seen as important occasions for asking favours of institutions and prominent regional administrators. This

Figure 5. The arrival of irrigation water at the Huillca Raccay tableland and terraces, showing the restored second drop structure in the background. Photo: A. Kendall.

inauguration achieved the distinction of attracting acceptances from sufficiently empowered dignitaries who were able to further ensure the future socio-economic success of the now irrigated terrace systems; these included the Prefect of the Region, the government head of the Ministry of Industry and Tourism, the local Mayor and agronomists from the Faculty of Agronomy for Agricultural Research (KAYRA) at the National University San Antonio Abad of Cuzco (UNSAAC). This led to two important commitments: the action group Cooperación Popular was sent to build a new bridge over the Urubamba River at Km 88 (distance on the railway from Cuzco), to enable the valley inhabitants to export their produce as well as to provide access for tourists to the famous Inca Trail to Machu Picchu; and KAYRA was to play a vital role in providing agricultural extension support, especially for the community in a pilot scheme for the rehabilitation of the terraces of Huillca Raccay.

In 1983, during the final year of the canal restoration work in which the Quishuarpata canal was extended back to the upper reaches of its original intake off the River Huallancay, it was the local people who took over and ran the implementation of the project with their own foreman supervising the 20–25 local workers. Work was coordinated with the INC for the clearance of vegetation, digging out, consolidation and restoration work, tasks which were accomplished without difficulty. In October the canal became operative in its entirety and has remained so to date.

1983–1985. REHABILITATION OF THE TERRACES: 'THE ANDEAN AGRICULTURAL PROJECT'

A pilot area of 7ha of terracing was initially set up as a trial. The general objectives were to be achieved through the support of tools and seed capital supplied by the project and KAYRA, technical assistance through the visits of agronomist, Andrés Peña and, most importantly, the community's own manual work to improve their quality of life by the appropriate cultivation and care of the newly restored terraces (Figs. 6 and 7). Improved production, agricultural job creation, diversification, improvement of dietary choice and commercialization of surplus production would result from their own endeavours, leading to increased earnings and socio-economic development.

The experiments supervised by Peña took place over three years on terraces that had been abandoned for over 20 years. Prior to this abandonment they had only been cultivated with barley on a fallow system, and prior to that had supported, under irrigation, the more intensive cultivation of crops such as maize from pre-Inca times until the 19th century. Six varieties of *kiwicha*, a highly nutritious native Andean grain under redevelopment at KAYRA, were introduced. This proved to be an ideal habitat for the crop, which came to be more widely re-introduced. Varieties of cleaned Andean cultivars of the tarwi bean, quinoa grain and potatoes were distributed to complement local maize in a carefully monitored crop rotation, also combining with colonial introductions such as barley and broad beans. KAYRA was also concerned to assess the need for fertilizers and pesticides in relation to performance results.

Figure 6. Community agriculture starting up on the Huillca Raccay terraces. Photo: A. Kendall.

Figure 7. Maize planted on a terrace at Huillca Raccay, 2000. Photo: A. Kendall.

Results and recommendations were obtained both for community use and feedback for the university (Peña, 1985, 1986, 1987). In summary, the monetary value of the seed capital and labour input value trebled in the first year, enabling the programme to be widened. In the second year, community conflicts began over sharing out land and keeping animals out. Some hybrids required more fertilizer and were not resistant to pests. There were also problems with transportation for exporting the surplus. The internal conflicts intensified during the year following completion of the restoration work of the project until the farmers realized that the responsibility was entirely theirs and tackled the problems themselves by dividing the land between the different extended family groups, creating boundaries to keep the animals out.

EVALUATION VISITS

In 1992 an evaluation visit, as one of the field trips associated with the Seminar 'Infraestructura agrícola e hidráulica prehispánica. Presente y futuro', was organized by Cusichaca Trust. This visit to Chamana was undertaken to see the state of the canal and the productivity of the lands on the terraces (Kendall, 1992) (Fig. 8).

It was appreciated that the entire upper tableland was under cultivation and the lands were divided between three extended family groupings. Each had constructed an enclosure to keep out free-roaming animals. The restoration of irrigation had resulted in a significant increase in the percentage of production of maize, potatoes, quinoa and broad beans, products that were being sold in Machu Picchu, Ollantaytambo and Urubamba. An Irrigation Committee, formed in 1983, had successfully maintained the canal, although an overenthusiastic use of cement was noted. The irrigation committee reported that they suffered from a lack of sufficient power to obtain adequate attendance of community members on communal maintenance days to do the work and collect quotas to buy the materials wanted. The Seminar group pointed out it was clear the cement reparations were already cracking and that this problem would be solved with a reduction of dependence on the use of this costly, brittle material and a return to the more appropriately flexible clay with stone, available locally. Further recommendations included reduction of the wear and tear in the main canal by

Figure 8. View of the agricultural rehabilitation of the Huillca Raccay tableland, 1991. Photo: D. Drew.

diminishing the flow of water when irrigation was not needed. The community was farming all the irrigated areas successfully and had plans to further extend them.

The community members' feedback focused particularly on the question of productivity versus costs and the role of fertilizers and pesticides. They said the rehabilitated lands on the tableland were more productive than the lower lands of Chamana (not in the rehabilitation programme). This was because fewer chemical fertilizers and pesticides were needed. Their input of work and investment on the rehabilitated lands was therefore more economic, but it was still relatively low because of low market prices and use of some chemical products. For this reason they wanted to know more about compost and other economic farming methods. The use of seeds appropriate to the area was recommended in preference to hybrids, which required the input of expensive fertilizers and herbicides.

An important measure of the success of the project and strengthening of the community over the period of the project was that the school expanded from a single-room thatched structure to the construction of substantial buildings comprising four classrooms. The 1992 visit also confirmed the overall stimulus generated by the rehabilitation project: in 1987 a new chapel was built beside the school by the community of Chamana and another canal was restored in a locally organized project activated by the largest single local landowner. Finally, it was reported that no one had migrated out of the area. On the contrary, local sons had brought home brides and daughters husbands, which contributed to an increase in population. The usual lack of resources and microeconomic problems (amongst others), which were combining with the problems of social unrest to provoke urban migrations throughout Peru at this time were not so apparent at Chamana. Unfortunately, though, a storehouse for potatoes provided with windows for diffuse light (based on Inca precedents) went through a major change of function – it was adapted for use as accommodation!

In 1998, a brief evaluation visit by the Agronomist Juan Guillén, found that the canal was still benefiting 13 families in Chamana and three families in Quishuarpata, with sufficient irrigation water and soil fertility to permit up to three crops a year, in some cases incorporating horticulture. These beneficiaries were intensively farming the terrace soils recovered from sporadic pasture. Even two crops a year is exceptional today in the Andes, here two crops a year had become the standard.

A minimal use of fertilizers was also recorded and local people were found to be following traditional agricultural practices, mixing plantings of maize with beans and quinoa with rotations practiced for nitrogen fertilization of the soil. There was limited use of modern fertilizer for mixing with natural manure for some improved cultigens, which were more demanding. The Irrigation Committee had been strengthened by being taken directly under the wing of the community directorate. They had introduced twice yearly cleaning and maintenance works along the entire canal. An impressive gesture of support had been made by the local office of the National Police at Corihuayrachina, who provided the traditional feast to the voluntary workers. Food security was assured by major crops of maize, followed by horticulture and wheat, and the market at Machu Picchu was a secure one for surplus early maize and potato crops. Local people reported that they could now afford improved medical treatment and education in local towns.

In 2000, a socio-economic study commissioned by Cusichaca Trust found the project to be 80% successful in completing its objectives. It was, however, disturbing to hear that as a result of a major landslide down the railway line there were transport restrictions on taking surplus produce to the preferred market in Machu Picchu. This was because the railway was prioritizing tourism under its new foreign ownership. Produce had to be taken further afield, up the line by pack animals and transport to the more competitive market of Urubamba. This is expected to be a temporary situation until local trains can be reinstated to reach the down-valley markets of Machu Picchu, Santa Teresa and Quillabamba; however, it could be restrictive if not resolved.

IMPLICATIONS OF THE REHABILITATION WORK IN THE CUSICHACA VALLEY

Indigenous pre-Hispanic technology in the Andes developed in economic and social circumstances very different from today. We must take account of these differences. Firstly, the workforce is no longer the same. In Inca times the *mit'a* workforce and water management was in operation, which demanded community participation; this continued to be enforced through laws during the colonial period and water 'judges' continued. However, both these systems of state organization for water management have collapsed, and local community structures for organizing work parties for canal cleaning and maintenance have deteriorated, particularly accelerating since Agrarian Reform when the migration to urban centres resulted in a major loss of infrastructure and community organization. Secondly, the interaction of community *faenas* with religious festivals for the agriculturalists, especially water maintenance with supporting rituals and feasting, has been broken down by the intervention of other interests, including Adventist religions in competition with Catholicism who denounce the consumption of alcohol resulting in reduced community sponsorship (Mitchell, 1991). Today, the organization of communal work parties is severely limited. Migration to urban centres, weakening rural infrastructure and community organization are continual problems. Loss of management is particularly noticeable in the lack of integral planning at the local level, leading to conflicts between animal husbandry and the needs of agriculturalists.

Better transport facilities providing greater access to markets are now becoming available in many, but not all areas, although these can be costly to use, limiting the economic benefits that this greater access to markets should bring. The facilitation of travel can also facilitate technical developments, although these are not always in the best interests of the rural poor. For instance the import of chemical pesticides and fertilizers is harmful to the biomass system inherent in the terraces, and cement is inflexible in seismic areas and not environmentally friendly in maintaining some humidity in the soil to support a diversity of flora generally below irrigation canals.

Two major constraints on highland farmers redeveloping their terraces are: firstly, the distance to markets – particularly for isolated communities with inadequate transport access to their terraces; and secondly, the low sale price for agricultural produce as a result of the government's importation policy of key basic foods, such as rice, pasta and even potatoes, which have sometimes also been subsidised or donated by 'Northern' countries. While these problems can be seen as almost insuperable for surpluses destined for commercialization, there are incentives for well-placed communities with irrigated terraces located between 2100 and 3600m a.s.l. to provide one main harvest a year. This is indispensable to ensure a healthy nutritious diet for family self-sufficiency. In addition, two different harvests a year using the rotation system are also possible in the right locations, but is a more risky strategy in exposed or relatively high locations and where the climate is more variable, being subject to frosts and hailstorms.

In the Cusichaca experiment to apply the lessons learnt about traditional technology from archaeological and anthropological investigations and related disciplines, there has been a considerable level of success. This could encourage further experimentation and development leading to an implementation model for agricultural restoration by rehabilitating the past infrastructure and traditional practices. Successes and demonstrated concepts resulting from this experiment include:

- The practical application of results from archaeological investigation has contributed to providing sustainable social and economic benefits.
- The technical feasibility of re-establishing irrigation in a pre-Hispanic canal using traditional technology was demonstrated.
- 17 poor farmers of Chamana received agricultural extension training, which they applied to achieve two, and sometimes three, crops a year using irrigation and rotation of crops on terracing.
- The sustainability of the project is demonstrated by socio-economic evaluations.
- A spin-off from the organization of community workparties for logistics and restoration was that local communities, especially Chamana, became more unified and developed stronger political entities.
- The evaluations also list the ways the economic and resulting social benefits have empowered the community and its leadership to take initiatives to improve their organization and quality of life: by improving the school and building a chapel.
- The restoration and rehabilitation experience can be considered a positive preliminary experimental step in addressing the wider redevelopment of abandoned pre-Hispanic agricultural systems in the Andes.

From the achievements of this initial experiment outlined above, the following discussion examines how the Cusichaca Trust has sought to and will continue to take the concept further forward.

FURTHER DEVELOPMENTS

It was hoped that the Cusichaca experiment would be an effective demonstration to encourage further rehabilitation of abandoned canals and terracing using traditional technology. But we soon learnt that this was to be only a first step to achieve this objective. It did, however, result in invitations from other communities to work with them on more ambitious projects involving hundreds of farmers, and a chance to continue learning and developing a model with which to interest government institutions.

In the Cusichaca Valley it was possible to support only one sector of farmers. Thereafter, the Cusichaca Trust developed projects with varied programmes extending more widely to poor farmers throughout valley systems, additionally involving potable water, health and nutrition, and technical workshop and cultural centres. Such a project was carried out between 1987 and 1997 in the Patacancha Valley based on Ollantaytambo, and subsequently from 1998 in the Pampachiri Project in Andahuaylas, Apurímac. In both locations it was learnt that when it comes to the social aspect, the degree of participation by the community in the agricultural restoration work, its management, budgeting for maintenance, foreseeing the potential production and income generation, is essential for efficiency and sustainability.

Since 1992 ten major three-day seminar workshops have been held in highland capitals and towns to disseminate the results, advantages and benefits of traditional agricultural technology. Since 1997 these events have sometimes been in partnership with the Ministry of Agriculture's active arm Programa Nacional de Manejo de Cuencas Hidrograficas y Conservacion de Suelos (PRONAMACHCS), who have extended their work on the prevention of soil erosion to terracing restoration projects working with local conservation committees since 2001 with the Programa de desarrollo rural del valle del Colca (DESCO) who have restored 8000ha of terraces in the Colca Canyon, specializing in working with the communities; and the International Center for Agricultural Research in the Dry Areas (ICARDA) who have contributed to the study of socio-economic aspects with Cusichaca and, since 2002, also with the experienced Andamarca Community. Many smaller one-day events have also been held.

Following the seminar-workshops and practical experience, it is now felt that the way forward is through counteracting the increase in general rural social disorganization by encouraging new initiatives for leadership training and social development. At the same time there needs to be an emphasis on prioritizing the strengthening of agricultural organization. The focus should be on re-introduction of the social 'irrigation culture' to manage and maintain the valuable infrastructure, clarifying and supporting property rights and responsibilities. Community cohesion is required to carry out the routine tasks of maintenance, allocation of pasturing locations and dates, and the repair of the irrigation and terracing works. The Cusichaca Trust will continue its seminar programme and focus on more demonstration projects. The local NGO, Asociación Andina Cusichaca, is being established independently and more energy will need to be directed to advocacy, market research and disseminating results to the government and NGO institutions.

It is intended to continue to work from 2003 in Ayacucho and the Apurimac regions, using the example of the Andamarca community, an indigenous community whose social organization and ritual calendar is geared to, and has successfully maintained, their intensive concentration of pre-Hispanic terracing systems. Interaction between indigenous communities, who can demonstrate different skills and management strategies to each other, is the best way to stimulate wider appreciation of Andean technologies and ensure their continuing relevance. In many areas of the highlands where farmers currently depend for cash more on herding interests (requiring relatively little input), integrated actions between agriculturalists' interests and herders will add to cohesion within communities.

Finally, from the original project and more recent experiences of Cusichaca Trust, PRONAMACHCS, DESCO and some other NGOs, Andean communities have demonstrated that they can apply their traditional technology with some social and economic innovations to restore the pre-Hispanic agricultural infrastructure of irrigation canals and terraces to significantly increase their economic potential. Questions remain concerning how to bring together the government institutions, NGOs and communities on resolving issues of procedure, technical standards, community participation and marketing. The most important players should be the INC and the Ministry of Agriculture, who need to define the steps and methods to be used for regaining this national agricultural heritage. In some locations there is a groundswell of interest in terracing restoration in Peru. Few NGOs work in this field, but it is expanding so standards and training are much needed.

CONSERVING ARTEFACTS AND MAINTAINING INDIGENOUS COMMUNITIES

In recent years the philosophy of archaeological conservation work has tended to be critical of projects that reconstruct ancient sites, there has instead been a much greater emphasis on preserving and displaying as much as possible of the original structures. The Cusichaca Trust's work to rehabilitate pre-Hispanic terraces and canal systems may be considered as a direct challenge to this conservation philosophy. Although, wherever possible, the stones were replaced in their original position after clearing and cleaning, and some special sections might be dismantled and carefully rebuilt, much of our work required reconstructing terrace walls and canal channels that involved adding new stones, mortar and clay linings.

However, without our interventions these structures would continue to deteriorate and to erode down the steep slopes of the valley. More importantly, our work was designed to rehabilitate these structures as part of a working agricultural infrastructure when functioning irrigated terraces are still the most productive agricultural use of the landscape, and this technology is ideal for the wider conservation of the environment. This draws attention to a potential distinction between conserving the ancient artefact as an original monument as opposed to maintaining the traditional technology within its live social context – it also raises the question of the incorporation of other technologies.

This latter theme was discussed at two seminars organized jointly by the Cusichaca Trust and the National Institute of Culture (INC in Cuzco) in 1992 and 1995. At both of these meetings the point was made that although the continual rebuilding and maintenance of canals and terraces may not be considered as the authentic, original artefact, nonetheless this maintenance work, which must also have taken place during pre-Hispanic periods, is essential to preserving the structures intact and maintaining Andean agricultural practices as a part of the living cultural tradition and constitutes a live patrimony.

The Cusichaca Trust produced a short guide exploring how to organize rehabilitation work using traditional technologies and including some appropriate modern solutions to specific structural problems. This booklet has been distributed for use by other NGOs and communities (Kendall and Green, 1997). The issue of appropriate levels of intervention and the degree to which traditional methods of construction should be used needs to be adequately clarified between all interested parties so that standards of consolidation can be understood and applied by non-archaeologists. Generally the standards of conservation work laid down for the preservation of ancient monuments need to be adjusted in relation to the active use of traditional and appropriate technology for the benefit of living communities in order to achieve the best solution for constructions where only a minimum of maintenance is possible and durability is essential. Non-archaeologists require an official guide for implementation of minimum standards that are acceptable to indigenous cultural heritage interests, but archaeologists and conservators also require guidance in the function of agricultural infrastructures and how best to work *with* local communities to maintain traditional technologies. The INC recently participated in a further seminar held in Andamarca in 2002, and it is hoped that there will be further progress in developing a more dynamic approach to the conservation of agricultural infrastructures as working examples of traditional technology so that they can maintain their social and economic role into the 21st century.

ACKNOWLEDGEMENTS

I am grateful to the staff and volunteers who have given their committed energy to the Cusichaca Trust, to the communities who have trusted us and shared experiences with us, and to Binnie and Partners, the National Institute of Culture and the National University of San Antonio Abad of Cuzco and all our funders in this first Cusichaca Project – particularly the Overseas Development Aid of the UK government, BP, the Baring Foundation and research funders including The Leverhulme Trust, The Royal Geographical Society, The Royal Society, The British Museum and many others. Finally, I would like to thank David Drew for reading the first draft of the manuscript and to express my appreciation to Bill Sillar for his encouragement and constructive comments in the preparation of the paper.

Ann Kendall completed her M.A. in Interdisciplinary Archaeology in 1970 at UCLA, USA, and her PhD in 1974 at the Institute of Archaeology, London, where she is currently a Research Associate of University College London, UK. Since 1977 she has been the Director of The Cusichaca Trust for research and rural development work in Peru and has been decorated in Peru and the UK for her contribution to Peruvian agriculture.

Contact address: The Cusichaca Trust, St Peters, Farm Lane, Crawley, Nr Witney OX29 9TL, UK. Email: eannkendall@hotmail.com; cusichaca@cusichaca.org

REFERENCES

Becerra, H. Canal Quishuarpata: Recomendaciones para uso. Cuidado y mantenimiento del canal. Binnie & Partners Unpublished Report for Cusichaca Archaeological Project (CAP) (1982).

Erickson, C.L. Applications of prehistoric Andean technology: experiments in raised field agriculture, Huatta, Lake Titicaca, Peru 1981–1983. In Farrington,

I. (ed.) *Prehistoric Intensive Agriculture in the Tropics*. British Archaeological Reports, International Series No. 232, Oxford (1987).

Farrington, I.S. The archaeology of irrigation canals, with special reference to Peru. *World Archaeology* 11 (1984) 287–305.

Flores Ochoa, J. and Paz Flores, P. La agricultura en lagunas (qocha). In De la Torre, C. and Burga, M. (eds) *Andenes y camellones en el Peru andino: Historia, presente y futuro*. Consejo Nacional de Ciencia y Tecnología, Lima (1986).

Green, D.W. Proyecto Cusichaca: Informe sobre la rehabilitación de las obras de ingenieria y el desarrollo agrícola. Binnie and Partners Unpublished Report for CAP (1978).

Isbell, B.J. *To Defend Ourselves: Ecology and Ritual in an Andean Village*. Waveland Press, Prospect Heights IL (1985).

Keeley, H.C.M. The soils and terraces of the Cusichaca Valley, Peru (11). Unpublished Report for CAP (1980).

Keeley, H.C.M. The soils and terraces of the Cusichaca Valley, Peru (11). Unpublished Report for CAP (1982).

Keeley, H.C.M. Soil studies in the Cusichaca Valley, Peru. In Kendall, A. (ed.) *Currrent Archaeological Projects in the Central Andes*. British Archaeological Reports, International Series 210, Oxford (1984) 323–343.

Kendall, A. Archaeological investigations of the Late Intermediate Period and Late Horizon Period at Cusichaca, Peru. In Kendall, A. (ed.) *Current Archaeological Projects in the Central Andes: Some Approaches and Results*. British Archaeological Reports, International Series 210 (1984) 247–290.

Kendall, A. *Los patrones de asentamiento y desarrollo rural prehispánico entre Ollantaytambo y Machu Picchu*. Cusichaca Trust and Universidad Nacional San Antónío Abad de Cusco (UNSAAC), Cusco (1991a).

Kendall, A. The Cusichaca Archaeological Project, Cuzco, Peru: a final report. *Bulletin of the Institute of Archaeolgy* 28 (1991b) 1–98.

Kendall, A. (ed.) *Infraestructura agrícola e hidráulica prehispánica presente y futuro*. Cusichaca Trust, Asociación Grafica Educativa, Cusco (1992).

Kendall, A. Obras de tecnología tradicional Andina en la restauración de la infraestructura prehispánica. In Kendall, A. (ed.) *Restauración de sistemas agrícolas prehispánicos en la sierra sur, Peru; arqueología y tecnología indígena en desarrollo rural*. Editorial Amauta, Cusco (1997) 76–84.

Kendall, A. and Green, D. *Irrigando el Futuro: Manual para la restauración de sistemas de irrigación prehispánicos en la sierra sur, Peru*. Cusichaca Trust, Amauta Press, Cusco (1997).

Kendall, A. and Rodríguez, A. Restauración agrícola en los Andes: Adaptación de los sistemas tradicionales de andenes irrigadas al contexto moderno. *Proceedings of SEPIA IX Meeting, Puno*, Peru (2001).

Michel, K. Trade and exchange in the Cusichaca Valley. Unpublished Report for CAP and dissertation in the School of Agriculture, Wageningen (1981).

Mitchell, W.P. *Peasants on the Edge: Crop, Cult and Crisis in the Andes*. University of Texas Press, Austin TX (1991).

Peña, A. Proyecto de Desarrollo Andino (Cusichaca). Unpublished Report for CAP (1985).

Peña, A. Proyecto de Desarrollo Andino (Cusichaca). Unpublished report for CAP (1986).

Peña, A. Proyecto de Desarrollo Andino (Cusichaca). Unpublished report for CAP (1987).

Renfrew, C. and Bahn, P. *Archaeology: Theories, Methods and Practice*. Thames and Hudson, London (1991).

Villafuerte, F. Campesinado y antropología: el caso de Cusichaca. Dissertation, Department of Anthropology, UNSAAC, Cusco (1981).

Villafuerte, F. and Saico, A. Informe Antropológico. Unpublished Report for CAP (1980).

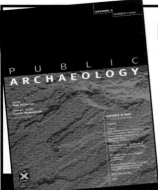

PUBLIC ARCHAEOLOGY
An international, peer-reviewed journal, setting archaeology in a global context

'A significant development... deserves to be immediately recognized as a key journal for the discipline' Times Higher Education Supplement

The only peer-reviewed journal to provide an arena for the growing debate surrounding archaeological and heritage issues as they relate to the wider world of politics, ethics, government, social questions, education, management, economics and philosophy.

ORDER FORM

Yes, please enter my subscription to **Public Archaeology** journal - ISSN 1745-2007 - Volume 4 (4 issues)

☐ Institutional subscription (£75 / US$135) ☐ Personal subscription (£40 / US$70)

☐ Please send by Airmail (optional - add £12 / US$20)

TOTAL (inclusive of optional 'Site Reburial' issue of CMAS journal) _____

☐ Please also include the special 'Site Reburial' issue of Conservation and Management of Archaeological Sites journal. Add £25/$40 (Vol. 6 Nos. 3&4)

☐ Please send me the Notes for Contributors

☐ Please send me further information on Earthscan books on Heritage Conservation

Delivery details

Name _____ Position _____

Company _____

Address _____

City/State _____ Post/Zip code _____

Country _____ E-mail _____

Telephone _____

Payment options

☐ I enclose a cheque/bankers draft payable to James & James / Earthscan (in sterling drawn on a UK bank)

☐ Please debit my credit/debit card as follows: ☐ Amex ☐ Mastercard ☐ Switch/Maestro ☐ Visa

Cardholder name _____

Card number ☐☐☐☐ ☐☐☐☐ ☐☐☐☐ ☐☐☐☐

Expiry date ☐☐ / ☐☐   Issue number (applies to Switch only) ☐☐

Signed _____ Date _____

☐ Please send me a pro-forma invoice (no issues will be sent until payment received)

☐ Occasionally we may send you information on our relevant publications. Please tick here if you do not wish to receive these updates.

☐ Occasionally we may pass on your details to other reputable companies for them to send relevant product information. Please tick here if you do not wish your details to be passed on.

Please post a copy of this form to: Earthscan Publishers Ltd, 8-12 Camden High Street, London NW1 0JH, UK
Or order by: Fax +44 (0)20 7387 8998   Tel +44 (0)20 7387 8558   E-mail earthinfo@earthscan.co.uk   Web www.earthscan.co.uk